MW01627175

Praise for
AdvisorSmart for the Individual Investor

"Anyone who's ever wanted to confidently select a financial advisor will absolutely benefit from the effective tools and guidance presented in this book."

—Ivan Illán, AIF®, CFS®, founder and chief investment officer of Aligne Wealth Advisors Investment Management (AWAIM®) (www.alignewealth.com), and best-selling author of *Success as a Financial Advisor for Dummies*

"Whether you are already working with a financial advisory firm or trying to decide on whether to hire one, *AdvisorSmart for the Individual Investor* is an extremely valuable tool. I highly recommend it."

—Larry Swedroe, head of financial and economic research, Buckingham Strategic Wealth (www.buckinghamstrategicwealth.com), and author of *The Only Guide to a Winning Investment Strategy You'll Ever Need*

"Slick relationship people can be very persuasive. Trust but verify. This book gives you the tools you need to get what you pay for when you hire a financial advisor."

—Ron Surz, president of Target Date Solutions (www.targetdatesolutions.com) and author of *Baby Boomer Investing in the Perilous Decade of the 2020s: How to Live a Dignified Retirement*

"Sales is the focus of many financial advisory and wealth management firms. However, there are a growing number of fee-only financial advisors who strive to be more focused on your needs. Reading *AdvisorSmart for the Individual Investor* will give you the knowledge to see through the Wall Street marketing and distinguish the good firms from the bad ones."

—Guerdon T. Ely, MBA, CFP®, AIFA®, ChFC®, founder of Ely Prudent Portfolios, LLC (www.elyportfolios.com), and author of *Lower Your Financial Handicap: Advice from the Financial Caddie*

"*AdvisorSmart for the Individual Investor* is a must-read for anyone who is looking for investment or financial planning advice that is truly in their best interest. It slices through the myriad mysteries and confusion found throughout the financial services industry. Both first-time and experienced investors will benefit greatly from its clear and concise explanation of how the investment advice world really works."

—Allan Henriques, JD, fiduciary consultant, FiduciaryPath (www.FiduciaryPath.com)

"*AdvisorSmart for the Individual Investor* offers a highly detailed process for selecting a financial advisor in the United States. David Bromelkamp uses examples and provides resources, making it an interesting read and a very practical guide. You would be wise to read this book before making a hiring decision."

—Carlos Panksep, vice president, CEFEX, Broadridge Retirement and Workplace (www.cefex.org)

"Decades of wisdom, vulnerability, honesty, humility, this book has it all. This is a powerful read for the individual investor and an even better mentorship read for the over 80 percent of advisors that are not real fiduciaries. The educational value of the text is enormous; thank you, David Bromelkamp, for putting it out in the world and fighting the good fight."

—Justin Sanderson, CFP®, CIMA®, CEO of Sanderson Wealth Management (www.SandersonLLC.com)

"This book will help you to greatly transform your approach to locating a financial planning professional to serve as your trusted partner. Your level of understanding concerning financial advisors can make the difference between sustainability or struggle, peace of mind or disaster. *AdvisorSmart for the Individual Investor* is infused with passion and loaded with transparent truth-telling. David Bromelkamp succeeds in 'pulling back the veil' on an insular industry, rendering us wiser and far better able to achieve the financial security we seek."

—Lori Crever, work culture evangelist, former international banking vice president, and author of *Protégé Power: A Roadmap to Mentorship* (www.protegepower.com)

"David Bromelkamp understands that, as investors, we bring more than just our money to the investor profile. We bring our whole selves—our fears, our values, our goals for ourselves and our families. And money is personal, whether you are investing a little or a lot. *AdvisorSmart for the Individual Investor* reflects Bromelkamp's investor-centered approach and gives practical advice for anyone navigating the world of financial advisors. He will change the way you seek out financial advice."

—Yvonne Hundshamer, president, Blue Grotto Inc. (www.bluegrottoinc.com)

"In my years cohosting the weekly PBS series *MoneyTrack*, many of our viewers have shared their personal horror stories about how devastating bad financial advice can be. They wished for guidance to find alternatives to brokers and salespeople. Individual investors are now starting to understand what real financial and retirement advice looks like and how seriously they should be taking the process of finding the right financial advisor. I'm beyond thrilled to see a widely respected investor advocate like David Bromelkamp valiantly join the quest to help people recognize and distinguish financial advice from sales tactics. In this incredibly usable resource, I wholeheartedly applaud David's bold and brave stance in exposing Wall Street's deceptive tactics and empowering people to take the search for better financial advice into their own hands. Anyone nearing retirement needs to read this book."

—Pam Krueger, founder and CEO, Wealthramp, Inc. (www.wealthramp.com)

"If you've ever wondered how to choose a financial advisor, you're not alone. It's baffling. And that's not by mistake: financial selling machines want to lure you in with ads claiming to provide what you need. They don't. They sell you what they need to sell. *AdvisorSmart for the Individual Investor* is the best guide I've seen to help you find genuine advice from an authentic fiduciary—someone who acts in your best interest with loyalty, care, and genuine advice. Buy the book and get out your highlighters and Post-it Notes, because you're going to refer to this guide time and time again."

—Kathleen M. McBride, ERISA 402(a) Named Fiduciary expert, Fiduciary Wise, LLC (www.fiduciarywise.com)

"For anyone wondering if they should hire a financial advisor and unsure how to get started, *AdvisorSmart for the Individual Investor* is an easy-to-read playbook that educates readers on how to make more informed and educated decisions while exponentially increasing their odds of choosing an advisor who will have their best interests in mind."

—Brian Thorp, chief executive officer, Wealthtender (www.wealthtender.com)

"Reading this book is THE first step for anyone considering whether (or not) to hire a financial advisor, as well as for individual investors who are not absolutely convinced that their current financial advisor is the right fit. *AdvisorSmart for the Individual Investor* provides you with an unbiased, comprehensive, and concise step-by-step guide to identify and then select a qualified, professional, and trustworthy wealth advisor from the multitude of self-described money managers and financial companies."

—Steven Klos, MD, associate professor of emergency medicine, University of Minnesota

"Choosing a financial advisor is an important step to obtain the peace of mind that comes with having a financial plan. The most difficult step is often finding a good financial advisor. *AdvisorSmart for the Individual Investor* breaks down the financial industry from an insider's perspective so that the reader can be better informed and thus feel more confident in choosing a trusted advisor."

—**Linda Wedul, CAE, president and CEO, Minnesota Society of CPAs (www.mncpa.org)**

"*AdvisorSmart for the Individual Investor* is an insightful book full of simple frameworks that can help hardworking people get the help they need. Amid all the industry jargon, financial salespeople, marketers, and designation collectors, this book will help cut through the noise and give you clarity on how to find a financial advisor who will truly represent your interests."

—**Steve Atkinson, managing director at CRA | Admired Leadership (www.admiredleadership.com)**

"This is a must-read for anyone struggling with the management of their finances, debt, investments, or retirement planning. David Bromelkamp makes a strong case for seeking professional financial planning help and provides a comprehensive and easy-to-read road map to find an independent, conflict-free, and well-qualified financial advisor. This book also serves the needs of those who already have a financial advisor but believe that it might be time for a checkup."

—**Roger L. Levy, LLM, AIFA®, managing director, Cambridge Fiduciary Services, LLC (www.cambridgefiduciaryservices.com)**

"Selecting a financial advisor is one of the most important financial decisions that you make during your lifetime. *AdvisorSmart for the Individual Investor* provides the reader with the knowledge needed to select a trustworthy financial advisor. Based on my experience, choosing the wrong financial advisor can have devastating results—such as a broker churning a client's account to make excess commissions. Verifying that an advisor has YOUR interests at heart will provide you with the confidence that you are taking positive steps for securing your financial future."

—**Debra Thompson, CPA, CFE, founder, HUGS 4 Business (www.hugs4business.com)**

"The movement for the best financial advisors to gain independence has been a boon to investors looking for investment advice that's free of so many of the traditional conflicts of interest. However, it's left a void where investors can no longer look to well-known, established brands as a mark of quality. *AdvisorSmart for the Individual Investor* is the sherpa that investors need to find a new trusted financial advisor."

—**Brian Hamburger, JD, CRCP, MarketCounsel (www.marketcounsel.com)**

"Given the thousands of investment opportunities available today, how do investors make smart decisions with their money? Seek professional advice, of course—but given the thousands of advisors out there, how do investors choose who to work with? David Bromelkamp answers this question comprehensively with cautionary tales that warn the reader of the pitfalls to avoid and checklists that speed the process of finding the perfect professional."

—Samuel Adams, CEO and cofounder, Vert Asset Management (www.vertasset.com), and coauthor of *Your Essential Guide to Sustainable Investing*

"Powerful, practical, and solid advice on selecting a financial advisor with confidence. David Bromelkamp is to be commended for providing this invaluable resource to the investing public."

—J. Richard Lynch, former fiduciary investment management instructor at Broadridge Fi360 (retired), former member of the CEFEX Registration Committee

"This is a must-read for investors wanting to cut through the noise and confusion of finding, selecting, and working with a professional financial advisor. I believe that investors at any stage of their financial lives will be better off following David Bromelkamp's straightforward advice on seeking fee-only fiduciary advisors who always put their clients' interests first."

—Allan Slider, founder, FeeOnlyNetwork (www.feeonlynetwork.com)

"David Bromelkamp has written the book that I have always wanted to write: a well-written, plain English, comprehensive book that truly guides the individual investor to an appropriate financial advisor to get better financial advice. This book's four parts and thirty-eight chapters provide a thoughtful, evidence-based approach and flow seamlessly toward the excellent appendices and glossary. I believe *AdvisorSmart for the Individual Investor* is a groundbreaking achievement—you will benefit by reading this book."

—Keith Loveland, Keith Loveland Consulting

"My wife and I went through the financial advisor selection process in our late forties and wish that David Bromelkamp had written this book fifteen years ago. His client stories are like those that we experienced prior to and during our search—and in the years since. *AdvisorSmart for the Individual Investor* is an easy read that provides you with a road map to conduct your search and, most importantly, choose and retain a trusted financial advisor."

—Mark McKeown, former vice president (retired), Circana (formerly IRI)

"In addition to being an easy read and pragmatic guide for individuals looking for guidance on how to vet and select financial advisors, *AdvisorSmart for the Individual Investor* offers some great insights on David Bromelkamp's personal journey that are sure to resonate with other fiduciary-centric financial professionals."

—John Faustino, AIFA®, PPC®, head of retirement products, Broadridge Financial Solutions, Inc.

"David Bromelkamp's new book, *AdvisorSmart for the Individual Investor*, is the go-to reference guide for individual investors looking to find and select a prudent financial advisor. It is chock-full of powerful and practical ideas that give investors the information they need to identify the financial advisor that will stand them in good stead throughout their investing lives."

—W. Scott Simon, JD, CFP®, AIFA®, former *Morningstar* columnist, and author of *Index Mutual Funds: Profiting from an Investment Revolution* and *The Prudent Investor Act: A Guide to Understanding*

"David Bromelkamp delivers a guide that is imperative to an individual investor's prudent selection of a new financial advisor. If an investor wants to find an advisor that is focused on making money *for* the client relationship instead of *from* the client relationship, *AdvisorSmart for the Individual Investor* provides the evidence-based tools that will be referenced time and time again."

—Michael Smith, managing partner, Insight Financial Partners, LLC (www.insightfpllc.com)

"David Bromelkamp unpacks his vast experience and study of investing and advice in plain words. He makes readers smarter by describing what to avoid and what to seek. My favorite tip? Keep it simple and only hire a fee-only (and fiduciary-always) advisor who puts their proud fiduciary status in writing."

—Knut A. Rostad, president, Institute for the Fiduciary Standard (www.thefiduciaryinstitute.org)

"In clear language and relatable stories, David Bromelkamp shares his personal journey from discovering that there's a better model of financial advice to championing that vision for investors. David has committed his professional life to educating investors and advocating for a transparent, client-centric advice model that puts their interests first."

—Dave Butler, co-CEO, Dimensional Fund Advisors (www.dimensional.com)

AdvisorSmart for the Individual Investor

Your Guide to
Selecting a Financial Advisor to
Get Better Financial Advice

David Bromelkamp

Visit the AdvisorSmart® website at www.AdvisorSmart.com
Visit the AdvisorSmart® book website at www.AdvisorSmartBook.com

ISBN 13: 978-1-63489-732-7
Library of Congress Catalog Number: 2025901706
Printed in Canada
First Printing: 2025
29 28 27 26 25 5 4 3 2 1

Cover design by Emily Mahon
Interior design by Shannon Plunkett
Author photo by Kyra Nygard, Kyra Nygard Photography
Edited by Kate Leibfried
Proofread by Caitlin Fultz and Zenyse Miller
Production editing by Lindsay Bohls

Wise Ink
PO Box 580195
Minneapolis, MN 55458-0195
WiseInk.com

Wise Ink is a creative publishing agency for game-changers. Wise Ink authors uplift, inspire, and inform, and their titles support building a better and more equitable world. For more information, visit WiseInk.com.

To order, visit ItascaBooks.com or www.AdvisorSmartBook.com. Reseller discounts available.

Contact David Bromelkamp at www.AdvisorSmartBook.com for speaking engagements, freelance writing projects, and interviews.

"Wall Street is the only place that people ride to in a Rolls-Royce to get advice from those who take the subway."

—Warren Buffett

To my father, Henry James Bromelkamp,
who was a man who understood the value of
education to make the world a better place.

Contents

Foreword

How does the average person find a trustworthy personal financial advisor? We might consult Uncle Steve, or a friend from the golfing or gardening club, or a coworker. A personal recommendation *could* bear fruit, but that approach is severely flawed (for reasons discussed in this book). The other obvious option is to consult the internet—our modern answer to nearly everything.

With limitless knowledge and resources at our fingertips, it is easy to assume we can find a suitable financial advisor without issue. After all, a brief online search can tell us the weather, the latest football score, or the molecular structure of table salt. But if we're searching for something *beyond* the basics, things become murky quickly. In my experience, this murkiness is especially present when searching for a financial advisor.

In online searches, priority is often given to those with the largest marketing budgets or the resources to manipulate and dominate search results. Because of this baked-in bias, Wall Street brokerage firms and lead generation websites tend to rise to the top of the internet search quagmire, even if their information is flawed, tainted, or does not align with the consumer's needs.

How can we navigate this labyrinth, teeming with misinformation and predatory tactics? How can individual investors make their way through the tangle of search results when looking for a personal financial advisor? One of the best ways is to arm ourselves with information.

When I was asked to write the foreword to *AdvisorSmart for the Individual Investor,* I saw it as an opportunity to promote a book that helps consumers navigate one of the most important decisions of their lives: finding a trustworthy and suitable financial advisor. Not only does this book provide straightforward, easy-to-comprehend advice, it is also written by a passionate consumer advocate with several decades of experience in the industry.

I met the author, David Bromelkamp, several years ago through the National Association of Personal Financial Advisors (NAPFA). This is a membership organization for fee-only fiduciaries—a type of financial advisor which is client-focused, highly ethical, and solely compensated by a set fee (rather than through commissions, bonuses, or hidden charges). David is a longtime NAPFA member and has been committed to the fee-only compensation model since 2005, when he rejected the principles of his longtime employer (a brokerage firm) and founded his own financial planning company. Though I have never been a personal financial advisor, I have worked closely with the industry for over twenty years, consulting with financial advisors on search engine visibility and online reputation management.

In 2008, I decided to utilize my tech and business background to make financial advice open and available to the public. With this goal in mind, I founded the Financial Advice Network. This company began as a way to compile the advice and insights that financial advisory companies were either publishing online or sending out through their email lists. Through the Financial Advice Network, I developed relationships with several different financial organizations, from large brokers to small firms, and financial associations like NAPFA.

At first, I worked with anyone who labeled themselves as a "financial advisor." At the time, I did not have a comprehensive understanding of the differences between commission-based, fee-based, and fee-only financial advisors (differences David explores in this book). I did not concern myself with the distinction between brokerage firms and Registered Investment Advisers (RIAs). I didn't understand what it meant to be a practicing fiduciary and why that was an important asset for consumers.

My understanding of these disparate worlds clarified gradually, and once I understood the differences, I could not ethically continue supporting and promoting financial advisory companies that were compensated through commissions, bonuses, or undisclosed charges. These companies were generally much more concerned about profits than people (essentially employing salespeople who masqueraded as financial planners), and they often made their millions (or billions) in underhanded ways—hiding fees, not disclosing conflicts of interest, burying payment terms in pages of legalese, and more.

If I thought about it much, my stomach would turn. I had to do something.

Eventually, I decided to tear down everything I had built and start fresh. I abandoned my brand, my logo, and my website. I started building something that would empower and support both fee-only fiduciaries and individual investors. I called the company FeeOnlyNetwork.com.

FeeOnlyNetwork is an online platform that exclusively lists vetted, fee-only financial advisors. My intention is to help fee-only advisors stand out among brokers and non-fiduciaries, both individually and collectively, while educating consumers on the importance of working with a client-focused, fee-only fiduciary. FeeOnlyNetwork is a single tool in the efforts against massive, multi-billion-dollar brokerage companies. *AdvisorSmart for the Individual Investor* is another such tool.

I often refer to fee-only financial advisors and their allies as an army of ants. Individually, a single ant can't do much, but together, we're capable of moving mountains. In the Amazon rainforest, leafcutter ants often carve tiny trails through the foliage—visible tracks of bare earth that they create by treading the same ground over and over and over. The same concept can be applied to the fee-only fiduciary movement. If enough people are united behind a single message, and a single mission, we can make a noticeable difference.

AdvisorSmart for the Individual Investor is an important tool for this "army of ants." In David's book, consumers will find uncomplicated, sincere advice from a well-respected expert in the financial planning industry. This book helps the reader recognize conflicts of interest, understand relevant terminology related to the financial advising industry, avoid biased advice, learn how to conduct an effective search for a trustworthy financial advisor, and much more. *AdvisorSmart for the Individual Investor* is a wealth of vital information that will benefit individual investors of all backgrounds and circumstances.

Above all, David is an advocate and an educator. Both these traits are crucial during this era of abundant misinformation and Wall

Street subterfuge. By empowering consumers and promoting financial literacy, we multiply the ant army.

In recent years, I've noticed encouraging signs of consumer empowerment and education. Individual investors are increasingly and specifically searching for fee-only financial advisors, as evidenced by their use of terms like "fee-only" and "fiduciary" in online searches and initial inquiries with potential advisors. This shift represents a significant departure from the past, where such qualifiers were rarely encountered.

Brokerage firms have also taken note of this growing consumer awareness and have responded with questionable tactics, such as redirecting online searches for fee-only financial advisors to their own websites. Despite these cunning tricks, I am hopeful that individual investors will eventually reject large brokerage firms entirely or, at the very least, demand greater protections and transparency.

AdvisorSmart for the Individual Investor is an important part of the push toward greater transparency and honesty within the financial advice industry. As you turn the page, I invite you to take notes, absorb the insights and practical tools within these pages, and take the necessary steps to improve your personal financial path. Then, pass along some of the knowledge you acquire. This is the only way to build the army of ants—one informed person at a time.

Allan Slider
Founder of FeeOnlyNetwork.com and advocate for fee-only fiduciary financial advisors (advisors that NEVER make commission)

Introducing AdvisorSmart®

When you, as an individual investor, sit down to talk with a so-called financial advisor, are you speaking with someone who is truly objective and disciplined? Does this person have your best interests in mind? Or are you really speaking with a professional salesperson masquerading as a financial planner?

In today's financial advisory industry, it can be difficult to parse the sheep from the wolves. Anyone can claim to be a financial advisor, even if that person is highly motivated to sell proprietary life insurance products, unnecessary annuities, or "in house" mutual funds. And when conflicts of interest and sales incentives exist, the consumer often loses. Even if the sales-driven "financial advisor" across the table is a perfectly decent person (and I know many brokers who are), it is difficult to ignore the tug of financial incentives like commissions and bonuses, and it's *impossible* for a financial advisor to completely reject a company's sales-focused approach (at least for long).

Years ago, when I worked for a large brokerage firm, I attempted to teach my clients about prudent, disciplined investing. My efforts were met with swift retribution. Education was never the goal; sales were. That's why I eventually parted ways with this company and started my own fee-only financial advisory firm (a story for chapter 1).

My experience with the dubious practices of investment securities brokerage firms is not unique. The vast majority of financial advisors work for a company—a brokerage firm or otherwise—that expects its people to make sales. When such pressures are in place, is it possible for financial advisors to be truly objective? Of course not. We see this exemplified in news stories of Wall Street investment firms misleading their clients (and, perhaps, receiving a slap on the wrist afterward). We hear about it from people who poured their life savings into a shady investment scheme, only to lose everything. Personally, I hear about this bad behavior regularly from investors who have been duped and misguided by salespeople acting as financial advisors. Many of these people have lost a lot of their hard-earned money in the process.

You might wonder why the federal government doesn't step in and stop salespeople from doling out bad financial advice. Why not regulate who can call themselves a financial advisor or wealth manager? Why not oblige salespeople to disclose every commission or bonus they make off a particular investment product? In the medical industry, not just anyone can call themselves a doctor. A medical doctor has to go through years of schooling, and once they *are* qualified to practice, they must regularly renew their license. Those types of requirements simply do not exist in the financial advisory industry. Why? Largely because big investment firms shell out a lot of money to ensure regulations remain lax.

How can we compete against the billion-dollar budgets of Wall Street firms? How can we resist the armies of lobbyists who are working to keep the system the same and to keep the average consumer confused and disadvantaged? In this David-and-Goliath-type struggle, the main rock we have in our slingshot is education.

For decades, I have been passionate about educating individual investors on how to find trustworthy, competent financial advisors (AdvisorSmart® is the product of that passion). In my own investment management firm, morality and ethical behavior are just as important as competence and maintaining a disciplined, evidence-based investment approach. We believe individual investors deserve transparency and professionalism, and we work tirelessly to make that happen.

Developing My Moral Compass

When I reflect on my life experiences, my deep commitment to ethical, people-centered work makes sense. My moral compass and my passion to help others started to form when I was quite young.

I grew up in a Catholic family, the sixth child in a family of nine boys. When I was about seven years old, my parents handed me a copy of the *Parable of the Talents*, a story that demonstrates how we can use our gifts to the best of our ability to do good works. The book's cover was dog-eared and the pages blemished, but I didn't mind. I was accustomed to hand-me-downs, and the lessons embedded in the story were more important to me than the book's sorry state. I started to think about how I could use my talents as a force for good.

Fast-forward to college. Growing up in a family that sometimes struggled to meet our basic needs prompted me to pursue a practical career path. I began taking business and accounting classes at Saint John's University in Collegeville, Minnesota, with the goal of becoming a Certified Public Accountant (CPA). Most of these classes were practical and straightforward, teaching me about balance sheets and cash flow, familiarizing me with profit and loss statements. However, one class diverged from the usual numbers-and-spreadsheets lessons, a course called Values in Business and Economics. We studied moral behavior in business and read several books on the topic, including *Readings in Ethics for the Analysis of Values.* This book of readings—and the class in general—was pivotal for me. It prompted me to think about how and why to put ethical behavior at the center of a business. Looking back, this course was foundational to how I would approach and think about business for the rest of my life.

But when I graduated from college, my focus was not on ethics but on paying back my student loans and making my way in the world. I was carrying about $8,000 in school loan debt, and I knew it was up to me to find a job, get to work, and start earning money (and, eventually, building wealth). My life had always consisted of hand-me-downs instead of handouts, so I knew I had to work hard to earn a living. I passed my CPA exam and landed my first job as a public accountant.

The work came naturally to me, and I enjoyed aspects of it, but I was disturbed by how little our clients knew about money and investing. At the time, I was gobbling up all the information I could about investing—reading books, browsing the *Wall Street Journal*, talking with others—and I couldn't help passing along some of this information to my accounting clients. Unsurprisingly, those types of discussions were frowned upon by the management of the accounting firm. Accounting typically addresses the past, not the future. We dealt with decisions people had already made; we didn't guide them on what to do with their money.

I stopped doling out investment advice, but I also made up my mind to leave. The summer after I parted ways with my employer, I read two books that solidified my decision to become an investment advisor: *Do What You Love, the Money Will Follow* by Marsha Sinetar and *Global Investing: The Templeton Way*, as told to Norman Berryessa and Eric Kirzner. The first book emboldened me to leave my practical, accounting-centered path so I could pursue my passions; the second book made me excited about the potential to help people through skillful financial planning.

After that summer in 1988, my life's trajectory changed. I began seeking work at money management firms but quickly learned I did not have the insider connections needed to land a position. I could, however, easily find work at a brokerage firm, so that's what I did.

For eighteen years, I worked in this world, earning commissions and bonuses when I convinced customers to purchase or enroll in certain financial products. I wanted to think I was acting in my clients' best interests, but I know sales incentives and contests influenced some of my decision-making. Not to mention the company itself had a way of pressuring brokers to push certain products. (Chapter 1 describes these pressures in more detail.)

For years, none of this sat right with me, but I didn't know what to do. I didn't know what other options were open to me. That's when I began taking classes and attending seminars to arm myself with enough certificates and knowledge to eventually chart a different course. I earned a Certified Investment Management Consultant (CIMC) designation. I joined the Investment Management Consultants Association (now the Investments & Wealth Institute) and attained a Certified Investment Management Analyst (CIMA®) designation from the Wharton School at the University of Pennsylvania. Interested in prudent investing and decision-making, I worked toward, and acquired, an Accredited Investment Fiduciary Analyst® (AIFA®) designation from the Center for Fiduciary Studies at the University of Pittsburgh to learn more about best practices for fiduciary investors.

Attending the Center was a tipping point for me in my career.

Everything I had been doing—all the independent study, coursework, and earning designations—had taught me what was practical and what was *right* when it came to guiding clients on investment decisions. I was becoming increasingly discontented with my investment securities brokerage firm and its "sales first" mentality. I was ready to put the client first.

But when I tried to pass along some of the knowledge I had learned through the Center for Fiduciary Studies, I was told by my brokerage firm's management, in no uncertain terms, that I couldn't do it. Sales trumped knowledge, and profit trumped people. This retribution was the straw that broke the camel's back. After talking with a mentor, I began figuring out how to leave my brokerage company and start my own customer-centric, fee-only financial advisory firm.

In 2005, I founded Allodium Investment Consultants, and I have been attempting to live out my purpose and passion through my company ever since. My path has not been a straightforward one, but my moral compass eventually guided me back to the values and principled living my parents instilled in me and that I learned in my college ethics course.

Why I Wrote This Book

For nearly twenty years, I have endeavored to do right by my clients by putting their interests first. I work with an incredibly talented, highly ethical, competent team of financial advisors who also believe in the fiduciary standard of care, which means all financial planning decisions are rooted in what's best for the client, not maximizing profit. Concurrently, I have also worked to educate my clients on the value of hiring a client-centric financial advisor (preferably a fee-only fiduciary). I do this so they can spread the word to friends and family members, perhaps preventing their loved ones from signing on with companies that are more focused on sales than people.

This educational work is a start, but it isn't enough.

I've grown tired of hearing stories about average people losing piles of money to hidden fees and commissions. I'm fed up with Wall Street flagrantly duping their clients *because they can*, because they've bribed

Washington to essentially look the other way. I'm sick of Goliath trampling the little guy time and again.

This book is my attempt to fight back, to spread my message, and to arm consumers with what they need most: knowledge. There is nothing more dangerous to the status quo than an educated public. If I could snap my fingers and teach everyone what I know about the inner workings of the financial advisory industry, probably 85 percent of investors would leave their current advisor.

I do not, unfortunately, have that superpower, so I settled for writing this book. In these pages, you will learn which types of "financial advisors" to avoid (and why), how to identify quality financial advice, and how to seek (and eventually hire) a qualified, competent, ethical financial advisor. You will also learn how to pay this knowledge forward so more people can become educated and empowered.

It takes a lot of effort to topple a giant, filthy rich system, but I believe it can be done. In my thirty-five-plus years in the financial industry, I have witnessed a shift in consumer savviness and consumer mentality. People are beginning to realize they do not have to be at the mercy of large Wall Street brokerage firms. There *is* another way.

Just as the wrongs of the mammoth tobacco industry gradually surfaced and resulted in the decline (although, unfortunately, not the demise) of that industry, so too can widespread awareness expose the backhanded actions of Wall Street. My hope is that this book will empower the everyday consumer and the individual investor to stand up for themselves, identify and reject salespeople as financial advisors, and help others do the same. A book such as this one may be a single rock in a slingshot, but you never know how that rock will land.

How to Read This Book

This book is divided into four distinct sections. Part 1 focuses on the types of financial advisors to avoid—the ones who are most likely to place profit over people. This section also lays some of the groundwork for the rest of the book. Part 2 revolves around the characteristics of good advice, in addition to defining and discussing the term *fiduciary*. Part 3 is all about searching for the right financial advisor (how to approach your search, which features to seek, what to avoid, etc.). Finally, part 4 puts it all together and addresses how to select and hire a financial advisor (and financial advisory firm).

Many readers will benefit from reading this book cover to cover. There is valuable information embedded in each section, and the material is laid out in a logical progression. However, some readers may already have a solid understanding of some of the information (e.g., which types of financial advisors to avoid) and can skip certain chapters or sections. Still others may have burning questions about a particular topic and will want to turn to that subject right away (the index in the back can help) before returning to the beginning of the book.

Approach this book in whatever way works best for you. Take notes if you'd like, flag the pages that are most valuable to you, or discuss the content with your significant other (or your friends, coworkers, book club, etc.). This is your journey, so use this book as a tool to navigate your unique financial situation.

Part One
SOURCES OF FINANCIAL ADVICE

In school, we learn our multiplication tables and how to analyze a sonnet. We study civics, chemistry, and world history. We're taught about concepts like centripetal force and the Pythagorean theorem. But what about financial management and investing? Most of us probably didn't learn the difference between a fee-only and a fee-based advisor or how to parse good financial guidance from bunk advice. We likely didn't learn the definition of a fiduciary or why a fiduciary standard of care matters. And I'm confident most of us never received instructions on how to effectively search for, hire, and compensate a qualified financial advisor who will fit your needs.

Because investing-related concepts are unfamiliar—or even completely baffling—for many Americans, it can be overwhelming to begin the hunt for a financial advisor. I get it. That's why I've designed this book to be as approachable as possible, starting with some essential information about which financial advisors you can trust, which you can't, and how to tell the difference. In this first section, I will also discuss some reasons for working with a **qualified, professional** financial advisor (not your uncle Tim!), how to recognize conflicts of interest, and the basic differences between fee-only and fee-based financial advisors.

Armed with these basics, you can start to recognize which financial advisors are on the side of the consumer—on *your* side—and which are mainly trying to make an extra buck.

Terms to Know

A comprehensive list of terms can be found in the glossary, but here are a few words and phrases we will be using frequently:

Broker: one that acts as an agent for others, as in negotiating contracts, purchases, or sales, in return for a fee or commission.

Fee-Based: a compensation model in which financial advisory firms receive sales commissions from the consumer based on specific financial products they sell.

Fee-Only: a compensation model in which financial advisory firms are compensated directly by their clients for advice, plan implementation, and the ongoing management of assets and do not accept sales commission compensation for their work.

Fiduciary: a relationship involving trust, especially with regard to the relationship between a trustee and a beneficiary.

Fiduciary duty: the relationship between a fiduciary and the principal (or beneficiary) on whose behalf the fiduciary acts.

Fiduciary standard of care: the overriding standard for a fiduciary financial advisor is called the fiduciary standard of care, which requires that a financial advisor act solely in the client's best interest when offering personalized financial advice.

Financial advisor: a professional who provides financial services to clients based on their financial situation. In many countries, financial advisors must complete specific training and be registered with a regulatory body to provide advice.

In this book, you might occasionally see the word *advisor* written as *adviser*, with an *-er* instead of an *-or*. The Investment Advisers Act of 1940, which defines what an investment advisor/adviser does and how they are regulated, spelled adviser with an *e*, which set an industry precedent for decades relative to investment advisers but not the more broadly defined group of advisors who provide financial advice. Today, it is more common to see the word advisor spelled with an *o*, especially by financial advisors who want to hold themselves out as providers of financial advice and are not legally allowed to use the term *investment adviser* to describe their services because they are not registered with the Securities and Exchange Commission as "Registered Investment Advisers." Regardless of spelling, if an individual is primarily paid to provide investment advice, they must register with the US Securities and Exchange Commission (SEC) (with some exceptions). While it is important to understand that the SEC has a very specific spelling of the word *adviser* for legal purposes, in this book I do not fight most of the population and have chosen to spell the words related to financial advisors providing financial advice in general with the *-or* spelling. I reserve the spelling of the word *adviser* (with an *-er*) to these two specific terms, as defined by the Securities and Exchange Commission:

1. Registered Investment Adviser (RIA)
2. Investment Adviser Representative (IAR)

Financial planning: a process that involves looking at a client's entire financial picture and then advising them on how to achieve their short- and long-term financial goals.

Investing: the process of committing money with the expectation of achieving a profit or material result by putting it into financial plans, shares, or property, or by using it to develop a commercial venture.

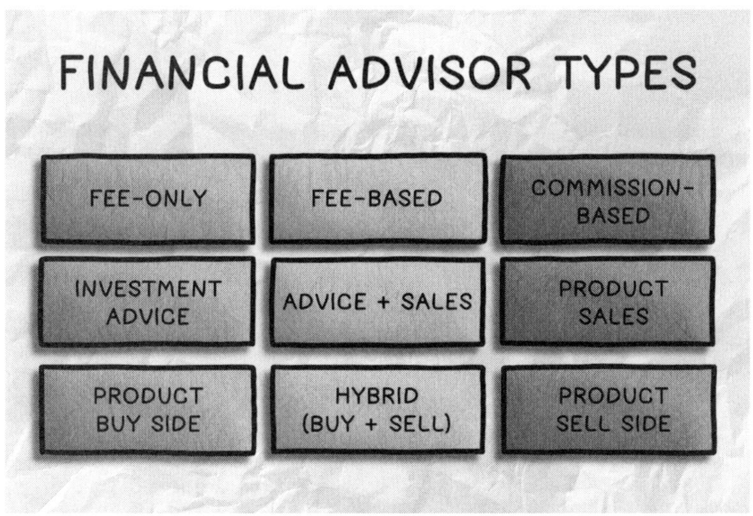

Chapter 1
Why I Rejected Commission-Based Brokerage Firms

Thirty years ago, I decided to change my life's trajectory and center my career around helping individuals make better financial decisions. Up to that point, I had been working as a Certified Public Accountant, which was an honest and steady job but not terribly inspiring. I wanted to be at the front end of financial decision-making; I wanted to guide others to make smart, evidence-based choices.

When I switched career paths in 1988, I had a vision of becoming something like a coach, a counselor, a trusted mentor. What played out was much different.

Bright-eyed and armed with a new investment securities brokerage license, I began working at a large brokerage firm in the Twin Cities. Like so many wealth management firms, this company had a commission-based fee structure, meaning it profited whenever a financial product or security was sold to a client. The financial advisor would take a slice of the profits, and the firm itself would also take a slice.

I didn't think about it much at the time, but this type of compensation structure can inevitably lead to conflicts of interest. Ultimately, the brokerage firm centers around profit, which can lead to pushing products or timelines that are not in the client's best interest. The firm does not have a fiduciary duty to serve the client first and the company second. The company and its profits take priority.

Regardless, when I began my work in the personal finance arena, I had no real reason to examine my company's fee structure. I was simply happy to be part of the team, and I reasoned that *I* would give unbiased, solid advice, regardless of earning incentives.

I was wrong.

The Mutual Fund Contest

Not long after I began my new employment as a commission-based financial advisor, my company announced an exciting new contest. Any advisor who sold $1 million or more worth of Templeton Growth Fund shares would enjoy an all-expenses-paid trip to the Bahamas and a chance to meet *the* John Templeton, visionary investor and founder of his namesake mutual fund.

That lit a fire under my shoes! To me, the tropical vacation was a bit of frosting on a much more substantial cake. The true prize, in my mind, was meeting John Templeton, a man I had admired for his visionary financial approach, investing philosophies, and philanthropy. From what I gathered (and I still believe this to be true), Templeton was not only a savvy investor but also an upstanding person who genuinely cared about humanity. Today, people might get excited about meeting Taylor Swift or a professional football player. For me, John Templeton was *that* big. He was something of a hero to me—a larger-than-life celebrity. So, when my company announced its sales contest, I got to work.

At every opportunity, I spoke to my clients about the Templeton mutual fund. I signed up so many clients that I easily met the contest goal and was soon winging my way to the Bahamas with my wife. At the time, I didn't consider the implications of the contest. I had simply risen to the challenge presented by my company and was enjoying the fruits of my labors. Only some time later, after I left the company and was able to reflect on my time there, did I realize that my actions had been borderline unethical.

Had the Templeton mutual fund been right for every single client?

No, almost certainly not. But I pushed it anyway.

And that's the danger of commission-based wealth management companies. When profits are the main emphasis, people inevitably come second. Does that mean every broker or financial advisor is crooked and driven purely by profits? Not at all! I know many decent people who work as commission-based advisors (and I'd like to think I used to be one of them). However, even decent people can be influenced by company pressure to sell more or less of a certain product.

When it comes down to it, the system is larger than the individual, and that can influence the way people dole out financial advice, whether they realize it or not.

Another Path

So, what's a person to do?

In my case, I eventually rejected the commission-based system and struck it out on my own. The decision was not an easy one. I pictured my new company crashing and burning within the year; I imagined having to pound the pavement, begging for new clients. But my fears were never realized. I successfully founded my own fee-only wealth management firm in 2005 and have been leading and growing the company ever since. At the heart of our mission is service to our clients through unbiased, evidence-based financial advice. The client's best interests will always come first.

I wish I could say I quit my job at the large brokerage company and founded my company shortly after the Templeton mutual fund contest, but that wasn't the case. I pressed on, serving clients as best I could within the company's parameters. As time passed, I grew increasingly disillusioned with the company's commission-based structure, but I didn't put up much of a fight. Instead, I quietly rebelled by striking out on my own to gain as many degrees and certificates and as much knowledge as I could, arming myself for an eventual exit.

In 2003, I attended the Center for Fiduciary Studies at the University of Pittsburgh to learn more about fiduciary responsibilities and client-focused investment practices. Through this program, I had the distinct honor of receiving one of the first published copies of the *Prudent Investment Practices* handbook. This handbook provides information and strategic guidelines to develop a legal, client-centric, practical fiduciary investment plan. It was cutting-edge at the time—chock-full of helpful, salient information.

However, in 2004, my company sent me an internal memo, forbidding me from sharing the information contained within the *Prudent Investment Practices* handbook with coworkers, clients, or the general public.

The move frustrated me and crystallized what I had long suspected: clients were to be treated as profit-generating machines, not as individuals to inform and empower. That ran counter to everything I believed. So, with this final straw, I began taking steps to cut ties with my company and forge my own path.

I might have left my company sooner, but I simply didn't know what other options were available to me. If I transitioned to another wealth management company, would it be any different? Would I face the same types of ethical dilemmas?

The infuriating memo made me realize that I *did* have a choice. I could choose to leave a brokerage company that operated around a commission-based structure in favor of a fee-only system. And that same option is available to you, too, as an investor. You have the power and capability to select a financial advisor who is honest, knowledgeable, and committed to putting their clients' needs first. And if you're already working with a financial advisory firm, you have the power and capability to walk away if that firm, and its people, are not meeting your needs. There's no need to stick with a firm that does not have your best interests at heart. It doesn't matter how long you've been with your financial advisory firm or how much money it is managing. It *is* possible to cut ties and choose a new path.

My goal is to help you do just that.

Empowering Investors

My purpose for writing this book is to educate and empower individual investors—no matter their age, circumstances, or net worth—to competently navigate today's investment management landscape and select a trustworthy financial advisor who fits their individual needs. If you follow along, you will pick up valuable information on topics such as:

- how to avoid biased financial advice

- identifying sources of financial advice
- identifying conflicts of interest
- where and how to seek trustworthy financial advice
- useful investing terminology
- learning the characteristics of good advice
- distinguishing between "fee-only" and "fee-based" companies
- how to find, interview, and hire a competent, honest advisor

By writing this book, I risk offending or even angering fellow financial advisors who work for commission-based organizations. So be it. My goal is not to win any popularity contests but to deliver unbiased, useful advice for the average investor. Specifically, I'd like to guide investors on how to identify impartial financial advisors and select the right one for their needs. I have noticed a distinct lack of information on this topic, and I aim to fill that gap.

Furthermore, I feel duty-driven to write this book. My goal has always been to use my God-given talents to make the world a better place. Leaving my brokerage firm and starting my own company was a start, but it wasn't enough. I want to reach as many people as possible—people who are uncertain, uninformed, or maybe even a little scared when it comes to investing. During my career, I have met dozens and dozens of this type of investor, and I know there are thousands more who are waffling over what to do with their assets because they are intimidated by the whole process.

Let me pull back the veil! In the following chapters, I aim to be as candid, transparent, and approachable as possible. If you ever have a question, feel free to leave a comment or contact me through my website. Let's create a more honest financial future.

Chapter 2

Do You Trust Your Financial Advisor?

I was approached a few years ago by an individual investor who had purchased a million-dollar life insurance product (variable annuity) and was questioning the purpose of this particular investment. He had some concerns, but his financial advisor was not interested in addressing his questions, so the investor developed some doubts about the real purpose of the investment. The lack of candor from his financial advisor led to a lack of trust in the financial advice and ultimately the financial advisor. In the light of day, the investor was enlightened about the percentage of sales commission that the financial advisor earned by the sale of this financial product (5% of $1,000,000 = $50,000) and the trust in the financial advisor dropped to zero immediately. Unfortunately, investors are taken advantage of by sales-commission-driven product salespeople every day, and this leads to a lack of trust in financial advisors as a group.

To function as a modern society, we must trust others. It's nearly impossible to gain *every* skill necessary to live a normal, productive life. We rely on others to perform surgery, fix a car engine, grow and process food, fix our teeth, and rewire the electricity in our homes. Even if you could grow a backyard garden or change the oil in your car, you'll likely have to rely on others to assist with a variety of basic tasks.

For many people, money management is among the tasks that get delegated to a professional. Just like auto repair, financial management is a practical skill that is rarely taught in school (or if it is taught, the depth is often lacking). According to the Milken Institute,* only 57 percent of US adults are financially literate, as measured by their

---

* Contreras and Bendix, "Financial Literacy in the United States."

familiarity with risk diversification, numeracy, inflation, and compound interest. Worldwide, the US is ranked fourteenth in financial literacy, and many people only have a tenuous understanding of basic financial concepts (such as the difference between stocks and mutual funds or the importance of a credit score).

In short, people need guidance when it comes to money management. The trouble, however, is that the vast majority of Americans do not trust financial advisors.

An Era of Mistrust

A survey by the Chartered Financial Analyst (CFA) Institute* found that financial advisors were among the least trusted professionals out of six different types of specialists. They were ranked slightly more trustworthy than auto mechanics and more trustworthy than politicians. In this survey, participants were more likely to trust doctors, accountants, and lawyers (who are often characterized as untrustworthy in TV shows, books, and even jokes!).

Other surveys revealed a similar level of wariness. The American Association of Individual Investors† found that 65 percent of individual investors mistrust the financial services industry, and only *2 percent* said they trust financial professionals "a lot." Another poll by Northwestern Mutual‡ found that only 26 percent of Americans view financial advisors as their "most trusted source of financial advice." Remarkably, this is an increase from years past!

So, Why the Rampant Mistrust?

Part of the hesitancy to trust financial advisors could come from the high-profile scandals we've seen in recent decades involving shady brokerage firms. The Bernie Madoff Ponzi scheme is one of the better-known examples, with Madoff posting fictitious earnings and defrauding investors of some $65 billion before he was outed by his

---

* Martin, "Advisors Rank Almost as Low as Mechanics on Trustworthiness."

† Backman, "Most Americans Don't Trust Their Financial Advisors. Should They?"

‡ Velasquez, "Americans Are Changing Who They Turn to for Financial Advice."

sons and sentenced to 150 years in prison. During that same time period, the Global Financial Crisis revealed many layers of unethical or fraudulent activity within the banking and investment industries.

Beyond newsworthy scandals, individual investors have a difficult time trusting wealth management firms due to a lack of transparency or confusing compensation models. According to CFA Institute findings,* 84 percent of polled investors stated that "full disclosures of fees and other costs is a determining factor in building a trusted relationship with an advisor." However, less than half of respondents thought their financial advisors were making those disclosures. Financial writer Kenneth Corbin expounded on the findings: "The mistrust expressed in the CFA poll stems from the increasingly elaborate compensation models and business structures in the industry," in addition to a "fractured regulatory environment."

In that same poll, the CFA Institute found that a paltry 35 percent of retail investors "believe their advisor puts their clients' interests ahead of their own." For institutional investors, that number drops to only 25 percent.

These figures are troubling, but, unfortunately, they are not terribly surprising. As a financial advisor, I have had to fight an uphill battle when it comes to trust. People are (often legitimately) concerned about being given biased advice, which happens all too often when brokerage firms have a commission-based compensation structure. I had one client remark, "I am cynical dealing with people who are dealing with my money. I constantly look to see what is going on. I have been burned once; I will never get burned again." Investors are forced to do their best when it comes to selecting a financial advisor and look for trust wherever they can find it.

How Do Investors Decide Who to Trust?

Steve Atkinson,† coach and former managing director of advisor relations for Buckingham Strategic Partners, says that it doesn't do to

---

*** Corbin, "Yikes! Clients Still Don't Trust Their Advisors, CFA Institute Finds."**

† Steve Atkinson is an author, coach, and podcast host who helps independent advisors. He is the former managing director of advisor relations for Buckingham Strategic Partners, LLC.

"hire an advisor just because you trust them. There should be a more thorough set of criteria beyond trust, since it's hard to define why you trust someone."* If I needed to pick a financial advisor, I would approach the process the same way I recently selected a new doctor. I would list all my possibilities, define my criteria, and begin eliminating names that did not fit those conditions. In my search for a doctor, I first began looking at all doctors that would be covered by my health insurance plan. Then I narrowed down the list by looking at each doctor's experience and background. When seeking a financial advisor, you might search for wealth management companies within twenty miles that use a fee-only compensation structure (those criteria alone will significantly narrow your options!).

Unfortunately, most investors are not so logical in their search. They rely on the advice of family members, friends, acquaintances from church or the golf club, or other even more dubious sources (strangers on social media, for instance).

One investor—let's call her Sandra—called me recently to inquire about investing with my fee-only financial advisory firm. She explained that she was having misgivings about her current advisor because he often talked over her head. "I don't know about stocks, bonds, or mutual funds," she said. "I don't understand that stuff!" She went on to say that one of her good friends was related to one of the financial advisors at my firm. Because of that familial connection, she felt she could trust this advisor and wanted to work with him.

I listened to Sandra's story (which was not at all out of the norm) and said we could certainly work with her if that gave her peace of mind. I did wonder, however, whether Sandra would feel the same type of mistrust and frustration if her new advisor gave her advice she didn't quite understand. In short, would she feel any better working with us?

Sandra assured me she would be more comfortable with us. Her friend trusted us, so she did too.

In an ideal world, Sandra would not have had to rely on a happenstance connection to find a new financial advisor. She would have had access to unbiased information about financial advisory and/or

* Atkinson, interview by author, August 10, 2023.

wealth management firms, their compensation structures, and their advisors. We do not live in an ideal world, but I still believe investment firms can endeavor to build trust among clients and potential clients.

Building Trust

In the financial industry, trust is more than a "nice-to-have" feature. To me, it is foundational. Building trust means being transparent, having high ethical standards, and putting clients first. But even those who don't put transparency, ethics, and clients first would be wise to emphasize trust. Frankly, a high level of trust is good for a company's bottom line. David Horsager, researcher, author, and founder of Trust Edge Leadership Institute, asserts that "without trust, leaders and organizations fail."* In his research, he has found that companies with a high level of trust are consistently higher performers than those that lack trust. Trust also creates a positive environment for employees and clients alike, increases revenue, and improves efficiency and performance.

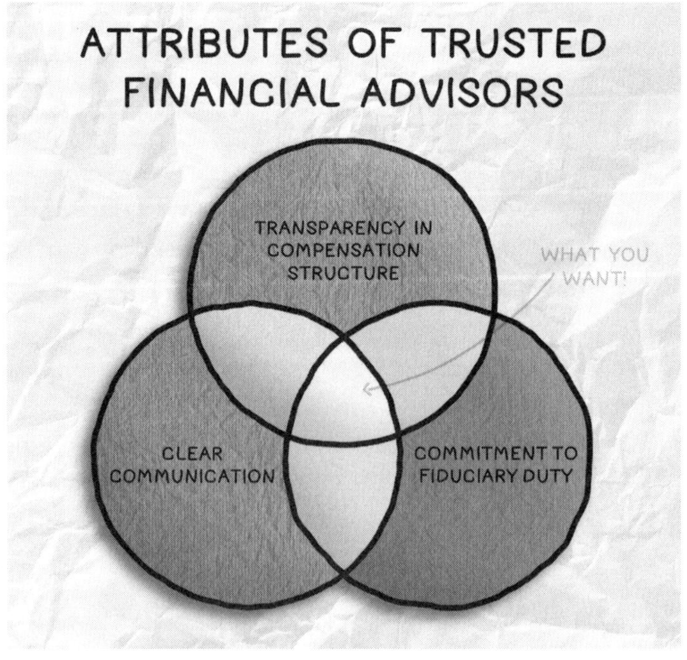

---

* Horsager, "Trusted Leader: 8 Pillars that Drive Results," https://davidhorsager.com/speaking/.

In finance, trust is critical. Clients must entrust financial advisors with the assets they have accumulated through long hours and decades of hard work. The character and integrity of a financial advisor could define the difference between an early, comfortable retirement and an uncertain retirement.

Trust matters. As an individual investor, it is in your best interest to seek financial advisory firms and financial advisors that emphasize trust across the board, including in the following areas:

1. Transparency in compensation structure

The compensation of financial advisors makes an enormous difference in terms of trust. Oftentimes, commission-based compensation structures are tied to inherent conflicts of interest. The financial advisors are strongly encouraged to sell certain products, even if those products are not necessarily in the best interest of the client.

Clients should always have a clear understanding of how the financial advisor is paid and what that means. I strongly encourage seeking fee-only financial advisors to avoid potential conflicts of interest.

NOTE: *This is a high-level overview of what it means to have a transparent compensation structure. We will discuss several of these terms and concepts in future chapters:*

Conflicts of interest: Chapter 8

Fee-only financial advisors: Chapter 14

Compensation structures: Chapter 35

2. Commitment to fiduciary duty

In essence, a fiduciary duty is the responsibility to act in the best interests of another person. For a financial advisor, that means treating the client's money with the same kind of respect and care as one might treat the assets of their own parents. It really boils down to the Golden Rule of treating others the same way you would like to be treated.

NOTE: *More information about fiduciaries and fiduciary duty can be found in chapters 20 and 21.*

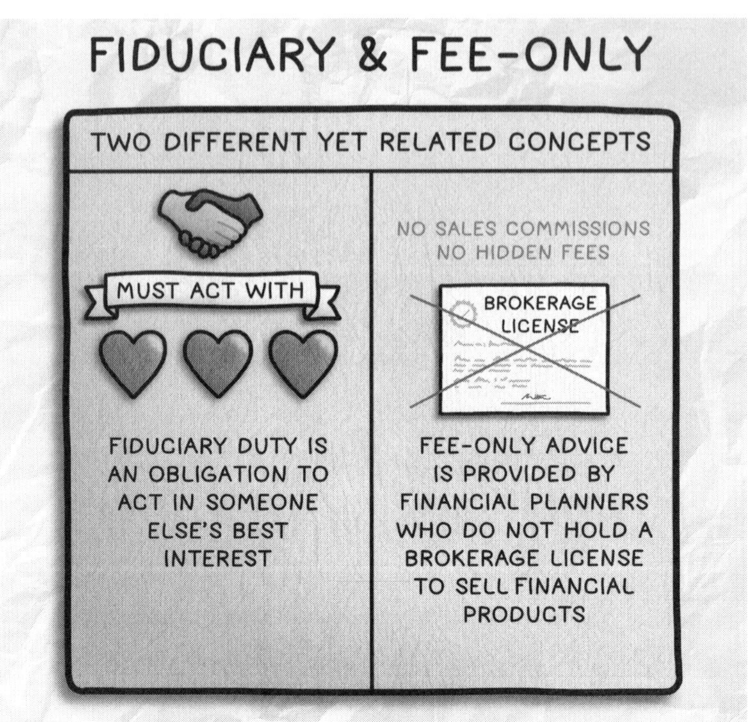

3. Clear communication

Compassionate financial advisors will endeavor to communicate clearly with their clients. They will avoid jargon, promote a dialogue, and encourage questions. Clients should never feel shy about piping up when they are unclear about something. This type of open, candid communication is helpful for building trust *and* demonstrating that the financial advisor has nothing to hide. It's easy to conceal bad motives behind dense language or confusing terms. Instead, opt for financial advisors who are straightforward and transparent.

Trust should be a core tenant of every financial institution. Until it is, clients will (rightfully) continue to be wary of brokerage firms and financial advisors. As an individual investor, I encourage you to place your trust in financial advisors and firms that commit to a culture of transparency, choose fee-only compensation structures, emphasize fiduciary duty, and practice clear communication. In our modern world, we have to trust all kinds of people . . . but we don't have to do it blindly.

Chapter 3

Should You Hire a Financial Advisor or Do It Yourself (DIY)?

Let's say your car's brake pads have finally bitten the dust. At this point, you really only have two choices: you can change the brake pads yourself, or you can hire someone else to do the job for you. You're not a mechanic, and you know very little about changing brake pads, so you'd have to do some research, order the parts, set aside time in your busy schedule, and go through the motions of changing the pads. Additionally, the stakes are high when you're dealing with brakes. If installed incorrectly, the brake pads might not engage, which could result in a car crash.

Given the options, most people (who don't happen to be trained mechanics) would probably opt to pay a professional for this service rather than attempt the do-it-yourself (DIY) route. Only those who have the time, interest, and skills (or potential to learn the skills) would choose to swap out the brake pads on their own.

This situation is analogous to financial planning. It is possible, of course, to develop and execute your own financial plan, but is it wise? Just as your car may end up in a wreck if you change your own brake pads, so, too, could your financial future be hindered (or even derailed) if you choose the wrong investment strategy or fail to take critical details into account.

In my experience, few people possess the necessary traits, knowledge, and time to masterfully plan their own financial path. This is why financial planning is a profession (as I discuss in chapter 19) and why so many people choose to pay for guidance rather than take a DIY approach.

Why Trust a Professional Financial Advisor?

In the last chapter, we discussed the pervasive lack of trust in the financial industry. Because of that, you might be thinking, "Right. Why *should* I trust a financial advisor?" Of course, it doesn't pay to put your faith in a dishonest or profits-driven financial advisor (just as you wouldn't trust a mechanic who is constantly trying to make unnecessary repairs). Later in the book, we'll talk about how to seek, interview, and hire a trustworthy and qualified financial advisor, but for now, let's talk about why to entrust a financial advisor or wealth manager with your money in the first place. Why *not* take a stab at your own investing?

Let me frame it this way: Unless you happen to have a very specific skill set, you probably wouldn't trust yourself to perform dental surgery, design a skyscraper, or produce a new multivitamin. These are specialized skills that take years of training and knowledge-building, practice, and development. The same is true for experienced Certified Financial Planners®.

Professional financial planners must go through extensive training, take exams, build experience over the years, and constantly sharpen their skills through continuing education. You can't simply read a Suze Orman book or watch a few online videos and call yourself an expert. Comprehensive financial planning often involves complicated calculations, a deep knowledge of rules and regulations, and a disciplined approach. These are skills that can't be picked up in an afternoon.

Although financial planning can be straightforward in some ways, it is also riddled with complications and conditions. The average everyday investor may not grasp the nuances of tax laws, for instance, or be familiar with the regulations involved with estate planning. What's more, rules and regulations often change, and financial planners must work to keep up with those changes. Because of all these factors, it can be extremely difficult for the average consumer to navigate their own financial planning. As I like to say, "You don't know what you don't know." There are many complex and less-than-obvious aspects of financial planning that the majority of consumers will not even entertain or consider, simply because they aren't aware such aspects exist.

In his book *Getting Started in Finding a Financial Advisor,** Chuck Jaffe says, "Finances and money are not like food, where failure to follow a recipe or simply using bad ingredients can leave a bad taste in your mouth. You can throw out a bad dish and forget about it by the time your next meal arrives, but bad financial mistakes will be with you for years, possibly as long as the rest of your life."

It's true. If you're not confident in your ability to master financial planning, it's far better to err on the side of caution and trust a *qualified* expert (we'll talk about what "qualified" truly means later in this book). Unfortunately, I've dealt with many clients and potential clients who are overly confident in their financial planning abilities, even though they lack essential skills and knowledge.

Years ago, a couple in their seventies approached me because they were looking for a financial advisor to help them plan for retirement. Up to that point, they had taken charge of their own financial planning but had little to show for it. They had few assets and had recently incurred a good deal of debt due to a home remodel. Their goal was to build a portfolio so they could cut themselves a check a month for the rest of their lives.

During the interview process, the couple asked several pointed questions, and I could tell they were wary of working with a financial advisor. Of course, I can't blame them, given the amount of deception in the industry, but if they had done their research, they would have known my company uses a fee-only model, believes in upholding fiduciary best practices, and prides itself on not taking commissions or charging hidden fees—all qualities that are desirable to the savvy investor.

Regardless, the couple's suspicions were apparent. At one point, they asked me, "What's been your company's typical performance?"

I didn't have an exact statistic to give them, but I pointed out that a diversified, long-term portfolio might have an expected return of

---

* Jaffe, *Getting Started in Finding a Financial Advisor.*

about 7 percent. When I relayed this information, they said, "Well, our Vanguard mutual fund is returning 8.5 percent, so why should we go with you?"

Why, indeed. To me, the answer was obvious. They were currently invested in a risky, 100-percent-stock portfolio that was narrowly diversified in one asset class of large cap domestic stocks. And they also hadn't considered the tax implications of moving their money from that portfolio. In their minds, investing was easy and straightforward—just pick the portfolio that yields the highest number—when in reality, there are dozens of other considerations involved in creating a truly effective and logical portfolio.

I can hardly blame this couple for not grasping the nuances of creating a diversified investment portfolio, but this is precisely why not everyone is cut out to take on their own financial planning.

Should Everyone Work with a Professional Financial Advisor?

The short answer to this question is "No, not everyone." The longer answer is "No, but many individuals would benefit from receiving personalized help from an experienced financial advisor." During my career, I've come to realize that people usually fit into one of the following four profiles:

1. No interest in financial planning/investing

These are the people who have no interest in finance at all. They would rather be on the golf course, baking a cake, or doing anything else besides thinking about financial planning or investing. They prefer a hands-off approach and are thus great candidates for working with a professional financial advisor.

2. No time for financial planning/investing

This group of people may be interested in DIY financial planning or investing, but they simply don't have time. These are the busy professionals, the parents raising kids or caretaking for elderly parents, the people who play an extremely active role in their communities.

Because of their busy lives, they don't have time to pay attention to financial planning and would benefit from professional assistance.

3. Lacking skills needed to master financial planning/investing

Because financial literacy is quite low in our nation (certainly not the consumer's fault), many people fall into this bucket. It's possible some of these investors could build their skill set, but that takes a good deal of time and commitment. The financial planning profession is a world filled with tricky terminology, acronyms, and subtleties, making it difficult for many people to fully grasp critical concepts. Not to mention, financial planning and investing can quickly get complicated, as we've discussed. If you have any doubts about your financial literacy or understanding, it would be prudent to hire a professional financial planner.

4. The Goldilocks types

Some investors do possess the Goldilocks combination of interest, time, and skills. They are willing to do the research, take on the responsibility, and stay disciplined. This is not an impossible combination, although I believe it's fairly rare. Sure, many folks can handle some basic financial planning, but the more specialized aspects of financial planning can require a deep level of financial acumen and industry knowledge.

Patrick Geddes,* cofounder of Aperio Group and author of *Transparent Investing*, does believe it's possible for some people to take a DIY approach. He says, "Financial planning doesn't have to be terribly complicated, but it's often challenging enough that paying for advice can be the right choice. Those willing to study up on financial planning basics or use online calculators can do this part themselves; for those who find such calculators intimidating or don't feel they have the time or confidence to master the essentials, paying a professional might be a smart move."†

---

* Patrick Geddes is the cofounder and former CEO of Aperio Group and former research director and CFO at Morningstar. He is one of the country's leading experts on after-tax investing. His book, *Transparent Investing*, is a no-nonsense guide to simple, data-proven investing.

† Geddes, interview by author, July 5, 2022.

It is certainly possible for motivated individuals with a little time on their hands to engage in personal financial planning. I would caution, however, to know your limits and admit if and when you're over your head. Even those who are just getting started with financial planning, or those with a small net worth, could benefit from consulting robo-advisors or virtual advisors. Though this route isn't foolproof (again, proceed with caution), it can provide a reasonable starting point.

When considering whether to hire a personal financial planner or trying to DIY your planning, I encourage you to think about the big picture. Financial planning is tremendously important for your future and the future of your family. It's not something to be taken lightly. If you're willing to pay a mechanic to fix your car or a plumber to fix your sink, why wouldn't you consider hiring an expert to guide you in making crucial financial decisions?

Chapter 4

The Average Investor Is Woefully Unprepared

It's an all-too-familiar story for financial advisors. A potential client comes in for an initial meeting, they share a few aspects of their financial situation, and then they ask some variation of the same question: "When can I retire?"

Some potential clients take the question a step further and ask, "Can I retire by next year?" or even "Can I retire by the end of the year?"

Many people expect a straightforward answer to these complicated questions. But the truth is, a retirement plan is multifaceted and takes a good deal of planning and consideration to put together. You might be able to take a five-minute test on the internet that tells you when you can retire, but there's no way a generic test can make a comprehensive assessment of your highly individualized life situation. We all have unique goals, different assets, and differing life circumstances, and sometimes it takes a good deal of digging by an experienced financial advisor to piece together a full picture of an investor's situation and begin developing a plan.

Not to mention, a person's financial situation tends to become more and more complicated as they age. A young adult in their early twenties has far different considerations than someone in their fifties who has worked in five different companies, has chronic health issues, owns two homes, and has kids in college. The twenty-something likely doesn't need a financial advisor to help them invest their first $10,000. With a little research, they can do it on their own. But the fifty-something with a laundry list of considerations could certainly benefit from some professional financial guidance.

In the last chapter, I profiled the three main types of people who should consider seeking help from a professional financial advisor. The last type of person I profiled—those who lack the necessary skills to master financial planning/investing—is probably the most common. That lack of knowledge can prompt people to make brash financial decisions, or it can cause them to shy away from hiring a financial planner (the process might seem daunting to them, or they may not understand the importance of hiring a professional financial planner).

Whatever their reason, many people tend to resist reaching out to a financial advisor until they've reached a breaking point. More often than not, they take a fairly hands-off approach to investing and get by with the basics (toss some money into the 401(k), set aside cash in an emergency savings account) until their circumstances change. Maybe they inherit some money. Maybe something happens to their spouse or their marriage dissolves. Or maybe they simply come to terms with the fact that they're aging and need to think about their next steps.

When lacking these external prompts—changing circumstances that require some financial planning—we tend to be a nation of procrastinators.

The Great American Delay

As a society, Americans tend to put off serious investing until we're older. Half of adults from ages eighteen to thirty-four* are not saving for retirement *at all.* And when we do begin to take retirement planning seriously, many of us greatly underestimate how much is needed to comfortably retire. This can lead to a lot of uncomfortable and, ultimately, disappointing conversations with financial advisors. If planning doesn't begin early on or isn't taken too seriously, it's very likely that the client will have some catching up to do in terms of retirement prep.

In many ways, putting off retirement planning is like ignoring a physical condition that will probably eventually require medical

---

*** Adamczyk, "This Is When People Start Saving for Retirement—And When They Actually Should."**

attention. You might be able to ignore that pain in your side for a while—and you might even treat it yourself with home remedies or over-the-counter medications—but if it keeps building and building (just as your personal financial situation grows increasingly complicated), the best course of action is to seek help from a professional.

Yet, too many Americans delay serious financial planning until they're feeling panicked (or their appendix bursts, to continue the medical analogy!). As of 2020, half of all Americans were struggling with retirement finances.*

Why are so many investors woefully unprepared?

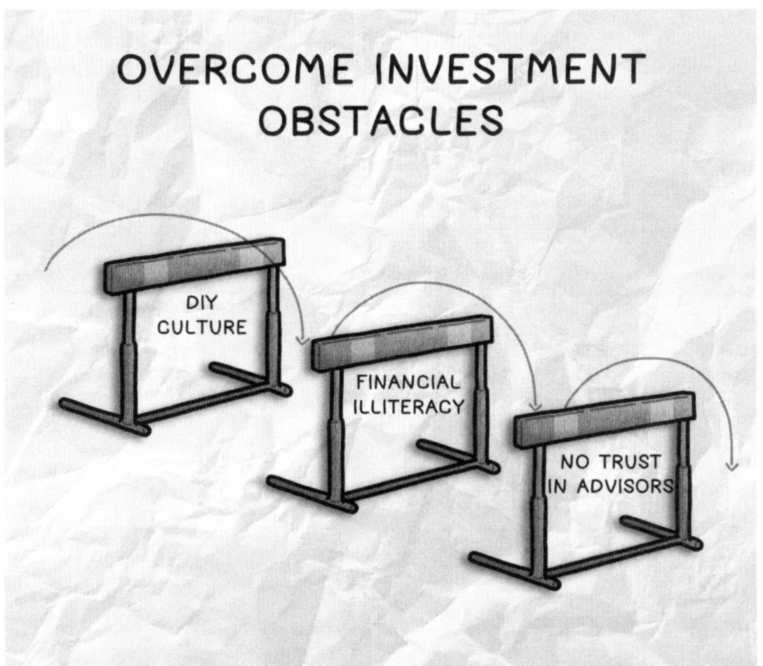

Investing Obstacles

When it comes to Americans' general lack of financial preparedness, a variety of factors are likely at play.

For one, we (as Americans) have a very DIY approach to life, and that carries over to investing (as I mentioned in chapter 3, the DIY

* Tretina, "Best Retirement Plans of 2023."

route is certainly not for everyone). We do the same thing with self-diagnosis. We tough out the pain in our side. We look up our symptoms and possible cures on WebMD. When we're finally in unbearable pain, we make an appointment to see a doctor.

If we're past the point of "DIY-ing" wealth management, we might seek help from a friend or acquaintance—*any* friend or acquaintance. Too often, I have heard stories of people turning to their daughter's soccer coach or their golfing buddy to help with some part of their investment strategy . . . just because that person claimed to have investment knowledge and happened to be a built-in acquaintance. This is frankly a lazy and dangerous approach, and it could lead to a lot of heartache and frustrations down the road. A wise investor 1) knows when DIY-ing is no longer the best course of action and 2) does their due diligence to find a reliable financial advisor.

Another reason Americans tend to delay investing/retirement planning is because of a general lack of knowledge or feeling overwhelmed or intimidated by the process. A Webster Bank survey* revealed that 36 percent of American consumers "don't know where to start" when it comes to investing.

Additionally, as previously noted, financial illiteracy is the norm. Most people do not learn about personal finance in school beyond what they might pick up from an Economics 101 class. Thus, the average investor is likely self-educated (or has received a financial "education" from questionable sources). Many people are told to contribute to a 401(k) or "invest in the stock market," but they do not necessarily grasp how these individual financial actions fit into a larger, comprehensive financial strategy.

A third reason Americans might delay turning to a financial advisor for support is that they are wary of advisors and do not necessarily trust them to act in their best interest. Unfortunately, that level of distrust *can* be warranted, and, in upcoming chapters, we'll discuss which types of financial advisors can be especially problematic or untrustworthy.

However, even though some financial advisors do not always act in

---

* Business Wire, "Webster Bank Explores Current State of Financial Inclusion with its Inaugural Financial Empowerment Study"

the client's best interest, there are plenty who do. As a savvy consumer, it is wise to do your due diligence and seek an advisor who is committed to upholding their fiduciary duty and who, preferably, works for a fee-only advising firm. We'll dive into these concepts in subsequent chapters.

Financial Advisors Can Help

Just as you would see a doctor when you're dealing with an increasingly painful medical ailment, so, too, should you enlist the help of a financial advisor when your financial situation begins to grow more complicated. Don't delay the decision! The earlier you seek financial guidance, the more freedom and flexibility you'll have when it comes to defining your financial strategy.

But why seek guidance from a financial advisor in the first place? What sets qualified advisors apart from internet articles, hobby investors, the news media, or your uncle Joe?

Quite a lot.

For one, qualified financial advisors have a wide variety of tools available to them *and* the training required to use those tools. Just as a doctor might have an X-ray or MRI machine at their disposal (and know when and how to use them), so, too, do financial advisors have analytical tools to aid in financial planning.

When creating a personalized financial strategy, advisors can take dozens of factors into account. How many children does the client have, and will any of them be attending college? Do they have a lake home they're planning to sell? Do they have a chronic health condition that significantly adds to annual expenses? Did they win the lottery? Do they enjoy taking lavish vacations? Asking these types of questions is like conducting a thorough medical examination. The doctor needs to understand the full range of the patient's symptoms in order to make an accurate diagnosis.

Another reason to turn to a financial advisor for guidance has to do with lived experience. Any experienced advisor will have dealt with a wide range of clients and financial situations. We've seen all manner of circumstances and have had to navigate many tricky cases. Because of this depth of experience, it's possible we will suggest an investing approach or propose a solution to a financial query that you may not have considered. Sometimes it's difficult to ask hyper-specific investing questions online, but financial advisors field these types of questions all the time and can usually come up with a satisfactory solution.

Lastly, when you call upon a financial advisor who upholds a fiduciary standard of care, that is similar to seeing a doctor who adheres to the Hippocratic oath. To put it simply, the client and their interests come first. By upholding a fiduciary standard of care, a financial advisor is duty-bound to treat their clients with the same fastidiousness and care that they would their own family members. When searching for financial guidance, be sure to seek those who are committed to this highest level of financial integrity.

Chapter 5
Why Is Wealth Management a Problematic Term?

Wealth management is a term that seems impressive on the surface. It sounds important and official. You'd probably work with someone whose business card read "wealth manager" over someone who billed themselves as an insurance salesperson. After all, someone who manages wealth for a living *must* be trustworthy, right?

Maybe . . . but maybe not.

Someone who purports to be a wealth manager *might* be a perfectly honest and capable individual, or they could be more concerned with turning a profit than emphasizing excellent client care. A person or company could provide any number of services—from estate planning to life insurance sales—and claim to be practicing wealth management. Why is that?

Ultimately, the reason wealth management services are so varied and disparate is because the term itself doesn't have teeth. No one is regulating its usage or stipulating the requirements to become a wealth manager. You don't have to pass an exam, take an oath, or adhere to a certain set of guidelines. And that can mean trouble for a lot of people who are seeking legitimate financial planning assistance. Before we dive into the potentially damaging effects of overusing the title "wealth manager," let's rewind and discuss some basics, starting with defining this ubiquitous term.

What Is Wealth Management?

Due to its nebulous nature, it is difficult to pin down an exact definition of wealth management. I have seen it defined as:

> *"the process of putting together a financial plan that supports you in achieving your life goals."* —Investec*

> *"a kind of financial advisory service for accredited investors and other people with high net worths."* —The Balance†

> *"an investment advisory service that combines other financial services to address the needs of affluent clients."* —Investopedia‡

> *"the science of solving/enhancing [one's] financial situation."* —Forbes§

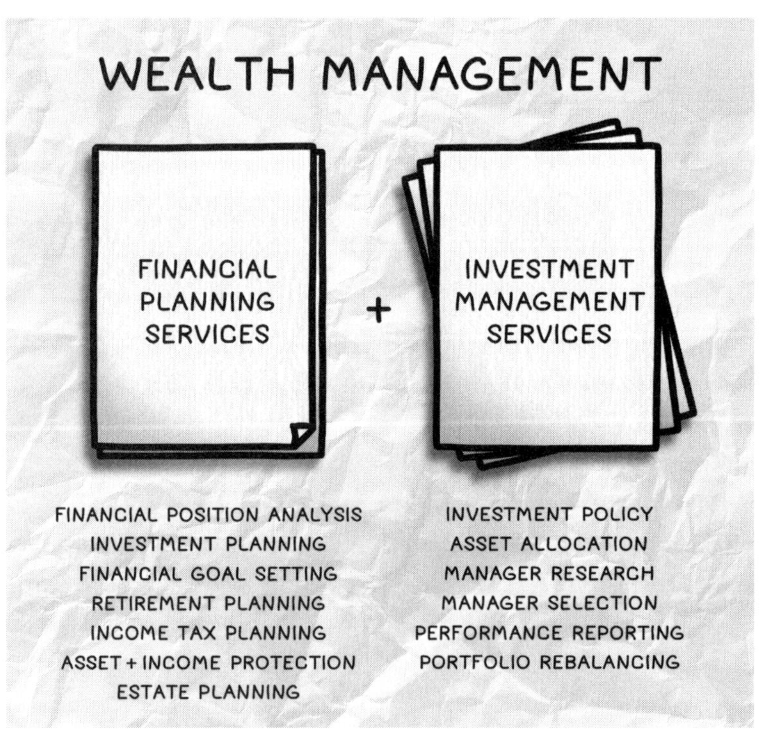

---

* Investec Wealth & Investment, "What Is Wealth Management?"

† Lemke, "What Is Wealth Management?"

‡ Ganti, "Wealth Management: What It Is and What Wealth Managers Charge."

§ Prince, "What Is Wealth Management?"

Many of these definitions are vague and not terribly helpful. Additionally, they do not necessarily agree. Is wealth management for anyone or just for high-net-worth clients? Is it about putting together a financial plan, improving one's financial situation, or simply "addressing the needs" of affluent clients?

When I think of traditional wealth management, I tend to divide the concept into two areas: *financial planning* and *investment management.*

Financial planning typically involves creating a personalized plan for a client to fit their unique needs and circumstances. Comprehensive financial planning services will include financial position analysis, investment planning, financial goal-setting, retirement planning, income tax planning, asset and income protection, and estate planning. Many people can benefit from hiring a qualified professional to aid in financial planning.

Investment management, on the other hand, involves the implementation of financial planning. Investment management services will include investment policy development, asset allocation strategy, investment manager due diligence research, investment manager selection, performance reporting, and portfolio rebalancing. In many cases, once someone has worked with a financial advisor to create an individualized financial plan, that individual will implement the plan on their own. They will buy the prescribed index funds, set up the necessary bank transfers, and so on. They will then monitor their portfolio on their own, in between meetings with their financial advisor.

These tasks, however, can be delegated to an investment manager/wealth manager. Because these services are costly, most people who hire a wealth manager are fairly wealthy. They've worked for decades, have several million saved, and simply want to take a hands-off approach to their finances.

So, if we're using my definition, it would be this: a wealth manager oversees both financial planning and investment management for high-net-worth individuals.

That doesn't sound so bad, right? Sure. Wealth managers have their place (my own company provides wealth management services to high-net-worth clients). Although most individuals do not need to hire someone to manage their investments, some individuals can certainly benefit from this service. It takes one more task off a person's plate and allows them to pursue other interests. This setup necessitates a good deal of trust, since a wealth manager handles many aspects of a person's finances, from implementation, to monitoring, to making necessary adjustments.

This setup is fine, and it works. However, problems arise when people *claim* to be wealth managers but have ulterior motives (such as profiting as much as possible) or provide services that fall well outside the above definition of wealth management.

How the Term Wealth Management Causes Trouble

Unfortunately, people can (and do) play fast and loose with the terms *wealth management* and *wealth manager.* A banker selling proprietary products might call themselves a wealth manager. An insurance salesperson could conceivably call themselves a wealth manager. So could an investment banker/stockbroker. All of these occupations might technically deal with "managing wealth," but they certainly do not fit most definitions you'll find online.

Why would a private banker at a major bank, for instance, call themselves a wealth manager? The reason is simple, really. This person wants to "soften" what they are actually doing. Instead of enrolling you in proprietary banking products, suddenly they're "managing your wealth." It's true that banking products relate to wealth, but is it fair to call a banker a wealth manager when they *really* can only offer one set of products, despite your financial circumstances?

To me, that's stretching the definition. It's like asking a Yoplait representative to sell you "the yogurt best suited to your tastes." Do you think they would ever point you toward a Dannon product or Chobani, even if you would probably prefer those products?

That's why, in my opinion, this title has become little more than a marketing term. It is used as an umbrella concept, loosely tied to wealth and finances. People take advantage of this prestigious-sounding title to falsely position themselves as qualified financial advisors. For instance, your former college roommate might label themselves as a "wealth manager" and arrange a meeting with you to discuss your fiscal future. At the end of the meeting, they offer one financial solution: a life insurance package. In the end, "wealth management" was nothing more than a guise to sell a single product.

It is worth mentioning that anyone who is in the business of providing investment advice does need to register as an investment adviser (the SEC spells this term with *-er* instead of *-or*), no matter what title appears on your business card. Michael Kitces,* a self-proclaimed "Chief Financial Planning Nerd," explains it this way: "The requirements to register as an investment adviser are based ultimately on what you *do*, and what kind of business you are engaged in. If you are engaged in the business of providing ongoing investment advice for compensation, you have to register as an investment adviser. Technically, there are three parts to the test of whether you're giving investment advice that would trigger registration. You have to be: Providing investment advice; As a business; For compensation."†

This definition becomes muddy, however, when so-called financial advisors (or wealth managers or investment advisors/advisers) are considered salespeople rather than true financial planners. Pam Krueger,‡ investor advocate and founder of Wealthramp, says, "Only independent registered advisers are regulated—and legally held to a fiduciary standard—by the SEC or the state. Those employed by a brokerage firm are not Registered Investment Advisers, but are (Series 7) licensed sales representatives or 'brokers' on behalf of Merrill Lynch, Raymond James, etc. Brokers do not work directly for the client; instead, as employees of the brokerage firm, they earn commissions to open new accounts and sell investment products for the brokerage firm. Under this model, whenever a brokerage rep is recommending an investment, the client's best interests

* Michael Kitces is the "Chief Financial Planning Nerd" of his company, Kitces.com. He is an experienced financial planner with many designations, including MSFS, MTAX, CFP®, CLU®, and ChFC®. He is passionate about learning everything he can about financial planning, and he passes much of that information on to the public through his *Nerd's Eye View* blog.

† Kitces, "Financial Adviser Vs Advisor—What's the Difference?"

‡ Pam Krueger is the founder and CEO of Wealthramp, a consumer-focused company which specializes in matching individual investors with thoroughly vetted fee-only fiduciaries. As an investor advocate and educator for over twenty-five years, she has delivered her message through several different mediums, including as a cohost of the popular Emmy-award-nominated PBS series *MoneyTrack*.

may not necessarily be the priority because the brokerage rep is financially incentivized to make a sale versus provide advice. The brokerage business model is a sales model. It is not designed as an advice model."*

Too often, I have worked with customers who have been duped by salespeople claiming to be wealth managers or financial advisors. To me, this is an egregious misuse of these titles, and it does a disservice to both the consumer *and* those who are *actually* engaged in financial planning and investment management. Unfortunately, the US government has no interest in regulating these job titles (why would it when it benefits from brokerage firms' lobbying efforts?), so it is up to the little guys—mainly consumers and consumer advocates—to build awareness around the misleading language brokerage firms use to discuss what their employees do.

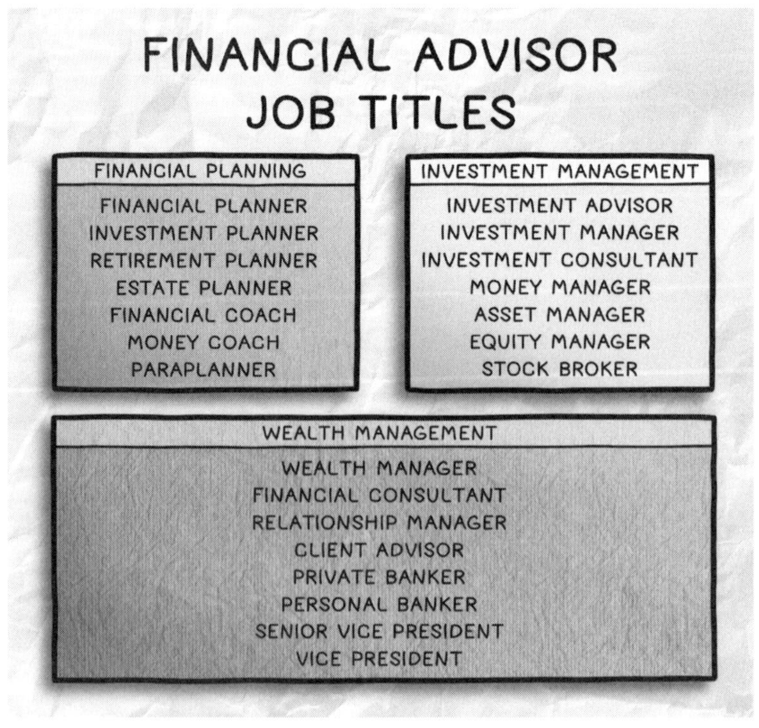

* Krueger, interview by author, August 7, 2023.

What Can We Do?

To combat the widespread overuse and misuse of the term *wealth management*, education is key. Consumers can take an active role in educating themselves on the ins and outs of wealth management (including whether or not it makes sense to pursue this service). Before agreeing to work with a purported wealth manager, it pays to conduct a little research into both the company and the individual. Look for transparent language and a clear commitment to a fiduciary standard of care. Reviews on third-party sites can also be helpful for determining the integrity of the wealth manager and the company they represent. Brian Thorp,* founder and CEO of Wealthtender, Inc., says that new SEC regulations (2022) permit "advisors to solicit client testimonials that can be shared on certain SEC-compliant online review websites (e.g., Wealthtender) that provide important disclosures to help consumers make more informed and educated hiring decisions." He goes on to speak directly to consumers, suggesting, "turn to online directories where you're empowered to filter by credentials, compensation model, and read online reviews to identify at least three fiduciary advisors you commit to interviewing before you make a final hiring decision."†

Financial advisors can also take an active role in education. I encourage individual investors to seek financial advisors who care enough to impart essential knowledge to their clients, including taking the time to explain what their company's version of wealth management entails *and* being candid about the fact that few people require this level of money management. Trustworthy financial advisors will also strive for clarity and transparency in every aspect of their business—everything from client contracts to website mission statements should be clear, accessible, and straightforward.

On a larger scale, consumers deserve a little more protection when it comes to investment management. Currently, independent regulatory agencies such as the US Securities and Exchange Commission (SEC), the Financial Industry Regulatory Authority (FINRA), and

* Brian Thorp is the founder and CEO of Wealthtender, Inc., a digital marketing platform that helps boost financial advisors' rank in search engine results.

† Thorp, interview by author, August 12, 2023.

US state governments regulate certain aspects of the investment industry. The SEC monitors companies that provide investment advice, while FINRA regulates broker-dealers, capital acquisition brokers, and funding portals. State governments monitor investment advisors who manage less than $100 million in client assets. However, the reach of these organizations and entities is not wide enough to protect consumers from so-called wealth managers who are less interested in managing wealth than they are in turning a profit.

Not to mention, it's difficult to impose new regulations on big banks and insurance agencies. These institutions have deep pockets, and they use some of that capital to sway politicians and lobby Congress on their behalf.

As an optimist, I *do* believe things are changing (albeit at a glacial pace!). If our nation could crack down on the mammoth tobacco industry, we can eventually increase protections for investors. In the meantime, it is imperative for consumers to do their research and seek financial advisors who focus on their clients, provide salient, straightforward advice, and are committed to a fiduciary standard of care.

Chapter 6

The Hidden Costs of Free Advice

It is said there's no such thing as a free lunch, and that's doubly true when it comes to financial advice. Plenty of people and companies dole out "free" information, but that information can be tainted by hidden agendas or bias or unsupported by reliable evidence. Additionally, free financial advice usually fails to consider people's highly personalized situations. Investing, after all, takes on an entirely different flavor for someone who is twenty-five years old with $10,000 than someone who is fifty years old with $10 million.

Yet, during my decades as a financial advisor, I have heard countless stories of people making major financial decisions based on a magazine article or advice from their uncle. Recently I talked with a woman who was persuaded by a gold salesman a few years ago to transfer her broadly diversified retirement account with a financial advisory firm to invest exclusively in a portfolio of gold bullion and gold collectible coins. The investor pointed to multiple websites that explained the risks of the stock markets and provided convincing evidence that gold is the only asset that will preserve wealth in the coming economic downturn. After a year of buyer's remorse, the woman has decided that maybe the advice to put 100 percent of a more than a million-dollar retirement portfolio into one asset class (gold) might have been misguided.

Sometimes the decisions to follow free advice turn out fine, but too often they turn into cautionary tales. And that's a shame, because good advice *does* exist and is widely available, but it's not always free. In this chapter, I will discuss the various sources of financial advice available to the public and illuminate some of the reasons these sources may be less than trustworthy. Although it *is* possible to encounter quality advice on TikTok or from your golfing buddies, it can be incredibly difficult to separate the wheat from the chaff.

Media

Today, more than ever, investors must be cautious with advice gleaned from the media, including social media. Anyone can create a YouTube channel or start an online advice column, and the popularity of content creators often has less to do with quality of information than it does with entertainment. And when social media is, in essence, a popularity contest, misinformation abounds. The problem is so pervasive that the SEC decided to release an investor alert* about advice gleaned through social media, which warns about fraudsters, misleading information, and market manipulation.

But false or misleading information is not limited to social media platforms. Other traditional media outlets are breeding grounds for iffy financial advice. Television, magazines, and newspapers are inundated with advertisements whose primary intention is to generate profit, *not* deliver impartial guidance. What's more, it can be difficult to parse the ads from the articles when publications allow advertisers to blend their "sponsored content" with normal content. This practice, known as native advertising, has raised ethical concerns because readers (or viewers, in the case of television) do not always know when they're seeing an ad. For an example, a company that sells massage chairs might write an article called "The Top 5 Ways to Cut Stress" and include its chair in the list. Is the massage chair *really* one of the top five ways to cut stress? The company has no incentive to tell you otherwise.

When you're scrutinizing sources of information delivered by the media, it's a good idea to ask yourself who stands to make money. Who sponsored or produced the content? Who might benefit from it?

Keep in mind that even if you do find unbiased, evidence-based content in a newspaper or YouTube channel, the advice may not fit your unique financial situation. It's tough to deliver one-size-fits-all content in a brief article or news segment.

---

* US Securities and Exchange Commission, "Updated Investor Alert: Social Media and Investing—Stock Rumors."

Friends and Family

When it comes to financial advice, I'd like to think that our friends, family members, and coworkers usually have our best interests at heart. They want to see us succeed and prosper, and they (probably) do not have any apparent conflicts of interest. However, numerous problems can arise from taking advice from family and friends.

For one, your acquaintances may not be aware of your precise financial situation. In polite conversation, we typically steer clear of talking about personal finance, which means your cousin Bill or the members of your gardening club probably do not know how much you have in your bank account or your 401(k). And that's just the tip of the iceberg. A number of other factors (personal debt/loans, costly health treatments, your mortgage, childcare expenses, target retirement date) comprise your personal financial situation and help define the best path forward. In normal circumstances, your friends, coworkers, and extended family members will not necessarily be privy to this information.

And then there are those who purport to be financial "experts" and love doling out advice. They might have found an investing method that works well for them and, thus, believe it will work well for everyone. Sometimes, these people are simply seeking validation for their decisions. If they invested in a particular stock, it is validating—and makes them feel safer—if others do the same. Strength in numbers!

Some individual investors will go beyond taking advice from their friends and actually *hire* a friend or acquaintance as their primary financial advisor. Larry Swedroe, head of financial and economic research at Buckingham Wealth Partners, explains why this can be a disastrous decision: "[Individual investors will] continue depending on the financial advisor even when their investments perform poorly. They won't fire them because they're friends. The truth is that they're only your friend because they're making commissions or other fees off of you."*

Unfortunately, I have worked with many clients who received faulty guidance from acquaintances who claimed to have an inside scoop or

---

*** Stotz, "ISMS 27: Larry Swedroe—Familiar Doesn't Make It Safe and You're Not Playing with the House's Money."**

access to "expert" financial guidance. The results have ranged from mildly annoying to disastrous.

On the disastrous end of the spectrum, I once talked with a client whose buddies advised him to pull all his investments from the stock market immediately. They claimed the market was going to tank and the smartest move was to convert all assets to cash. Additionally, this client had been reading a "doom and gloom" online newsletter which predicted an 80 percent decline in the stock market due to excessive government debt in the United States. Driven by fear, the client converted all his investments to cash.

This was the year before Donald Trump was elected president of the United States, and the stock market rallied over 40 percent in less than two years. Since then, the market has had its ups and downs, but it has continued a steady upward trajectory and continues to set new record highs. With such a strong performance, the client would likely have to buy back into the market at higher prices. Plus, there's the matter of pride. If he did decide to buy back in, that would be an admission of his previous poor decision-making, and no one likes to eat crow.

Financial Advisors and Companies

Another prominent source of financial advice is, of course, financial institutions and advisors. In 2021, 38 percent of Americans, or some 125 million people, used the services of a financial advisor.* While that's not the majority, it is certainly a significant portion of the population. On the surface, this source of financial information seems far more reliable than the media or friends/family. After all, we tend to share sensitive financial information with advisors that we do not normally divulge to friends and family. That means they are better equipped to put together a personalized investing plan (something we would never get from a random newspaper article, an online video, or your coworker Tina). However, financial institutions and advisors are not immune to bias and conflicts of interest, especially if their fee structure is based on commissions.

---

* Statista Research Department, "Share of Americans Who Work with a Financial Advisor in 2022."

As I've discussed in previous chapters, this type of commission-based compensation structure incentivizes advisors to push certain products, which can lead to putting their own interests before the client's. Individual investors must keep on their toes because "professional" financial advisors come in many forms and flavors. Someone calling themselves a financial advisor may also be an insurance agent, a securities broker, a bank representative, or a hybrid advisor. Instead, it is best to seek financial advisory firms that are fee-only (not fee-based or commission-based), transparent, and committed to fiduciary duty. If you're uncertain of what these terms mean, hang in there! We'll discuss them in detail in later chapters.

In addition to paying attention to firms' compensation/incentivization structures, it's a good idea to be wary of financial institutions that offer free services or guidance. Ask yourself how the company is making money if they purport to be 100 percent free. How do they pay for employees, an office building, office supplies, and marketing? These companies are not running charities, so they *have* to make money somehow. Companies such as Robinhood and Charles Schwab have recently been charged with misleading customers and violating fiduciary duty. This, unfortunately, illuminates the true cost of "free" services.

When it comes to wealth management, expect to pay in one way or another. Free advice may be associated with conflicts of interest at best or be downright wrong at worst. Savvy investors understand that the maxim "there's no such thing as a free lunch" holds true when it comes to obtaining quality financial advice and guidance.

Chapter 7
Avoid Bias and Protect Yourself from Wall Street's Media Propaganda

If an individual investor is searching for a financial advisor, where will they go? More than likely, they'll turn to the internet and conduct a search for the "top financial advisors near me" or "best financial planners." When the search results pop up, they might breeze past specific firms in favor of a more "neutral" source—an article from a major news outlet, a column by a financial writer, a database of financial planners, or a report from a financial publication. As they scroll through these articles, the same names—or, at least, the same companies—might keep cropping up. The investor may think, "That's a good sign; clearly these are the top performers in the industry."

But are they the top performers or merely the top spenders? Are these the most competent and trustworthy financial advisory firms and advisors or simply the ones with the largest marketing budgets? We established in the last chapter that it is not always prudent to obtain investing advice from the media. Let's look at this source of advice from a different perspective and examine how Wall Street leverages the media to its advantage.

The Media Can Be Bought

At this point, few people will probably be surprised to learn that much of the news media—including financial media outlets—can be bought. Though the average consumer might, in theory, be aware of this, they may not realize the extent of the deception or know who to trust. It can be difficult to discern between factual articles and sponsored content. And it can be hard to know how a media company went about compiling lists of "top financial planners" or "best investment companies."

Financial writer/commentator Bob Veres* discusses how sponsored content can appear under the guise of objective reporting in an article he wrote for the *Inside Information* newsletter (it's worth subscribing if you are a financial planner seeking succinct, insightful financial planning guidance). Veres points out that every single financial advisor in a recently published "top 40 under 40" list hailed from a wirehouse brokerage firm (a broker-dealer with multiple branches that provide a variety of services). The same was true in a recent Barron's "top 100 financial advisors" list.

How were these financial planners selected? And why did thousands of financial planners in independent financial advisory firms fail to make the lists? It *could* be that the wirehouse brokers really are better and brighter, but I highly doubt that's the case. Far more likely, the big brokerage firms backing these brokerage-firm-licensed financial advisors are doling out thousands—if not millions—of dollars to appear in big-name publications and at the top of "best of" lists.

On this topic, Veres says, "Firms with enormous profit margins, who are gouging their clients and fighting a fierce lobbying battle NOT to have to be held to a standard of putting their clients' interests first, will inevitably have a lot more marketing money lying around than would a firm that charges reasonable fees and recommends investments with tight expense ratios." He goes on to say, "There's a reason why the brokerage firms can advertise on national TV."†

In other words, big brokerage firms have marketing budgets that are many, many, many times larger than those of independent financial advisors. This gives them an advantage when it comes to shaping their public image and influencing the media. They can hire public

---

* Bob Veres is an editor and publisher of the *Inside Information* interactive guide to trends and innovations in the profession. He is a professional speaker and the author of *The New Profession* and four novels.

† Veres, interview by author, June 2, 2022.

relations firms to create positive press releases and secure media appearances for their people. They can also buy advertising space in financial publications or pay to sponsor articles.

Consume with Caution

It's worth pointing out that not *all* media articles are false or misleading. Financial writer Wendy J. Cook* published a poignant article on the topic titled "Who Is 'the Media'?" In this article, she sums up the media's relationship with and portrayal of the financial industry by eloquently stating, "Among the financial press, you'll find an ocean of noise, islands of common sense, and rare voices of reason that rise clearly above the din."†

But how do you find those "islands of common sense"? Where do you look?

If you're unsure if you can trust a financial publication, do a little research to determine the publication's owner and its funding sources. A publication that is owned by a large corporation or funded by a financial firm may have a bias toward promoting its own interests. Additionally, look for articles that are written by reporters rather than sponsored content (sponsored content is usually labeled as such). It's also a good idea to read a few different sources to get a well-rounded perspective. Remember to consume financial news with caution and use critical thinking to separate fact from fiction.

How to Protect Yourself as an Investor

So how can individual investors protect themselves? For one, approach all articles and reports from major news outlets and financial publications with a healthy dose of skepticism. Question the sources of their information and be aware of the marketing tactics of big Wall Street banks and brokerage firms. Additionally, it's a good idea to look for

---

* Wendy J. Cook offers writing, editing, and related services to fee-only, evidence-based financial advisors through her company, Wendy J. Cook Communications. She is an advocate for the inherent value of a fiduciary, evidence-based advisory model.

† Cook, "Who Is 'the Media'?"

independent sources of information, such as blogs written by financial experts or forums where investors can share their experiences with different financial advisors.

Keep in mind, not all journalists or media outlets are acting maliciously or trying to deceive you. Sometimes, these news outlets profile active or risky investing simply because it's interesting. As journalist Robin Powell articulates in a recent *Money Marketing* article, "Indexing, frankly, isn't much of a story." He goes on to say that readers "have to beware [of] the inherent conflicts of interest in investment journalism, and remember that the voice with nothing to sell is often the hardest to hear."*

Considering journalists are often on the hunt for compelling, edgy stories, it may be best to skip the news media entirely when seeking a financial advisor and, instead, use a trustworthy search database to find a suitable fee-only fiduciary (I will go over several of these databases in chapter 14). Fee-only fiduciaries are financial advisors who are legally bound to act in their clients' best interests. These advisors typically charge a straightforward fee for their services, and they do not accept commissions or bonuses or charge hidden fees. Fiduciaries are also subject to strict ethical standards, which require them to disclose any potential conflicts of interest.

If you do choose to read financial publications, take the information you consume with a grain of salt. You likely won't have time to research every single publication you read or look into how each reporter obtained their information, *but* you can use critical thinking and common sense. Ask yourself: Who has something to gain from this article's publication? Who may benefit monetarily?

As an investor seeking financial planning guidance, it's wise to be cautious of the marketing tactics of big Wall Street banks and brokerage firms. Their marketing budgets are many times larger than independent financial advisors, giving them an advantage when it comes to shaping their public image and influencing the media. When consuming financial news, it's important to question the sources of information and read multiple sources to get a well-rounded perspective.

---

* Powell, "Robin Powell: The Voice with Nothing to Sell Is Hardest to Hear."

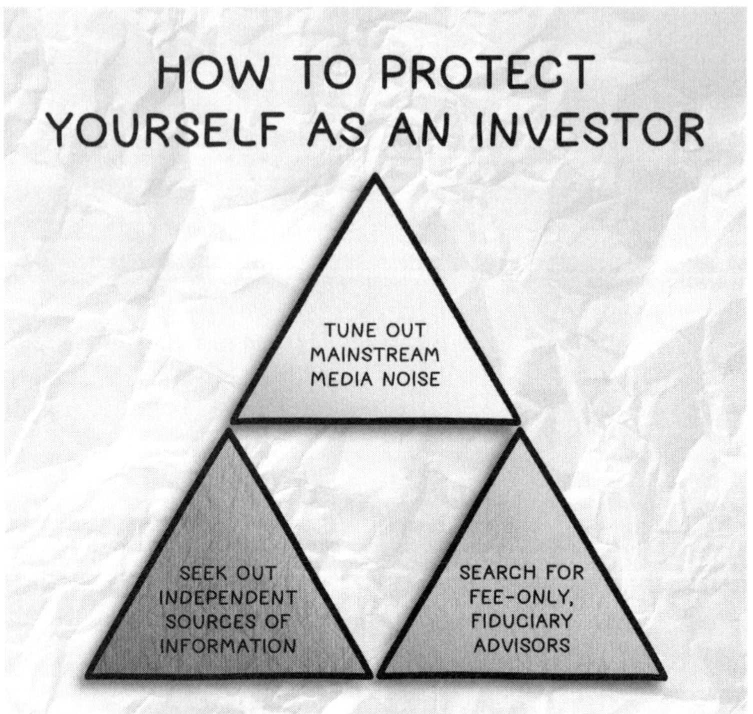

To me, all this information boils down to three key recommendations:

1. Tune out the noise from the mainstream media.
2. Opt for independent sources of information.
3. When you're searching for a financial advisor, place your trust in fee-only fiduciaries who are legally bound to act in their clients' best interests.

Beyond those three straightforward recommendations, it's a good idea to pay attention, question articles' sources, and seek guidance from a variety of trusted resources. When it comes to consuming information from the media, the more you practice discretion and actively explore the motives for the content, the easier it will become to spot the wolves in sheep's clothing.

Chapter 8

Financial Advice: Recognizing Conflicts of Interest

In the US, about half of all medical doctors accept some form of payment or gifts from pharmaceutical or medical device companies. If you suspect these payments influence doctors' recommendations to patients, you are correct. The results of thirty-six individual studies all showed the same thing: "industry cash influences how doctors treat their patients."* The same type of influence affects politics (through lobbying), magazines and newspapers (through sponsored content), and social media influencers (through paid sponsorships). It also, unfortunately, affects the financial industry.

When financial advisors are offered incentives—commissions, bonuses, paid vacations—in exchange for promoting a specific product, their lens becomes clouded. Even if they don't intend to, they will likely be swayed by those incentives. That was the case for me when I worked for a commission-based brokerage company. Even though I tried to act in my clients' best interests, there was always company-wide pressure to push certain investment products. And that created an inherent conflict of interest.

How Can You Recognize Potential Conflicts of Interest?

For the average investor, the signs may not be terribly obvious. Companies might expertly conceal fees or obfuscate their sponsors.

---

* Mitchell and Korenstein, "Drug Companies' Payments and Gifts Affect Physicians' Prescribing. It's Time to Turn Off the Spigot."

What, then, is the everyday investor to do? I recommend taking the following five warning signs into consideration:

1. Unclear sources of revenue

Where does a company make its money? What are the sources? With fee-only wealth management firms, income is generated through its clients' fees (often charged by the hour or taken as a percentage of the client's assets under management). For other financial companies, the answer isn't always so simple. Companies could generate income through commissions, by charging fees for buying or selling securities, by earning interest on clients' uninvested cash, or a combination of many different revenue streams.

The investing app Robinhood has gained popularity as a commission-free service with no minimums for investing. While that might be true, doesn't it have to make money somehow? After all, it *is* a publicly traded company and, thus, beholden to its investors (who are counting on its continued growth). So, how does it do it? Mainly, it sells customers' orders to high-frequency trading firms (firms that use powerful computer programs to facilitate numerous orders in milliseconds). This controversial practice relies on sophisticated computers and complex algorithms, which can edge out the average trader or cause extreme fluctuations in the market if an algorithm is triggered. The practice itself is not illegal, but removing humans from trading and relying solely on machines can cause plenty of trouble. For Robinhood, that trouble culminated in the Financial Industry Regulatory Authority (FINRA) slapping it with a $70 million fine because "algorithmic bots had approved thousands of customers for options trading, even if those users weren't eligible or had red flags in their account that would have prevented them from taking part in the advanced trading strategy."* This is the largest penalty that FINRA has doled out to date—a clear sign that Robinhood was not acting within the best interest of its customers.

The lesson here is to be cautious with companies whose revenue sources are unclear. An honest company has nothing to hide.

---

* Davis and Taube, "Robinhood Review 2023: Pros, Cons and How It Compares."

2. Vague language or hidden terms

When it comes to avoiding companies with clear conflicts of interest, clarity is key. Does the company clearly outline its fees, terms, and the cost of its services? Or is all of that buried in dense legal jargon in the terms of services? As explained previously, if financial advice is advertised as free, be wary! The company has to make money somehow, and those sources of revenue are likely hidden away in thirty-page user agreements.

3. An offer or performance that's too good to be true

In 2008, one of the most elaborate Ponzi schemes in history collapsed, and its mastermind, Bernie Madoff, was brought down with it. For years, Madoff hoodwinked investors into believing they were making consistently high annual returns by investing with his "exclusive" wealth management company, Bernard L. Madoff Investment Securities, LLC. Madoff attracted throngs of investors with his high returns and image of exclusivity and by earning trust and respect in the financial community. However, his clients' assets were not invested in a variety of blue-chip stocks (as he claimed) but were instead funneled into a single bank account, which Madoff could access at will. In the meantime, he funded investors' payouts through capital gained from new clients. The scheme fell to pieces during the Great Recession of 2008 when investors began trying to draw on their investments and, eventually, Madoff's sons reported his activities to authorities.

The Madoff Ponzi scheme was a hard lesson for the many investors who were, collectively, defrauded out of tens of billions of dollars. The crux of the lesson is this: if something seems too good to be true, it probably is. In the case of Bernie Madoff, investors were consistently realizing higher-than-average returns, even when the market was down. This is an extreme example, but it applies to other situations as well. Those who claim "exclusive" or "insider" knowledge that isn't verifiable are likely spinning yarns and are ultimately looking out for their *own* interests (making a profit) above yours.

4. Commissions/personal stakes

If a company or individual stands to gain some form of compensation through selling a particular product, that is a clear sign of a conflict of interest. Brian Hamburger,* chief counsel at Hamburger Law Firm, LLC, says, "Quite simply, humans tend to demonstrate bias toward those who are paying them. It's been said that if you're not paying for it, you become the product. And that's why investors that seek advice should always insist on being the sole form of compensation that their advisor receives."†

Commissions can occur in wealth management or brokerage firms (incentivizing teams with sales contests or pushing them to sell a certain product), as well as in other financial institutions. Bankers might receive a commission for opening a certain number of accounts in a given quarter. Insurance salespeople earn commissions for any new clients they enroll in their company's program. Credit card representatives earn bonuses for getting new members to sign up for their card. The list goes on.

A few years ago, Wells Fargo found itself in hot water because of the widespread fraudulent behavior of its employees. Bankers had opened approximately 1.5 million unauthorized bank accounts and issued 565,000 credit cards without customer consent.‡ Why? Because they were incentivized to do so. Wells Fargo offered quarterly bonuses if, and only if, the bankers met the company's ever-increasing standards. To receive their payout, the bankers had to provide a certain number of "solutions" to customers each quarter. "Solutions" could consist of any combination of new bank accounts, credit cards, lines of credit, loans, etc. As long as the quota was met, the banker received their bonus. Driven by this monetary incentive and sky-high company standards, desperate bankers began opening bogus accounts.

Although this questionable behavior may be difficult to detect, a savvy consumer will recognize when someone is pushing a product.

---

* Brian Hamburger is an attorney, business strategist, public speaker, and a counselor to "the country's preeminent wealth managers." He is the president and chief executive officer of MarketCounsel, as well as the chief counsel at Hamburger Law Firm, LLC.

† Hamburger, interview by author, August 9, 2023.

‡ Corkery, "Wells Fargo Fined $185 Million for Fraudulently Opening Accounts."

If a banker is prompting you to open a second or third bank account when you've already said no, you have to wonder, "What's in it for them?"

Additionally, if you're working with anyone who earns a commission—from used car salespeople to those selling insurance—it's a good idea to question their true motives.

5. No accreditation

Medical doctors are required to take board certification exams every few years to prove their medical expertise meets the current standards. Though the process has recently been called into question, the intentions of medical boards are valid. These exams aim to verify whether a physician is as knowledgeable and up-to-date as they should be. And that can, quite literally, mean the difference between life or death for a patient.

Financial advisors are not necessarily required to carry specific certificates (although various securities licenses are necessary for selling certain investment products), but it is telling if they *do* choose to pursue accreditation.

A **Certified Financial Planner®** (**CFP®**) designation is earned through rigorous coursework, professional experience (at least six thousand hours), and an in-depth exam. Ethics is a core pillar of the coursework and is emphasized throughout the process.

An internationally recognized **Chartered Financial Analyst®** (**CFA®**) designation is earned through intensive coursework, hands-on experience, and a three-part exam. Adherence to ethical guidelines is also part of earning one's CFA®.

Personal Financial Specialist (**PFS™**) accreditation, sponsored by the American Institute of Certified Public Accountants®, is yet another financial industry designation that indicates a high level of commitment to education, ethics, and experience. Though this accreditation is geared toward accountants, it is meant to expand participants' knowledge base to include financial planning and wealth management.

The **Accredited Investment Fiduciary®** (**AIF®**) designation is issued by Fi360 and demonstrates that the individual has achieved the organization's educational, ethical, and competence standards, in addition to committing to a fiduciary standard of care which prioritizes the client.

If your financial advisor has earned any of these accreditations, this usually demonstrates a high level of interest in the field and care for the customer. Look for one or more certifications in addition to a commitment to the fiduciary standard of care. This fiduciary commitment requires that a financial advisor act solely in the client's best interest when offering personalized financial advice. Many financial advisors, me included, take this commitment seriously.

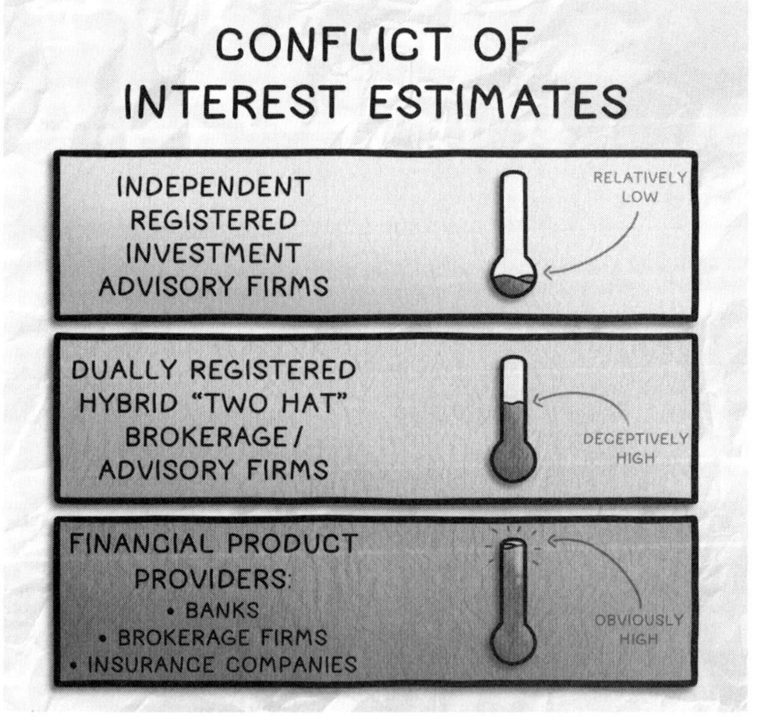

When it comes to obtaining financial advice, it is imperative to look for any conflicts of interest. Is the person across the table paid a commission? Do they have a personal financial stake in your choices? Are you staring down an offer that seems too good to be true? Are the terms of service opaque or hidden in pages of legalese? Know the warning signs and be on the lookout for conflicts of interest.

Chapter 9

Searching for a Financial Advisor? Try the Process of Elimination

Picture yourself in a grocery store. You've grabbed a bag of tortilla chips, and now you're on the hunt for salsa. You step over to the salsa section and find yourself staring at thirty different varieties. There are green salsas and red. There's original or chunky. They come in mild, medium, hot, and set-your-mouth-on-fire varieties. And then you must consider the brands, the prices, the size of the jars. If you want to compare every feature of the salsas, you'll be there for hours. What do you do?

Mostly likely, you make a gut decision and pick the first salsa that seems appealing. You might know what you like from experience, or you might simply pick whatever looks appealing at the time. Whatever the case, you probably don't overthink it. Doing so would make every trip to the grocery store a nightmare (just think of the cereal aisle!).

People often rely on this type of qualitative decision-making to move through life. It's how we decide what to wear in the morning, what to eat for breakfast, or even which pen to use when signing a document. Decision-making based on emotion is largely governed by a part of the brain called the limbic system, and when this region is damaged or inaccessible, daily life can become overwhelming. In one famous case, part of a man's brain was removed during neurosurgery, which damaged his emotional processing center and turned him into something akin to *Star Trek*'s emotionless Mr. Spock. And that affected his decision-making abilities. As *Harvard Business Review* explains, "In effect, he was doing the organizational task too well, considering every possible option—but at the expense of achieving the larger goal."*

It is, perhaps, because of our natural impulse (and daily need) to make "gut-based" decisions that we, as a species, do not always do our due diligence when it comes to major decisions. We might select a new physician or dentist based off the recommendation of a friend, or we might choose a mechanic because they offer a cheap oil change with every visit. Sometimes our quick decisions don't make much of a difference, but other times they can have enormous, lasting effects.

In the financial industry, I have witnessed the enduring effects of quick decision-making time and again. When investors put little thought into selecting a financial advisor, they may end up paying for services they don't need, receiving flawed advice, or working with someone who is more concerned about sales than customer care.

I was approached by an investor a few years ago that had concerns about the fees she was paying her financial advisor at the bank. As the investor had a very large account, the fees being charged on the account were also very large. An analysis of the account revealed that the investor was indeed paying high fees relative to the competition—in fact, the fees were much higher than what was even being disclosed by the bank. Naturally, this information angered the investor. When I asked how she had selected this financial advisor at the bank, she replied that when she sold her business, the sales proceeds were wired into her checking account at the bank. The bank teller noticed the large cash deposit and recommended that the investor walk down the hall to talk with the bank's investment department. This is how she was introduced to her new financial advisor at the bank. Thinking that all financial advisors are the same, her thought process seemed logical to her at the time. In hindsight, she felt misled by the bank and the bank teller. Fortunately, she was able to exit the high-cost financial advisory arrangement and engaged a fee-only financial advisor to reduce her investment management fees.

Impulsively selecting a financial advisor can potentially cost the investor thousands of dollars and set them back from achieving their

---

* Morse, "Decisions and Desire."

goals. How can we resist the compulsion to make rapid decisions based on qualitative reasoning?

Use the Process of Elimination Method

Though many of us are loathe to put in the legwork to make data-based decisions, there are a few notable exceptions. People tend to do their homework when it comes to finding a new job, purchasing a car, or buying a house. Most people realize these are big-ticket, high-stakes items, and they deserve careful research and attention. If you fail to properly vet a workplace, for instance, you might find yourself in forty-plus hours of weekly misery.

An effective way to make major life decisions is to employ the process of elimination method. Essentially, this means eliminating subpar options until you're left with only a handful of good choices.

NOTE: *This introduction to the process of elimination method is a high-level overview of how to find a competent, ethical financial advisor that fits your unique circumstances and criteria. This topic is covered in greater depth (over several chapters) in part 3.*

A good illustration of the process of elimination method can be found in house hunting. When you begin searching for a new home, you might first narrow your search to a certain city. That will drastically reduce your pool of options right away. Then you might take the criteria a step further and choose a certain part of the city to conduct your search. After that, you might take other factors into account, such as your budget, the size of the house, the number of bedrooms and bathrooms, access to public transportation, the size of the yard, etc. With each new criterion you introduce, you will likely whittle down your pool of viable options.

Keep in mind, it's a good idea to begin with the important "must-have" criteria. If there are still quite a few options after you've run through that list, you can move on to optional "nice-to-have" features.

Eventually, you'll be left with only a handful of houses. From there, you can compare and contrast their features and start touring the homes to get a sense of how they "feel" (something that is impossible to glean from a house listing). At the end of this process, you can make an informed decision and, hopefully, end up with a house that matches your most important criteria.

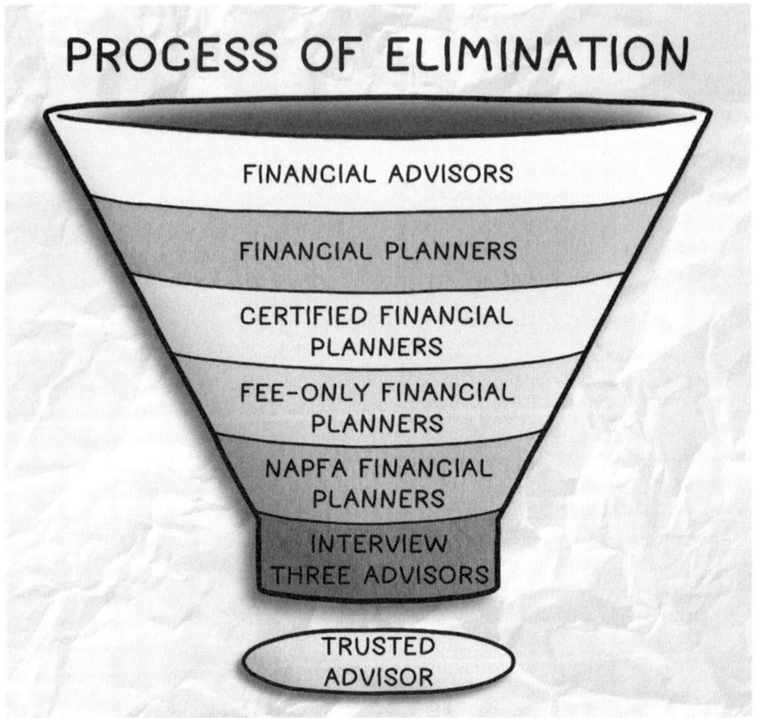

The Process of Elimination and Financial Advisors

Now, let's apply this approach to choosing a financial advisor. There are nearly four hundred thousand financial advisors in the United States,* and you're expected to pick one. Good luck! While that may seem daunting at first, it *is* possible to whittle down the list using the same methodology as our house-hunter in the example above.

Start with the most important criteria first, and continue to narrow down your list of advisors until you're left with only a few viable candidates. You might consider factors such as the size of an advisor's company, whether or not an advisor is a CFP®, their geographical location, their compensation structure, or whether the advisor is NAPFA registered (we'll address this particular criterion soon).

* Data USA, "Personal Financial Advisors."

You might be tempted to narrow down your search right away according to geographical location. I understand that temptation. There's a certain amount of comfort that comes with having a financial advisor close by. However, with today's communication technology, geographical location is less important than it used to be. It's far better, in my opinion, to choose an agent that's right for you, regardless of their location.

With that in mind, I suggest a different starting point: eliminating all agents whose work is commission-based. As we've discussed in past chapters, any financial advisor who receives a commission to sell products has an inherent conflict of interest. It's unavoidable. Even if the advisor is a good person with good intentions, they are ultimately incentivized to sell certain products—products that may or may not be in the client's best interest.

If a financial advisor is also working as a broker, they are incentivized to sell brokerage products. If an advisor is working through a bank, they will likely earn a commission by selling the bank's proprietary products. And the same is true for any financial advisor working through an insurance company—they have a strong incentive to sell their company's products. (I will discuss each of these groups—brokers, bankers, and insurance salespeople—in upcoming chapters.)

If you agree with the basic premise that it's best to seek financial advisors who are not incentivized to make a sale, what then? How do you begin striking agents from the list who do not meet this standard? You *could* examine financial advisors one by one, but that would frankly be a tedious and exhausting process. Instead, it's a good idea to use online search tools.

BrokerCheck is a handy tool facilitated by the Financial Industry Regulatory Authority (FINRA). Through BrokerCheck, you can type in the names of individuals or firms to determine if they are licensed brokers (an instant red flag). You can also find out if a person is barred by FINRA, get a brief glimpse of an advisor's employment history, and see if they have formal complaints on their record.

Another way to use the process of elimination to find a financial advisor is to use the National Association of Personal Financial

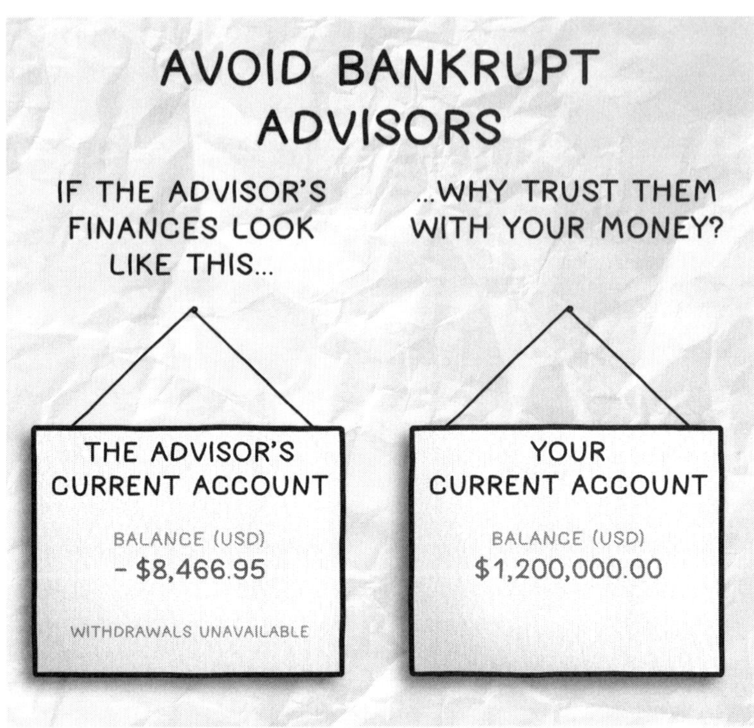

Advisors (NAPFA) as a measuring stick. NAPFA is a professional association of fee-only financial advisors who are client-focused and comply with rigorous membership standards. As articulated on their website, "each advisor must sign and renew a Fiduciary Oath yearly and subscribe to our Code of Ethics."*

Fortunately, it's easy to find NAPFA-Registered Financial Advisors. NAPFA's "Find an Advisor" tool allows you to search for advisors in your area that adhere to the organization's standards. By using this tool, you *are* taking geography into account, but, most importantly, you are eliminating commission-based financial advisors and narrowing your search to advisors who

- are fee-only,
- adhere to to a fiduciary standard of care (i.e., vow to work in the client's best interest),

---

* The National Association of Personal Financial Advisors, "About Us."

- provide independent, objective advice, and
- meet NAPFA's organizational standards.

It is worth noting that NAPFA's search platform is a good starting place, but it is not necessarily the most selective or discerning online matching tool available today. Other platforms have winnowed down the list of fee-only fiduciaries even further, considering factors such as the financial advisory company's assets under management (AUM), customer retention rate, specialties, and availability to take on new clients. Wealthramp, founded by investor advocate and educator Pam Krueger, is an example of a matching platform with a stricter vetting process for financial advisors.

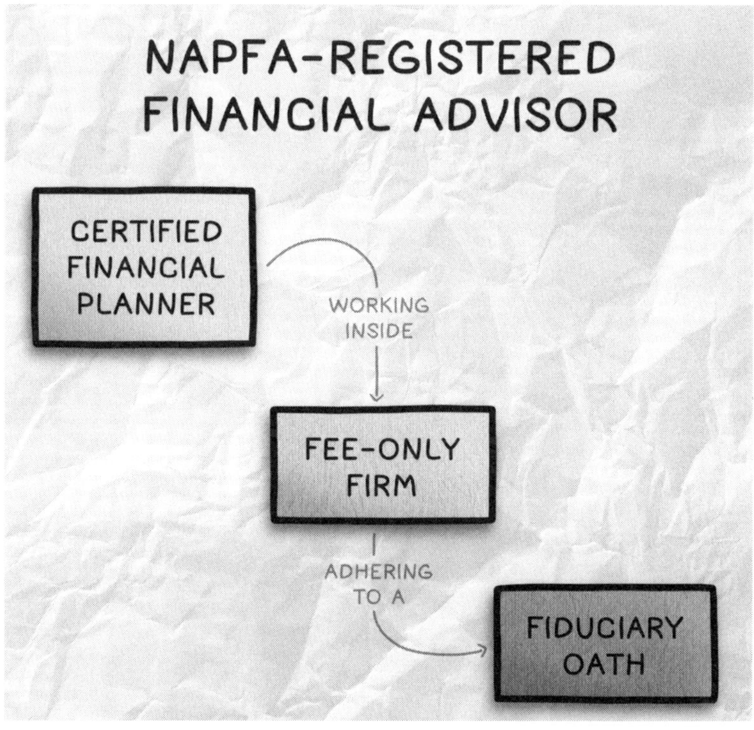

Once you have a list of qualified financial advisors, you can start thinking about other considerations. Would you prefer to work with a solo practitioner or a team? Do you prefer a male advisor or female? Is the office location important to you?

Browse company websites, read over mission statements and customer testimonials, and begin to gain a sense of each company. Once you've honed your list to a manageable number (say, three or four), you can begin conducting interviews. At that point, your emotion-based decision-making can kick in. You already have a few very good options, so your decision will likely boil down to your comfort level with the advisor. Did you have a good rapport? Did they listen to you and ask thoughtful questions? Did they communicate clearly?

Then make your selection!

The whole process is a bit like highly organized dating. You start with a few basic criteria, you whittle down the pool of contenders, and you eventually "hand your rose" to the person of your choice. The front end of the process is informed and logical, but the final decision usually comes down to a gut feeling. And that's okay! By that point, you have three or four solid contenders, so you'll probably be in good hands.

Chapter 10
Why to Avoid Brokers When Searching for a Financial Advisor

In the not-so-distant past, stockbrokers provided a somewhat valuable service. They acted as a bridge between wealthy individual investors and the market. Investors would call their broker to place an order for securities, and the broker, in turn, would charge a commission for facilitating the sale. But this model quickly went the way of the dinosaur when the average investor gained easy access to the stock market through the internet. Suddenly, investors could buy and sell securities without paying a middleperson to arrange this financial "handshake."

Because of this, brokers were forced to become inventive and rebrand their services. Instead of emphasizing sales, they played up their roles as financial advisors. Brokers had always been doling out financial advice to some degree, but this side of the business became more important as consumers realized they could (in many cases) facilitate securities sales on their own.

That doesn't sound so bad, until you realize that financial advice from brokers could easily be tainted by conflicts of interest.

Why is that?

I'll answer that question later in this chapter (and provide some advice on how to weed out brokers from your search for a financial advisor), but first let's talk about some basics.

Differences Between Brokers and Investment Advisors

Those who provide financial advice go by a variety of titles: financial advisor, wealth manager, full-service broker, asset manager, investment advisor, etc. Many of these titles are loosely defined (see chapter 5 on why *wealth management* is a problematic term), which can create quite a headache for investors. Since anyone can call themselves a "financial advisor" or a "wealth manager," it's impossible to tell if the person providing financial advice is a) qualified and b) honest simply by glancing at their title.

You must do a little more digging.

One of the most important factors to consider is how the individual is licensed. First of all, *are* they licensed? If not, that's a major red flag. Both licensed stockbrokers and Registered Investment Advisers must pass a series of exams *and* regularly renew their licenses. This alone requires a certain degree of competence and an obligation to keep one's financial knowledge current.

Additionally, Registered Investment Advisers and licensed stockbrokers must comply with certain federal regulations. Investment advisors are regulated by the US Securities and Exchange Commission (SEC), while brokers are regulated by the Financial Industry Regulatory Authority (FINRA). However, while both groups are required to uphold certain laws and standards, their rules of conduct are quite different. In the words of writer and investment advisor Zaw Thiha Tun, "[investment advisors] are held to a higher legal standard than brokers."* Tun goes on to explain that in the US, investment advisors must "adhere to the Investment Advisers Act of 1940, which calls on advisers to perform fiduciary duties in regards to their clients' accounts."

As I've touched on earlier, a fiduciary standard is the gold standard of care in the financial industry. It means putting the interests of the client above one's own interests or the interests of the firm.

On the other hand, licensed stockbrokers are required to comply with FINRA's Rule 2111, which states that the broker must "have a reasonable basis to believe that a recommended transaction or

---

* Tun, "Investment Adviser vs. Broker: What's the Difference?"

investment strategy involving a security or securities is suitable for the customer."'* In other words, the broker must aim to provide financial services and strategies that suit the customer. This sounds great on the surface, but it can be difficult to ascertain what a "reasonable basis" is and what "suitable" actually means.

Such a vague definition inevitably leaves room for conflicts of interest. And those potential conflicts of interest are nearly unavoidable when brokers are part of a commission-based payment structure.

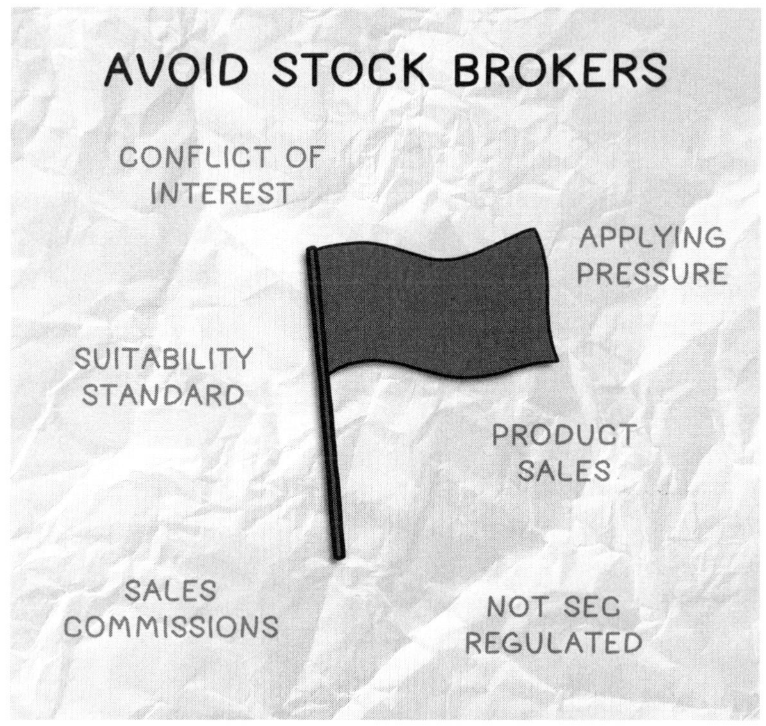

Brokers and Conflicts of Interest

As a former employee at a commission-based brokerage firm, I have firsthand experience with the pressures and influences brokers face selling financial products. As explained by the Consumer Federation of America (CFA), "commission compensation creates an incentive to maximize transactions. In the brokerage model, the firm and financial professional get paid only if a recommendation results in the

* Financial Industry Regulatory Authority, "FINRA Rule 2111 (Suitability) FAQ."

completion of a transaction. Therefore, a broker-dealer has an incentive to recommend that an investor complete a transaction, regardless of whether doing so is in the best interest of the customer."*

And that's problematic. Even if a commission-based broker has good intentions (and I know many brokers who do!), their compensation structure creates an inherent conflict of interest. If someone is incentivized to sell a certain product, they can no longer be bias-free.

The CFA puts it this way: "When financial professionals' pay and firms' profits vary significantly based on what investments they recommend, conflicts of interest are multiplied and magnified."† That's right on the money (so to speak). How can a financial advisor possibly remain neutral when their firm is incentivizing them to sell specific products?

For protection against potentially damaging conflicts of interest, a prudent investor will avoid commission-based advisors and institutions altogether. Instead, they will seek financial services from fee-only investment advisors who are committed to upholding fiduciary standards.

Finding an Investment Advisor

When searching for a fee-only investment advisor (keep in mind, their actual title may vary), it's a good idea to approach your search somewhat scientifically by using the process of elimination. This logical approach can help you narrow the vast pool of financial advisors to a manageable number. One of the ways to significantly whittle down your list is to eliminate all brokerage firms and broker-dealers.

While that sounds daunting, there is actually a relatively easy way to do this—a method I touched on briefly in chapter 9. The search engine called BrokerCheck, operated by FINRA, allows you to type in the name of an individual financial advisor or institution to determine who is licensed as a broker and who is registered as an investment advisor.

---

* Consumer Federation of America, "A Framework for Addressing Broker-Dealer and Investment Adviser Conflicts of Interest When Providing Retail Investment Advice."

† Ibid.

When you try out the tool, you may find that some people hold both types of licenses. So, does the investment advisor license negate the broker license? Does it mean this individual is automatically more client-focused and free of conflicts of interest?

Absolutely not.

These "dual registrants" or "hybrid advisors" are beholden to the same types of conflicts of interests as regular brokers. That's because the same sale pressures and incentives still exist; becoming a Registered Investment Adviser doesn't make them magically disappear. A 2019 study by Egan, Matvos, and Seru found that "dual-registered advisers are 50% more likely to commit misconduct than standalone brokers. Further, among dual-registered firms, those that advise individuals more often engage in misconduct, and firms advising individual clients more often hire advisers with misconduct records, consistent [with] these firms taking advantage of less sophisticated investors."*

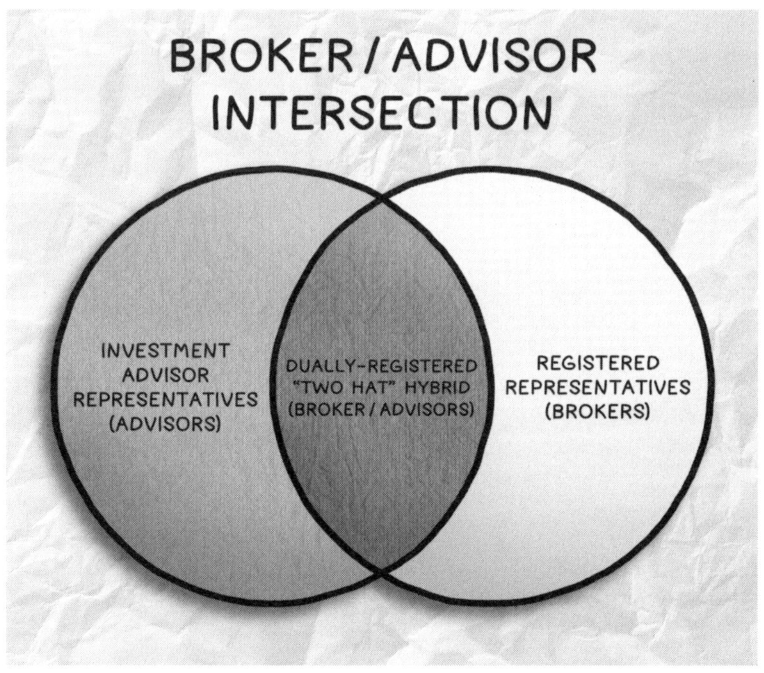

---

* Boyson, "The Worst of Both Worlds? Dual-Registered Investment Advisers."

So, be cautious. If someone claims to be an investment advisor, that may be true . . . but it may not be the full story. If someone is working as both a broker and an investment advisor, the broker side of the practice still carries weight. Use BrokerCheck to investigate, browse through a prospective advisor's website, or simply ask them if they are a licensed broker.

Thorough research is important when choosing a financial advisor. After all, you're entrusting this person with your financial goals and aspirations, in addition to some potentially difficult financial decisions. When it comes to advisor-client relationships, trust is foundational. Ask yourself: would I *really* trust someone who is paid a commission and incentivized to make sales?

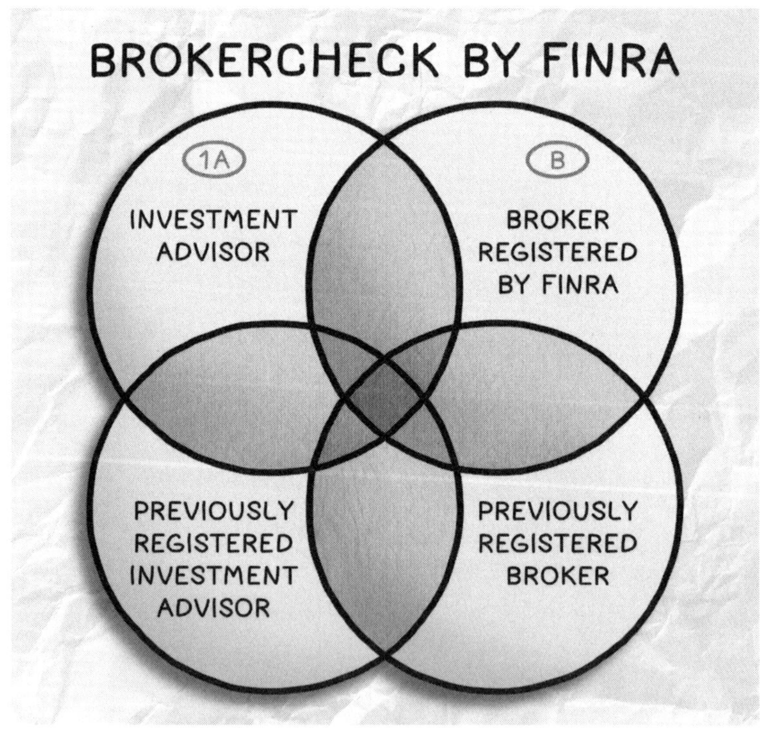

Chapter 11
Why Avoid Life Insurance Agents for Financial Advice?

If I told you most life insurance agents do not offer objective financial advice, you'd probably nod and agree. It seems obvious that someone with a license to sell products and plenty of incentives to make a sale (commissions, bonuses, etc.) would have inherent conflicts of interest. Why, then, do we continue to make "investments" with these professional salespeople? Mostly, it boils down to a simple reason: these folks—and the companies they represent—are *good* at what they do.

It's hard to resist the allure of a nicely packaged product peddled by a skilled salesperson. I'll admit, even I—an experienced investment advisor—have been convinced to purchase life insurance products that were not necessarily suited to my needs. It's easy to be pulled in by smooth talk, polished presentations, and offers that seem too good to be true.

But that's the thing. Too often these services *are* too good to be true. In this chapter, I'll address the dubious practices of life insurance companies (particularly those that tend to package their services as *investments*), how the line between life insurance agents and financial advisors has blurred, and how to avoid partnering with a life insurance agent in the first place.

Let's start by discussing life insurance agents' barriers to objectivity.

Life Insurance Agents and Objective Advice

In past chapters, I've discussed the problems that arise when people are incentivized to make a sale. Essentially, objectivity goes out the window. Even if someone has good intentions, they will still feel pressured by their company to sell certain products, *and* they will be motivated by commissions or bonuses. To make matters worse, life insurance companies occasionally offer sales contests, which pit agents against each other and add even more pressure to make a sale, regardless of the consumer's best interests. In short, when working within a commission-based system, you're fighting an uphill battle for objectivity.

This sales-focused atmosphere is especially pervasive in life insurance companies that offer an array of packages with extra trimmings. You might not find this sales-driven environment in all insurance companies, but it is prevalent in many.

Built around Sales

If a company is built around sales, it's logical to assume that more time will be invested in sales training than in educating sales reps about the products or building a personalized financial plan for a customer. The typical life insurance salesperson, for instance, will not have the training or qualifications necessary to fully capture and comprehend a person's financial picture, analyze it, and deliver sound financial advice. Even if they had the right background and tools to do so, they are limited by their company's premade financial packages.

Insurance companies can spend a staggering amount of time, money, and effort to design attractive packages to lure potential clients. Some of these packages are marketed as investments, and some even promise a guaranteed return. These investment opportunities can seem incredibly attractive on the surface (9 percent back! Guaranteed to beat the S&P 500!), but they are often accompanied with pages and pages of fine print. An incredible deal may be less than incredible once you start digging into the terms and conditions. But most of us don't read the fine print, and, if we do, we probably wouldn't understand the jargon.

Aside from their attractively packaged products, life insurance companies behave like sales machines through the efficiency and attitude of their sales reps. They are highly motivated to close on a deal, and, after that, they have little or no stake in what happens to the customer.

Unlike reputable financial advisors, life insurance agents do not regularly check in with their customers to see how their financial products are affecting them. In fact, in my experience, as soon as an insurance rep closes a deal, you'll never hear from that person again. In one instance, I had a life insurance agent calling and emailing me for an entire year, urging me to sign up for a particular plan. He gave a convincing pitch, and, eventually, I decided it made sense to purchase what he was offering.

This guy acted like my best friend for a year, but do you think I heard from him again after I signed the papers? Of course not. Why would I? Once the sale was made and the commission collected, the insurance agent had every reason to move on and pursue his next sale. This lack of follow-up is another indication that insurance salespeople are not objective and are largely motivated by "making their numbers" and earning a share of the profits. If they truly cared about their clients' well-being (rather than a nice commission), they would regularly check in *after* the sale to make sure the product was still fulfilling their clients' needs.

But what happens if you're not working with an insurance agent, per se, but a financial advisor or broker who is licensed to sell insurance? That's where things start to become murky.

Financial Advisor or Salesperson?

Investors may not realize many financial advisors are also licensed to sell life insurance products. This is common in brokerage firms where selling products can be prioritized above client care. Having a license to sell life insurance products is simply one more arrow in their quiver. It represents another opportunity to earn additional commissions.

This can catch clients flat-footed because they may not associate their wealth manager/investment advisor/financial advisor with insurance sales. People want to trust their advisor. They want to believe that when a life insurance product is offered to them, it is in their best interest. But that may not be the case, and all investors should be cautious when dealing with a financial advisor who is licensed to sell life insurance products.

It's worth noting that some advisory firms state they do not sell insurance products when, in truth, some of their advisors *do* sell these products. They can get away with this statement because the advisors may be acting in a "separate capacity" as insurance agents.

I've spoken with some financial advisors who argue that they acquired an insurance sales license "just in case." If a client brings up a request for insurance, they'll be prepared to match them with a product. However, from my perspective, this is a lot like buying a fishing license. You wouldn't purchase a license unless you intended to go fishing. Similarly, you wouldn't bother to obtain a license to sell insurance products unless you planned on selling them to clients.

I acknowledge that this isn't a perfect analogy, and there are certainly some exceptions. One of my colleagues—a financial advisor who firmly believes in upholding a fiduciary standard of care—is

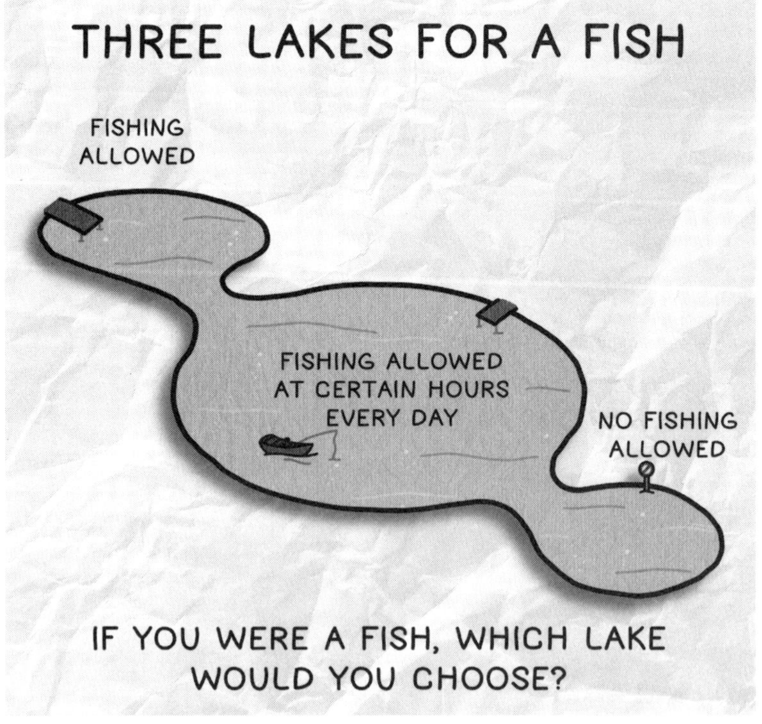

licensed to sell insurance products because the state of Wisconsin will not allow her to even discuss insurance product options unless she holds the correct licensure. She does not intend to sell products, but she is prepared to go over life insurance–related options with her clients if that's what they wish.

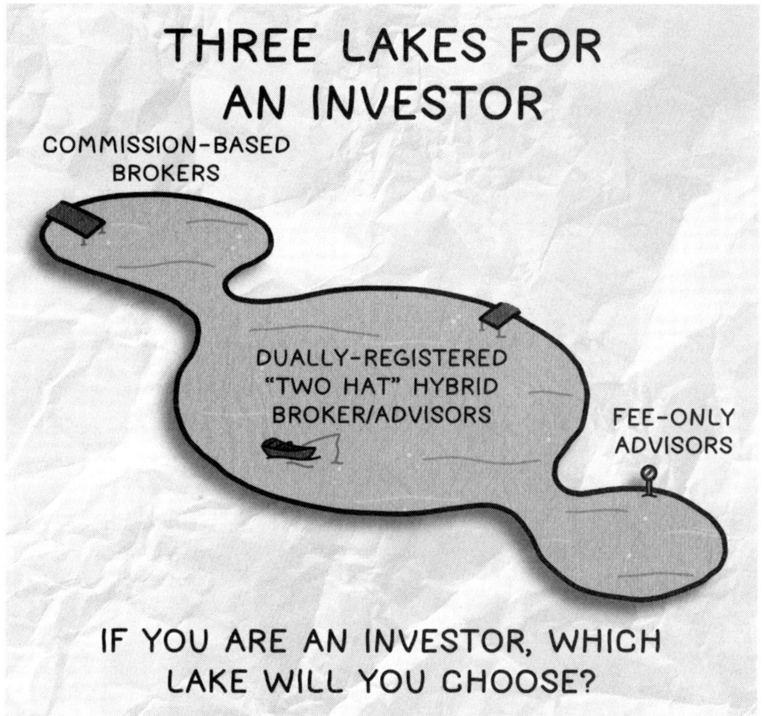

Protecting Yourself

The truth is the life insurance company—not the consumer—is designed to "win." How else would these companies remain viable, let alone profitable? That's not to say elective life insurance coverage is inevitably bad or not worth the cost. In some cases, it absolutely makes sense to purchase additional coverage. However, it's wise to proceed with caution and remember that insurance companies are designed to be profitable.

One way to protect yourself from falling for disadvantageous life insurance products is to work with a financial advisor who does not carry a license to sell insurance. As I mentioned above (in the case of my colleague in Wisconsin), not *all* advisors who carry this licensure are out to sell unnecessary insurance, but looking up a potential advisor's various licenses is a good place to start. All insurance agents must be licensed through their state government, so you should be able to search for a particular agent in your state's records. If you find that the advisor *does* carry an insurance sales license, do a little more digging to determine if that person works in a fee-only advising firm and is committed to a fiduciary standard of care. These two factors can tip the scales back in their favor.

Another way to protect yourself from purchasing unsuitable life insurance products is to have a neutral third party assess the costs and benefits of a particular plan. At my investment advisory firm, we have the tools and training to run the numbers and figure out if the proposed insurance plan is likely to be cost-effective. Sometimes they are, but often, these plans will likely be more expensive than helpful in the long run. If that's the case, we can work with the client to figure out alternative investment avenues to build up their emergency fund(s).

When it comes to life insurance products and salespeople, it's best to exercise an abundance of caution. Too often, those who push life insurance products are less interested in the good of the client and more interested in lining their own pockets. Do your research, seek advice from a neutral third party, and move with caution when working with anyone who carries a license to sell life insurance products. And remember, if an offer seems too good to be true, it probably is.

Investors can take action to protect themselves by following three simple steps:

AdvisorSmart Action Items

1. Ask the financial advisor if they are licensed to sell life insurance.
2. Ask the financial advisor for their state life insurance license number.
3. Look up the financial advisor's name in the state's list of licensed life insurance agents.

Chapter 12
Should We Trust Banks with Our Investments?

Even after several scandals and poor decision-making in recent years, people still tend to trust banks. According to a national survey in 2020, "U.S. adults trust banks more than any other entity—including healthcare providers, non-bank payment providers and the government—to keep their information secure and private."* Another survey shows that 73 percent of consumers believe financial institutions have their best interests in mind when it comes to personal finance (compared to a 51 percent trust rate in the federal government).† Perhaps this trust is built upon strict government regulations for banks and oversight by the Federal Deposit Insurance Corporation (FDIC). Maybe our trust is built on the view that major banks are "too big to fail." After all, several large financial institutions were bailed out by the US Treasury Department after the 2008 financial crisis, to the tune of $245.1 billion.

Whatever the case, we largely see banks as a trusted institution, and, by extension, we trust the people who work within them. Bankers, tellers, loan officers, mortgage consultants—we trust these individuals to guide our decision-making and offer us practical solutions to financial needs.

But do banks and bankers deserve our full trust? Are there instances when we should be skeptical of bank services and conduct

* American Bankers Association, "Americans Trust Banks Most to Keep Their Information Safe."

† McNair, "Survey: Consumers Trust Banks More Than the Federal Government."

some independent research to figure out if the products they offer are *well-suited* to our needs?

I *do* believe banks serve a valuable purpose and are a necessary part of any investor's financial portfolio. However, I also believe that banks are best suited for certain financial services and not others. If you're hoping to open a savings or checking account, take out a small business loan, or exchange foreign currency, a bank is a great fit for those services. But if you're hoping to engage in major financial planning (retirement planning, estate planning, insurance planning, etc.), a bank may not serve your needs.

Why? Let's dig deeper.

Banks and Bias

The 1980s and 1990s were an era of extreme growth, deregulation, and consolidation for banks. Big banks kept growing bigger (with over 4,300 bank mergers in the '80s and over 6,000 in the '90s), and several regulatory laws were overturned. Notably, the Glass-Steagall Act and Bank Holding Company Act of 1956 were undermined by the Gramm-Leach-Bliley Act of 1999, which paved the way for commercial banks to engage in investment banking and insurance services. Banks, of course, rejoiced. They were now free to create proprietary investment products and portfolios, which could be easily packaged and sold to commercial banking customers. Bankers, who may or may not have had any formal financial advisory training, were trained to sell a limited selection of products to customers (sometimes earning a commission for their efforts).

The result?

Too often, customers were sold products that didn't fit their unique financial situations. That is bound to happen when a) you must choose from a limited selection of financial portfolios and products or b) you are working with a bank rep that isn't trained to conduct an in-depth analysis of your financial situation and make wide-ranging recommendations.

Another major issue with entrusting a bank with major financial planning stems from banks' compensation structure. Oftentimes, bankers or wealth managers in major banks are incentivized to sell products. You might not think of opening a line of credit or starting a mutual fund as "buying a product," but that is how these actions are interpreted by banks. Thus, banks will incentivize their employees to steer customers into opening new accounts or making certain investments.

If you've read the prior chapters in the book, you are well aware that incentives inherently lead to bias. An individual may have decent intentions and may truly want to do right by the customer, but that is exceedingly difficult when their company is pressing them to make sales. That pressure could come in the form of carrots (sales contests, commissions, bonuses) or sticks (minimum sales standards, peer pressure, disciplinary action, or warnings from managers). Regardless, the pressure in a sales environment is very real and difficult to resist. I speak from experience.

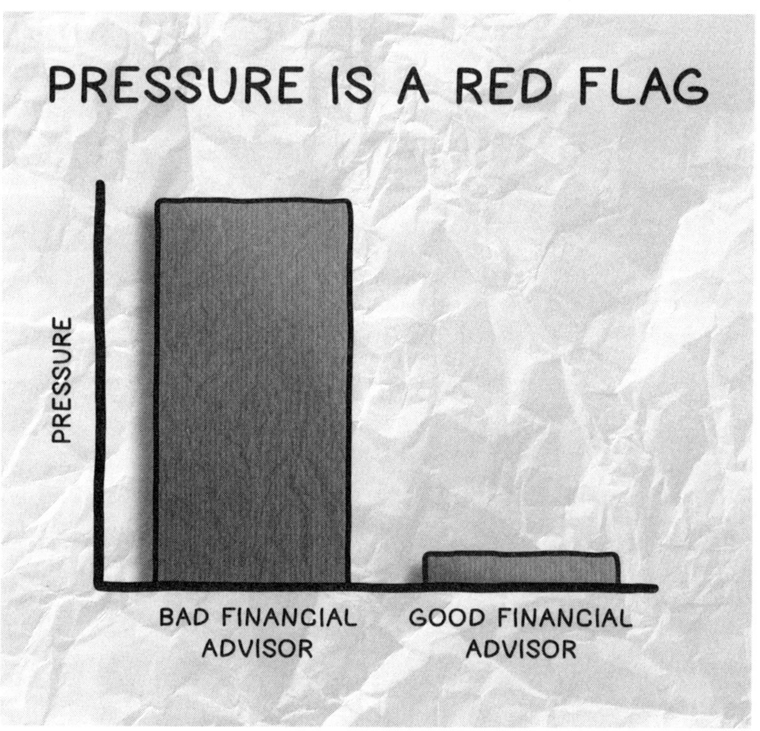

When Sales Go off the Rails

The unintended consequences of a sales-driven environment became apparent a few years ago when Wells Fargo got into hot water for the questionable actions of its employees. We touched on this scandal in chapter 8, about conflicts of interest, but it is worth reiterating the main points here. In short, the pressure Wells Fargo exerted on its bankers, tellers, and other financial professionals was immense, and its employees became desperate. To meet the bank's stringent sales standards, bankers began opening accounts without customer permission, and tellers looked for any possible excuse to send their customers over to bankers. This went on for well over a decade.

Why did customers go along with this questionable behavior for so long?

It's hard to say, but this may relate to the statistics I mentioned at the beginning of this chapter—people trust banks and believe they are in good hands when working with bank employees. Another reason this behavior passed without much notice for so long may have to do with the fact that no one person was culpable. Large financial institutions are a labyrinth of responsibility and decision-making. Do we blame the tellers and bankers for their actions? Or the branch managers? Or corporate decision makers? Or the shareholders for demanding constant growth? When responsibility is split among so many parties and people, why would a single banker feel guilty? When people are "just doing what they're told," the customer is swept along for the ride and will likely perceive that this is all business as usual.

However, the dubious actions of Wells Fargo inevitably reached a breaking point. Customers eventually caught on to the fishy behaviors, and legal action was taken by various regulatory bodies. In the aftermath, the bank had to pay significant penalties, the CEO stepped down, and actions were taken to reform the aggressive sales culture.

Reform is a positive step, of course, but the sales culture (in this and other major banks) still persists. Banks continue to sling proprietary investment products, and bankers continue to dole out financial advice that they may or may not be fully qualified to make. It takes years of training to gain a solid comprehension of investment advising, and there's always more to learn. Everyone's financial situation is unique, and many are extremely complex and could be approached with any number of investment solutions. Therefore, it's best to look outside a bank for investment advice.

It's also worth noting that just because a bank has a branch called the "personal finance division" or "private wealth group," it doesn't mean you'll be working with a qualified investment advisor. These are simply labels and, as we discussed in chapter 5, anyone can call themselves a financial advisor or a wealth manager.

What to Do?

To reiterate, banks have their purpose, and I'm not suggesting we abandon them altogether. However, it's best to proceed with caution and a healthy dose of skepticism when it comes to purchasing investment products through a bank. To protect yourself from investing in less-than-optimal products, I suggest taking one or more of the following steps:

- **Consult a neutral third party.** Ask a qualified financial advisor to "run the numbers" to determine if an investment opportunity is worth pursuing.
- Do some research to **find out if a particular banker is licensed to sell life insurance products** (see chapter 11 for reasons to exercise caution with life insurance agents).
- **Avoid "too good to be true" offers.** Chances are, they *are* too good to be true.
- **Go directly to a qualified financial advisor** and avoid investing at banks altogether. As always, I suggest working with a fee-only advisor who is committed to upholding a fiduciary standard of care.

Investing with a trustworthy financial advisory firm has myriad benefits. Qualified advisors have the abilities and tools to create customized strategies and portfolios that make sense for *you* and your unique financial situation. They also can oftentimes offer greater flexibility when it comes to fees. While a bank might offer a set fee for managing a particular investment or portfolio, fee-only financial advisory firms have the freedom to negotiate lower fees for their high-net-worth clients. Even if banks (or commission-centered brokerage firms, for that matter) *could* reduce the percentage they charge, why would they? Their commissions might depend on those fees.

Ultimately, banks serve many vital functions for consumers, but investment facilitation is not necessarily one of them. Always approach banking with caution, consult a third party to analyze your options, and be aware that *someone* is likely making a commission from your investments. Lastly, keep in mind that most bankers cannot provide the same kind of in-depth strategy and customization that reputable financial advisory firms can.

AdvisorSmart Action Items

1. Google your bank using the word "scandal" to see what you can find.
2. Research your bank to see how much they have been fined by regulators in recent years.
3. Ask your bank advisor if you own any proprietary bank products in your portfolio.

Chapter 13
Examining the Criminal Activity and Penalties of Wall Street Banks

The bad behavior of banks—especially large banks—goes beyond selling subpar or unsuitable investment products to clients. Criminal activity and shady practices have become pervasive in many different banking departments, from mortgage to insurance. Up to this point, I have only highlighted the criminal activities of one specific Wall Street bank—Wells Fargo—but dozens of other banks deserve to share the same spotlight.

We're told that bigger banks and brokerage firms are safer. They have greater protections in place for the consumer; they have better technology. We're told they are more reliable than the little guys and that they have the means to offer a more personal customer service experience. When lists of the "top" brokers or investment bankers are published, they are often exclusively filled with people representing large companies—Wells Fargo, Merrill (formerly Merrill Lynch), Citigroup, JPMorgan Chase, Charles Schwab, Goldman Sachs, Bank of America, and others.

But how safe are these mammoth Wall Street firms and investment banks? Do they really have the consumer's best interests at heart? If we solely looked at these organizations' criminal activities, the answer would be a firm and resounding no.

You may be thinking, "But all major organizations are going to run into legal issues. Is this *really* a fair assessment?" It's true that other industries face occasional legal battles. Doctors are sued for malpractice. Automobile manufacturers are sued for defective products. Tech companies are sued for infringing on intellectual property rights. However, the extent and frequency of legal issues faced by Wall Street firms are much higher and more severe in nature.

Criminal Activity Normalized

Despite marketing themselves as reputable and reliable, Wall Street firms have repeatedly demonstrated that they prioritize profit over the well-being of their clients. From insider trading to mortgage fraud, these firms have engaged in a wide range of illegal activities that have resulted in massive financial losses for their customers and the broader economy.

A recent study by Diggity Marketing analyzed the violations of a wide array of industries to determine that "businesses in the financial sector were by far the most likely to find themselves in trouble."* The numbers speak for themselves. During the last twenty years, the financial sector paid a staggering $331 billion in fines. Compare this to the other contenders over the same time period:

Pharmaceutical: $50.3 billion

Oil and gas: $45.5 billion

Motor vehicles: $31.1 billion

Utilities: $22.4 billion

The numbers aren't even close. What's more, the bulk of the financial industry's $331 billion in fines—over $100 billion—was for toxic securities abuses. Toxic securities are investments that are extremely difficult to sell because the market has no demand for them.

Though this was a particularly poignant problem during the 2008 financial crisis, it continues to be an issue to this day. And large Wall Street firms have clearly not learned their lessons.

Take JPMorgan Chase, for example. In September of 2020, the company agreed to shell out $920 million to settle allegations that it engaged in highly suspicious and manipulative trades centered around Treasury

* Fischer, "The 10 Most-Fined Financial Services Firms."

bonds and precious metals.* This was its third criminal case in just a handful of years. Not only that, the 2020 case demonstrated that the company had blatantly violated the terms of both its prior criminal cases.

One of the prior cases against JPMorgan Chase had to do with its knowledge of and involvement in Bernie Madoff's infamous Ponzi scheme. The other recent criminal case had to do with manipulating foreign exchange markets. A Better Markets special report explained, "The Department of Justice stated that JPMorgan's most recent criminal activity [in 2020] went on for 'nearly a decade,' which overlaps with both the prior DPA [deferred prosecution agreement] and probation."†

Clearly, the zebra didn't bother to change its stripes. And why would it? The Better Markets report goes on to state that despite JPMorgan Chase's disregard of past court rulings, the DOJ "never mentioned the prior cases or the fact that JPMorgan Chase apparently violated both agreements—without any penalty."

The behaviors of JPMorgan Chase are far from an isolated incident. To illustrate how widespread and deep the corruption goes, let's touch on the ten largest bank settlements in history. Despite paying billions of dollars in fines, these banks are still active today. And, given lax oversights, there's no guarantee that they won't continue to engage in illegal activities.

Keep in mind, all these institutions also sell investment securities in addition to banking products. They claim to employ "financial planners" or "wealth managers," but as I've already discussed in chapter 5, those labels don't mean much.

Top Ten Biggest Bank Settlements

10. Credit Suisse, $5.3 billion

In early 2017, the giant Swiss bank Credit Suisse was hit with a $5.3 billion fine for illegally selling toxic mortgage securities in the lead-up to the 2008 financial crisis. A Department of Justice article eloquently sums up its discretions: "Credit Suisse made false and irresponsible

---

* US Department of Justice: Office of Public Affairs, "JPMorgan Chase & Co. Agrees to Pay $920 Million in Connection with Schemes to Defraud Precious Metals and U.S. Treasuries Markets."

† Better Markets, "Special Report: Wall Street's Crime Spree 1998–2020: 395 Major Legal Actions and $195+ Billion in Fines and Settlements Over the Last 20 Years."

representations about residential mortgage-backed securities, which resulted in the loss of billions of dollars of wealth and took a painful toll on the lives of ordinary Americans."*

9. Wells Fargo, $5.35 billion

Wells Fargo has gotten in a lot of hot water in recent years for bankers creating "phantom accounts" to meet sales quotas. But before that, the banking giant was fined $5.35 billion in the aftermath of the 2008 financial crisis. You might think such a hefty fine would put an end to shady activity, but as of 2020, the bank has paid more than $18 billion in fines for various violations.

8. Goldman Sachs, $5.4 billion

During the 2008 financial crisis, Goldman Sachs was thrust into the national spotlight for potentially misleading investors and mismanaging funds. But its biggest fine was issued years after the 2008 debacle. In 2020, the firm agreed to pay $5.4 billion for its role in a Malaysian money laundering scheme, carried out by insiders in the Malaysian government.

7. Deutsche Bank, $7.2 billion

Deutsche Bank is a big name in the banking industry, with headquarters in Germany but operations across the globe. In 2016, this institution was fined $7.2 billion for knowingly selling toxic securities that it suspected would be harmful to the US housing market. Since then, it clearly hasn't gained any scruples and has knowingly loaned money to disreputable figures, including corrupt Russian oligarchs.

6. Bank of America, $8.5 billion

Since the 2008 financial crisis, Bank of America has paid an astonishing $76.1 billion in fines—more than any other bank during the same period. A small portion was the $8.5 billion it shelled out in the aftermath of the 2008 financial crisis to amend for the $174 billion worth of subprime mortgage-backed securities sold by Countrywide, its subsidiary.

---

* US Department of Justice: Office of Public Affairs, "Credit Suisse Agrees to Pay $5.28 Billion in Connection with Its Sale of Residential Mortgage-Backed Securities."

5. BNP Paribas, $8.97 billion

BNP Paribas, a French bank, was fined $8.97 billion for violating US sanctions against Sudan, Iran, and Cuba. The bank was also found to have conducted business with entities associated with terrorism. As the DOJ reports, "BNP Paribas went to elaborate lengths to conceal prohibited transactions, cover its tracks, and deceive U.S. authorities."*

4. Thirteen US Banks, $9.3 billion

This entry is a little different because it involves the conduct of thirteen different big banks in the US. Collectively, banking giants Wells Fargo, JPMorgan Chase, Bank of America, and ten others were fined a total of $9.3 billion in 2013 for foreclosure abuses in years prior. Unsurprisingly, all thirteen banks are still in business today.

3. Bank of America, $11.8 billion

A frequent flyer on this list is Bank of America, which racked up an $11.8 billion fee in 2012 as part of the National Mortgage Settlement.

2. JPMorgan Chase, $13 billion

Second on the list is JPMorgan Chase's $13 billion settlement with the DOJ, which occurred in 2013. This settlement was linked to its sale of toxic mortgage-backed securities leading up to the 2008 financial crisis. At the time, it was the largest settlement in US corporate history. But, as we discussed earlier in this chapter, this penalty did not stop its illegal activity. Since 2008, JPMorgan Chase has paid $43.7 billion in fines.

1. Bank of America, $16.65 billion

Bank of America holds the dubious distinction of paying the largest bank settlement to date. This penalty, assigned in 2014, was linked to illegal activity related to the sale of subprime mortgage-backed securities. But, as we've seen with other big banks, Bank of America hasn't exactly changed its ways. Since 2008, it has incurred an astonishing $76.1 billion in fines.

---

* US Department of Justice: Office of Public Affairs, "BNP Paribas Agrees to Plead Guilty and to Pay $8.9 Billion for Illegally Processing Financial Transactions for Countries Subject to U.S. Economic Sanctions."

This list illustrates why I am concerned about the culture of greed and corruption that seems to pervade the banking industry. Despite paying billions in fines, these banks continue to engage in illegal activities, and there is no guarantee they won't continue to do so. With the lion's share of fines (about one-third) in the last two decades involving toxic securities abuses, I have a direct concern about the conduct of these institutions. They are representing the financial industry, and that includes legitimate financial planners and fiduciaries who are trying to do right by their clients.

My hope is that individual investors will continue to do their research, educate themselves about the companies they choose to use for financial advice, and hold their financial advisors accountable. It's important to not just blindly trust that institutions are acting in your best interest. Aside from individual efforts, government regulators need to hold these banks accountable and continue to enforce strict penalties for illegal activity. Hopefully these collective actions will enable a shift toward a more ethical and responsible banking industry and greater protections for the individual investor.

For two excellent in-depth reports on the criminal activity conducted by and steep fines imposed on Wall Street banks, look at the 2021 Better Markets special report and the 2016 Good Jobs First investigative report based on information by Violation Tracker.*†

---

* Better Markets, "Special Report: Wall Street's Crime Spree 1998–2020: 395 Major Legal Actions and $195+ Billion in Fines and Settlements Over the Last 20 Years."

† Good Jobs First, "The $160 Billion Bank Fee: What Violation Tracker 2.0 Shows about Penalties Imposed on Major Financial Offenders."

Chapter 14

How Do Fee-Only and Fee-Based Financial Advisors Differ?

Many investors come to me with a similar story. They've read an article or watched a news program about fee-only financial planning, and a light bulb goes off. They realize their personal financial planner (or wealth manager or investment advisor . . . the terminology varies) is *not* a fee-only advisor and is probably earning a commission whenever they sell a financial product.

Oftentimes, the investor had a feeling—almost a sixth sense—that they were taken advantage of, but they couldn't put their finger on what was wrong. Something didn't feel quite right about their relationship with their financial advisor—too much product-pushing, too little personalized advice. After learning about fee-only advisors, they realize not all financial planners fall into the same category and that, in fact, some advisors are inherently more concerned with earning commissions and making sales for their firm than providing objective financial guidance.

The investor hops online and starts exploring their options. And that's when I get a call.

This story has repeated so often, I sometimes wonder if I'm in the Matrix. Clients experience a pivotal moment when they realize they have other options—other routes they can take—when it comes to working with a financial planner. This moment is liberating for them.

The second part of the story involves gratitude. My clients are often deeply grateful for the objective counseling they receive and the transparency that goes hand in hand with fee-only financial advisory firms. Their gratitude is extremely rewarding, but it's also a reminder that we have a long way to go in terms of educating investors on their choices.

One foundational piece of knowledge all investors should understand is the difference between a **fee-only** and a **fee-based** financial advisory firm. If the distinction between the two was more commonly understood, that might put an end to the same old story of frustrated investors contacting me after learning they have other, more attractive options. And I know I'm not the only one. Allan Slider, founder and president of FeeOnlyNetwork,* says, "Even though we are a directory of strictly fee-only financial advisors, we often receive messages from people saying they want to work with a 'fee-based financial advisor.' They're confused about the terminology because the financial industry has intentionally made it confusing."†

Fee-Only versus Fee-Based Confusion

What *is* a fee-only financial advisor? What about fee-based? And how are the two different?

If you ask a dozen financial advisors to define these terms, you'll likely get a dozen slightly different answers. When thinking about the meaning of a **fee-only advisor**, I tend to defer to the National Association of Personal Financial Advisors' (NAPFA) definition: "a Fee-Only financial advisor [is] one who is compensated solely by the client with neither the advisor nor any related party receiving compensation that is contingent on the purchase or sale of a financial product."‡

In other words, a fee-only advisor is not a salesperson. They are not incentivized with commissions or third-party compensation.

On the other side of the coin, **fee-based advisors** can be

* Allan Slider is the president and founder of FeeOnlyNetwork, a directory that exclusively lists vetted, fee-only financial advisors. He is a consumer advocate and is committed to elevating the visibility of fee-only financial advisors. Allan is also a twenty-plus-year veteran of search engine visibility and online reputation management for financial advisors.

† Slider, interview by author, August 30, 2023.

‡ The National Association of Personal Financial Advisors, "Our Standards."

compensated through several avenues. They may charge an hourly rate or take a fee as a percentage of a client's assets under management (AUM). That might sound harmless, but fee-based advisors don't *have* to stop there. They can also earn revenue through commissions or bonuses by selling financial products on behalf of their company. That's where conflicts of interest can arise. A fee-based financial planner is not necessarily 100 percent beholden to their clients. They are also often beholden to their financial advisory firm and its sales expectations. And when they can earn a commission from sales, they are, of course, incentivized to sell products.

The term *fee-based* is confusingly similar to *fee-only*. Geoffrey Brown, president and CEO of Illinois CPA Society (and former CEO of NAPFA),* says that "fee-only is a straightforward term," whereas the term *fee-based* was "developed by some industry participants to intentionally confuse the public." And that's problematic. Brown warns that "consumers should be wary of advisors that hold out as a fee-based. It's a clear signal that the relationship has a sales-based component."†

Learning the distinction between the terms *fee-only* and *fee-based* is a good start, but, unfortunately, the confusion doesn't end there. Some advisors might seem like traditional fee-only advisors—claiming to uphold a fiduciary standard, offering financial guidance, charging a set fee—but they are actually dually registered as *both* an investment advisor *and* a broker. This dual registration inevitably creates myriad conflicts of interest.

Beyond that, *anyone* can call themselves a fee-only financial advisor, even if they are not. There's no law or regulation against it. If there were rules governing the use of the terms *fee-only financial planner* or *fee-only investment advisor*, that would certainly help alleviate some investor confusion. Unfortunately, the federal government has no real incentive to make this happen, especially when brokerage firms have no issue with hiring lobbyists to mold financial regulations to

---

* Geoffrey Brown specializes in strategic and operational planning, coalition building, and fiscal management. He is the president and CEO of Illinois CPA Society and former CEO of the National Association of Personal Financial Advisors (NAPFA).

† Brown, interview by author, May 24, 2022.

their liking.

Though it's difficult to go up against the deep pockets of brokerage firms, I'm optimistic that consumers are becoming savvier and will eventually demand change. Geoffrey Brown agrees, saying, "Because of their focus on the client, fee-only planners are fast becoming the professionals of choice for many consumers."*

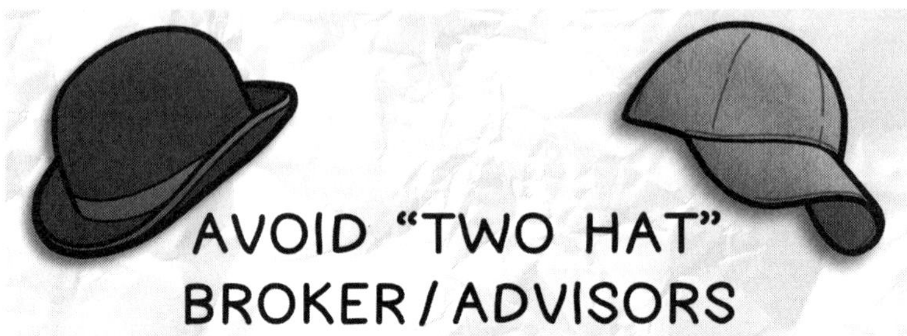

Consumer awareness and advocacy is how the tobacco industry eventually succumbed to stringent regulations—a true David and Goliath story, considering the power, money, and influence the tobacco industry once had—and I believe the same grassroots change can occur in the financial industry. In the meantime, investors must be diligent and do their homework before opting to work with a financial planner.

---

* Ibid.

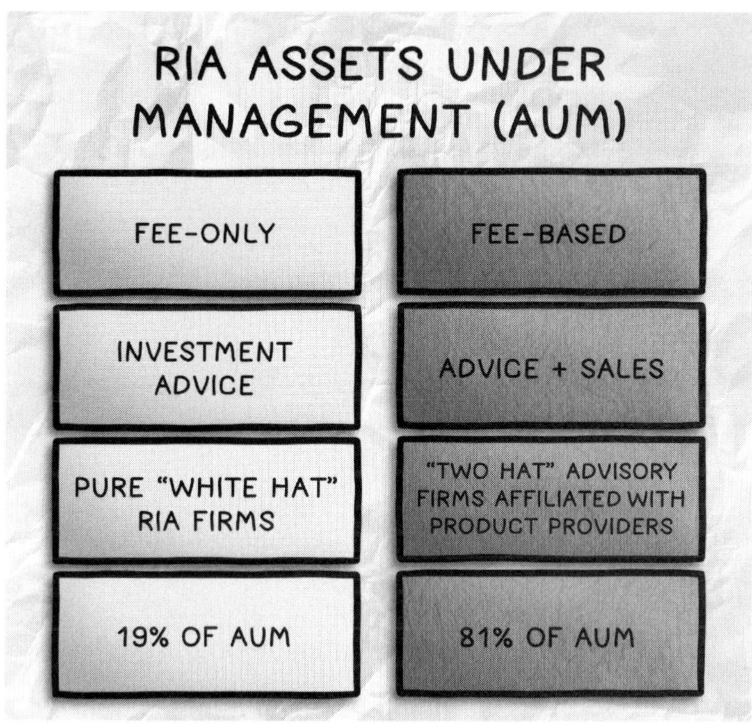

Three Steps to Identify Trustworthy Fee-Only Advisors

How do you determine if an advisor is *actually* operating under a fee-only model? There are several steps you can take to investigate both individual financial planners and financial advisory firms. Here are three action steps:

1. Search a reliable database.

In my experience, the best way to search for fee-only financial advisors is through a reliable online matching platform. To conduct a more narrow, highly curated, and highly vetted list of fee-only financial advisors, I recommend visiting the websites of Wealthramp or FeeOnlyNetwork. To conduct a broader search, visit NAPFA's Find an Advisor platform. There, you can search for fee-only advisors in your area who are part of NAPFA's association (the largest professional association of fee-only financial advisors in the nation). Any financial advisor who wants to join NAPFA must comply with a strict code of ethics, renew a Fiduciary Oath every year, and, of course, operate under a fee-only model. NAPFA's former CEO Geoffrey Brown explains, "Since the association is made up of fee-only planners, [the investor will] know that every professional is committed to working in their best interests."*

As you're searching NAPFA's database, keep in mind that not every advisor will be a good fit, even if they *are* members of this exemplary organization. Advisors may have different specialties, and it's imperative to match your financial goals with the financial advisor's unique areas of expertise. Narrowing your search (potentially by using Wealthramp or FeeOnlyNetwork) can help.

2. Do a deep dive.

Once you have a list of potential fee-only financial advisors, it's prudent to conduct a thorough search for information about the advisor and their firm. Read over their mission statement, look through any disclosures posted on their website, and look for adherence to a fiduciary standard of care. Search for reviews from past clients on the advisor and their firm (preferably posted on an independent website).

Brown advises, "Before contacting an advisor, [investors] should visit their website to learn more about them and their services. They should also review the advisor's ADV and disciplinary history which can be highly informative and help narrow the field."†

3. Pay a visit.

After conducting thorough research, you'll likely have whittled down your list of potential advisors to two or three. At this point, it's a good idea to pay each person a visit to see if you feel comfortable with them. Even if someone looks perfect on paper, you may not have great rapport.

Part 4 of this book will detail how to interview and select a financial advisor (and financial advisory firm), but here are some basics: Come prepared with a list of questions, sit down and have a chat, and trust your instincts. If you feel uncomfortable with someone, that's not a great sign. You may be working with this person for several decades, so comfort and trust are key!

Once you select a financial advisor, Brown suggests reviewing

---

* Ibid.

† Ibid.

the relationship "with a focus on the big picture to reconfirm [your] decision."* Think about your goals and if they align with the financial advisor's expertise and fit with the firm as a whole. Are you comfortable with the size of the firm? Maybe you prefer a larger firm in case your chosen advisor retires; maybe you like the feel of a smaller firm where advisors can potentially lend you more time and attention. Does the location work for you? Do other financial planners at the advisory firm also have a good reputation?

If it seems like a lot of work to select a financial advisor, you're absolutely right! This is a major decision and should not be taken lightly. An important step to finding a trustworthy financial advisor is developing a clear understanding of the differences between a fee-only and a fee-based advisor. Once you're aware of the benefits of working with a fee-only advisor, you're well on your way to finding someone you can trust and work with for many years to come.

* Ibid.

Part Two

THE HUNT FOR GOOD ADVICE

It's easy to find advice. Your relatives, coworkers, children, friends, hairstylist, and the cashier at the grocery store might all offer you advice on any given day. That doesn't mean it's any good. You might be receiving heaps of rotten oysters, with few pearls of wisdom. In my experience, this is especially true when it comes to financial advice.

How can you determine if you're receiving quality financial advice and avoiding guidance that will lead you astray? This section of the book will discuss the characteristics of good advice and where you're likely to find it.

From my thirty-plus years of working in the financial planning industry, I believe good advice is:

- objective
- comprehensive
- independent
- disciplined and continuous
- professional
- fiduciary

But what do these adjectives *really* mean when it comes to financial guidance? Let's dive into each concept to find out.

Chapter 15

Five Steps to More Objective Financial Advice

In many areas of our lives, we encounter biased advice. When your friend recommends eating at a restaurant her brother owns, you understand she *might* be influenced by her family connection. When a Nike employee touts the benefits of Nike sneakers, you know they probably have an allegiance to their employer. When a salesperson at the Subaru outlet presents all the areas in which Subaru outperforms other vehicles, it's a safe bet this person has something to gain when you make a purchase. The list goes on.

Many of us have learned to detect bias in our daily lives. However, it's still possible to be duped, especially if you're dealing with an area many people do not fully understand, such as financial planning. Unfortunately, some financial planners take advantage of this lack of knowledge and use questionable approaches or push unnecessary products.

The reason unscrupulous financial advisors can so effortlessly lead clients astray often boils down to the average investor's financial education, awareness, and acumen. As Daniel Solin remarked in his book *Does Your Broker Owe You Money?*, "Most investors are not stupid. My clients certainly are not. Many are quite intelligent. However, by and large, investors are ignorant of the realities of investing, of how stock markets work, and of how brokers and brokerage firms operate."*

This lack of knowledge is, perhaps, why many people would rather avoid investment firms altogether than risk falling victim to a

---

* Solin, *Does Your Broker Owe You Money?*

Madoff-esque Ponzi scheme or simply be exposed to exorbitant fees. We are innately predisposed to fear the unknown, which is possibly why so few people trust financial advisors.

If you have a bad experience with a financial advisor, you may not be eager to work with another advisor anytime soon. That's a shame because many people *could* benefit from the services of a credible investment advisor. In other areas of our lives, we wouldn't give up completely after one negative experience. If someone, for instance, receives a bad restaurant recommendation from a biased friend, they probably won't say, "That's it, I'm never eating at another restaurant again!" Instead, they'll opt for a different restaurant next time.

Investors, however, may not know how to find an investment advisor they can trust. My advice is simple: seek someone who will deliver objective advice.

Defining Objective Financial Advice

Objectivity is the opposite of bias. We've already established that biases can be problematic, but how can you avoid them? In other areas of our lives, we might seek objectivity by reading reviews on Yelp, Amazon, or Google. We might look up surveys or studies. Or we might test a product for ourselves to judge its quality. But how can you apply this same kind of diligence to the financial arena?

First, it's a good idea to understand what objective advice means when it comes to investing.

In essence, objective financial advice is provided by an advisor who is **free of conflicts of interest** and **upholds a fiduciary standard of care**.

Conflicts of interest are inherently problematic. Your friend who works for Nike will likely only recommend Nike sneakers, no matter if they're presented with evidence that Adidas are the superior shoe. Their conflict of interest stems from the fact that Nike is their employer, they're loyal to that employer, and they may even earn a kickback if you purchase a pair of Nike shoes.

Similarly, certain types of financial advisors have unavoidable conflicts of interest. Any advisor with a brokerage license is, at least in part, a salesperson. They are licensed to sell brokerage products for which they can earn commissions. It is possible for a licensed broker-dealer to also be a Registered Investment Adviser, which commits them to a fiduciary standard of care (a commitment to put the client's interests first when offering financial advice). As I mentioned in part 1 of this book, this dual registration is quite common and can be a source of endless confusion and frustration for consumers. How can a person who is licensed to sell products (and *expected* by their financial advisory firm to sell products) give objective financial advice?

The answer is, they can't. Even if they aim for objectivity, at the end of the day, they are still in the sales business. Sure, a dually registered broker *can* provide quality, objective advice at times, but it's difficult to know when they are acting as a broker (expected to make sales and earn a profit for their company) and when they are acting as an investment advisor (expected to uphold a fiduciary standard of care). In the morning, they might offer you objective retirement planning advice, but in the afternoon, they might steer you into buying a less-than-optimal mutual fund that their advisory firm happens to be pushing. It's impossible to know which person you'll be talking to—the broker or the investment advisor.

Avoiding Bias

Now that you have a good handle on what objective financial advice looks like, you may be wondering how to seek it. I strongly suggest doing your homework to determine if a financial planner is likely to provide advice that is data-driven and as objective as possible. Ask questions, conduct investigations, do your due diligence, and come to meetings prepared with some background knowledge and a list of questions.

Here are five steps to help your investigations:

1. Identify sources of compensation.

When considering working with a financial planner, it's crucial to determine how they are compensated. A **fee-only investment advisor** who is employed by an independent Registered Investment

Adviser (RIA) firm is typically compensated with a salary to provide advice to the investor. They do not sell securities and, thus, do not receive commissions. The investment advisor may charge an hourly rate, a project fee, an annual retainer fee, or an asset-based fee determined by the assets under management (chapter 35 covers financial advisor compensation in greater detail).

On the other hand, a **commission-based or fee-based financial planner** who is working for a securities brokerage firm may charge a commission every time a transaction occurs or a financial product is purchased. They benefit from sales and are often incentivized by their company to push certain products.

It is possible to determine a financial advisor's source(s) of compensation by asking them directly, looking for disclosures on their company's website, or conducting an investigation on the BrokerCheck database (see point two, below).

2. Avoid brokers and brokerage firms.

Individuals who are licensed to sell investment securities are "registered representatives" of the securities brokerage firms they sell for. While these registered representatives may have good intentions, they will always be saddled with conflicts of interest due to the inevitable pressure to make sales. Determine if a financial planner has a brokerage license by heading to FINRA's BrokerCheck website, typing in the name of a financial advisor (or institution), and seeing what information crops up. If an individual is a registered broker, I urge you to steer clear (with some exceptions—refer to chapter 10 on registered brokers for more information).

3. Seek fee-only financial advisors.

As discussed above, fee-only financial advisors are not incentivized to make sales, which means they are *much* less likely to have conflicts of interest. A good hint that your financial planner operates under a fee-only model is if they work for a Registered Investment Adviser (RIA) as an Investment Adviser Representative (IAR). This registration is not a foolproof way to determine if someone is a fee-only advisor, but it's a start.

Fee-only financial planners must also provide a Form ADV Part 2 upon request (see chapter 30 for information about this disclosure form). Don't be shy about asking for this documentation, which shows the advisor is registered with the Securities and Exchange Commission (SEC) or state regulators.

Other great tools I've mentioned in previous chapters are platforms, such as Wealthramp, that match investors with fee-only fiduciaries or directories of fee-only financial advisors, like FeeOnlyNetwork and NAPFA's Find an Advisor search function. As a reminder, NAPFA is the foremost professional association of fee-only financial advisors in the nation, and all three of the aforementioned search tools feature NAPFA-registered advisors. To join NAPFA, a financial planner must be strictly fee-only, adhere to a set code of ethics, and renew a fiduciary oath every year.

4. Trust your instincts.

Many investors I've worked with have a strong gut instinct when it comes to trusting financial advisors. They often tell me that something "didn't feel right" with a past advisor or that the advice they were given felt "off" or "wrong."

Geoffrey Brown, former CEO of NAPFA, advises investors to trust their instincts when working with financial advisors. He says, "Conversations that focus on performance, purchasing products, or ones that are not personalized may be cause for concern. If the advisor is vague or unresponsive, that can be a red flag too."* If your advisor-client relationship feels off, it's a good idea to investigate further.

5. Ask about the fiduciary standard of care.

We've already talked about the importance of an advisor living up to a fiduciary standard of care, but how do you determine if a financial advisor is committed to this standard?

One way is to simply ask about it. If the advisor is hesitant or dodges the question, that's a definite warning sign.

If an advisor or advisory firm practices fiduciary duty, this commitment will often appear on their website. Look for that when conducting

* Brown, interview by author, May 24, 2022.

your search for a financial advisor. Additionally, Registered Investment Advisers are obligated to uphold this standard, so simply determining if an advisor is an Investment Adviser Representative (IAR) is a great way to figure out if they center their work around a fiduciary standard of care.

As an investor, the best way to determine if you're receiving objective financial advice is to educate yourself on what to look for, and then begin your investigations. There are no shortcuts here. It's critical to do your homework when seeking a financial advisor. As Geoffrey Brown says, "Selecting an advisor is one of the most significant decisions some of us will ever make. These relationships can last for decades which is why it's important to get it right."*

---

* Ibid.

Chapter 16
The Merits of Comprehensive Financial Advice

If you're buying a suit or dress for a special occasion, you'll be faced with many different considerations and will likely whittle down your choices by asking yourself a series of questions. Is the event formal, semiformal, or casual? Are fun colors permissible (or even expected)? Are any colors or styles taboo? Is the event themed? Will outdoor weather be a factor in your decision? And once you've purchased your suit or dress, you may have to pay a visit to a tailor to have it properly fitted. They will take your measurements and rework the fabric so it fits just right.

This same type of care and forethought goes into delivering comprehensive financial advice.

There is no such thing as a one-size-fits-all financial strategy. People are multifaceted and have many different goals, interests, circumstances, assets, debts, and on and on. A business owner might also be a parent, a world traveler, and a wine connoisseur. That same person might have inherited a large sum of money and their family home, or they might have a modest nest egg and a good deal of debt.

Since everyone has a unique financial story, it's vital for financial advisors to take as much relevant financial information into consideration as possible when dispensing advice. Additionally, in order for the advice to be truly comprehensive, the advisor must consider many different avenues their client could take to achieve a successful financial future. In addition to general financial planning, this could involve investment planning, banking, insurance, estate planning, and more.

Depending on their expertise, the financial advisor could facilitate some of these areas, or they could recommend trusted experts.

Why Is Comprehensive Financial Advice Important?

Before we get too far ahead of ourselves, let's back up momentarily and talk about why it's important for financial advice to be comprehensive. At its heart, comprehensive financial planning is all about goal achievement. We all have different monetary-related goals, and an all-encompassing financial strategy can help us obtain those goals.

A comprehensive financial approach gives investors a direction—a path to follow. And that can help reduce stress and assist in finance-related decision-making.

When financial advice is comprehensive, it's holistic. It takes the investor's "big picture" into account. A person's big picture could include kids in college, a new home, plans to retire in San Francisco, or lingering credit card debt. When financial advice is comprised of a mosaic of factors, it can lead to solid financial planning that is more complete and less prone to surprises.

Comprehensive advice goes hand in hand with having a comprehensive investment strategy. Patrick Geddes, cofounder of Aperio Group and author of *Transparent Investing,* discusses the merits of engaging in a wide-scope investing plan by saying, "Great investing for individuals almost always requires a long-term perspective, and a comprehensive investing strategy can help keep an investor anchored in a disciplined plan, hopefully avoiding flitting from one bright shiny object to another as interesting-sounding investment ideas appear on the horizon."*

As a longtime financial advisor, I believe comprehensive advice is foundational when it comes to smart investing. But how does this happen from a logistical standpoint? How do financial advisors piece together the information they need to build a logical, customized plan for their clients? Let's discuss.

---

* Geddes, interview by author, July 5, 2022.

How Do Financial Advisors Engage in Comprehensive Financial Planning?

To provide comprehensive financial advice and holistic planning, a financial advisor must be something of a detective. It's important to ask dozens of questions *and* ask the right questions.

When I work with a new client, I tend to start the process by asking about their goals. Client goals are the crux of each comprehensive financial plan. An advisor might come up with a sensible financial plan for a client, but if it doesn't match their goals, it's ultimately useless. A person's investment approach will change dramatically if they're aiming for early retirement, hoping to buy a multi-million-dollar mansion, or planning on selling their home and living in a recreational vehicle.

It's also worth noting that a person's goals might change over the years. A responsible financial advisor will periodically check in on their clients' goals and work with them to adjust their strategy accordingly.

After determining client goals, most financial advisors will begin gathering relevant information during a (fairly lengthy!) diagnostic meeting. This is not a random process. Any competent financial advisor will have a go-to list of questions to determine a client's unique financial situation. These questions typically fall into seven subject areas, as outlined by the Certified Financial Planner Board of Standards, Inc. (CFP Board):

1. Financial statement preparation and analysis
2. Insurance planning and risk management
3. Employee benefits planning
4. Investment planning
5. Income tax planning
6. Retirement planning
7. Estate planning

Other categories come to mind (such as developing a comprehensive philanthropic giving strategy), but these seven areas cover a lot of ground.

The questions a Certified Financial Planner® (CFP®) asks will typically relate to one or more of these seven categories, thus guiding the advisor to address their areas of focus. A person may urgently need retirement planning, for instance, but have little use for estate planning. That doesn't mean this individual will never require estate planning services, but it *does* mean these services can be put on the back burner for a while (or be considered "long-term concerns").

During this process, the financial planner will likely ask dozens—maybe even a hundred or more—questions and collect volumes of data from the client. While this process may seem lengthy and complicated to the average investor, a CFP® should have no trouble making personal recommendations based off the data collected.

At its core, this information revolves around a client's balance sheet—their assets and liabilities (and projected assets and liabilities). In a way, a financial advisor is a balance sheet steward. A good steward will have both a broad and deep understanding of a client's balance sheet and make recommendations accordingly. A not-so-good steward will overlook or ignore certain areas of the balance sheet and make recommendations that do not necessarily serve the client.

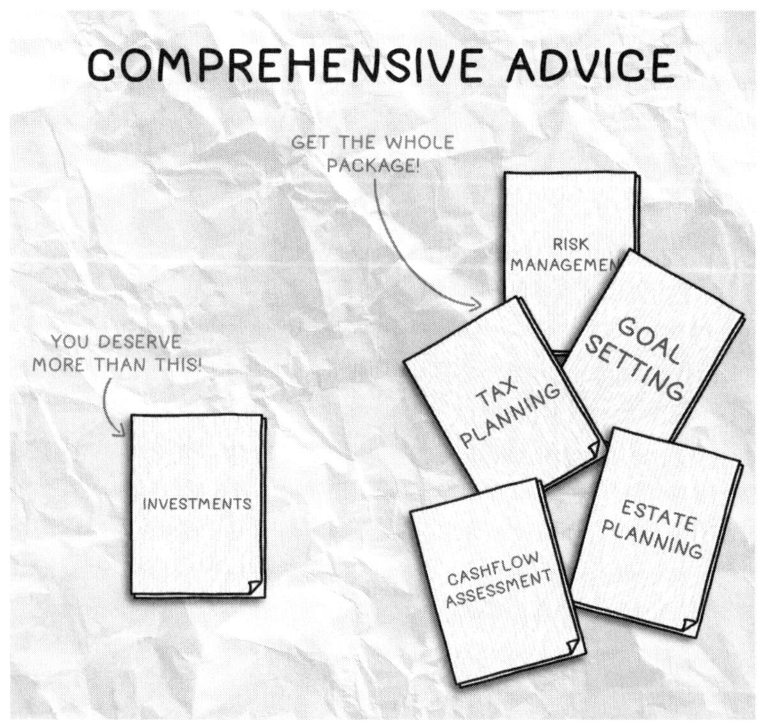

If a client is working with a financial advisor who asks minimal questions, glosses over certain financial areas, or neglects to ask about client goals, those are major red flags. As a consumer, be wary. Make sure your financial advisor sets up a diagnostic meeting to discuss your financial situation and goals in depth. And, once the advisor produces a financial plan (or *plans*, preferably), make sure it is comprehensive and aligns with your current situation and aspirations.

A Comprehensive Investment Plan

When a financial advisor creates an investment strategy for a client based off comprehensive, thorough data-gathering, the plan should be relatively accurate. The advisor has taken many variables into account, conducted detailed research, and applied their findings to financial best practices. In the end, comprehensive advice can directly translate to a comprehensive investment strategy.

Such a strategy is, admittedly, not terribly sexy. A comprehensive plan will likely involve a diversified portfolio, so all the investor's proverbial eggs are not placed in the same basket. When it comes to investing, a comprehensive approach is often a lower-risk approach.

Most of my clients understand the wisdom of pursuing a comprehensive investment strategy. However, not everyone is patient or prudent. Years ago, I worked with a young client who had made it big during the dot-com era. He had invested in tech stocks, made $5 million, and pulled his money from the market right before many tech stocks took a tumble (a risky decision, but one that happened to pay off for this young investor).

Many people would envy this person's position. With a prudent (and comprehensive!) investment strategy, he could have been set for life. However, the client was not enamored with the idea of pursuing the comprehensive investment route. He decided to ignore my advice and invested nearly all his money in real estate. Not only that, but he also secured another $5 million from a bank in the form of a loan.

There's an axiom in the investing world that goes something like, "The only way a wealthy person can become poor is through leverage." In other words, taking on unnecessary debt can be a risky and, ultimately, costly endeavor. That was the case for my young real-estate-focused client.

The client bought up land in Arizona and began developing housing . . . right before the housing market went belly-up. He ended up losing almost everything due to three critical mistakes:

1. He funneled all his assets into one asset class.
2. He funneled all his assets into one deal.
3. He relied on leverage (debt) for his investing endeavors.

His strategy was not comprehensive but narrowly focused. This recklessness was catastrophic for the young investor, and he ended up returning to me for advice with his tail between his legs.

The lesson here is that it pays to approach wealth planning holistically and prudently. A trustworthy financial advisor would never tell a client, "Bet all your money on red." Instead, they would take time to gain a deep understanding of the client's financial situation, make comprehensive recommendations based on their assessment, and create a comprehensive investment strategy to make that advice actionable.

Chapter 17

Why Independent Advice Matters

Let's say you own an Italian restaurant. That restaurant is beholden to a variety of health and safety standards, federal regulations, and state (or even city) regulations. Your restaurant will be periodically checked by a licensed food service inspector, who will make sure your perishable goods are properly refrigerated, your chefs are practicing good hygiene, your cooking equipment complies with safety standards, and a host of other considerations. In addition to these occasional inspections, any food that enters your doors will have undergone its own set of inspections, which have to do with how your food is harvested, packaged, or processed. The poultry must be antibiotic free; the tomato sauce needs to be properly sealed in its packaging.

All these inspections and regulations have been put in place to give your diners a safe and enjoyable experience. No one should have to worry about catching a salmonella infection, eating expired food, or being exposed to an allergen due to mislabeled food. Their only concern should be whether or not to splurge on the tiramisu for dessert.

The restaurant is an independent entity, and all the standards and regulations related to it are upheld by outside regulatory bodies. Could you imagine if you, as a restaurant owner, had to inspect each food item that passed through its doors for quality, safety, and proper packaging? The likelihood of something slipping through the cracks is extremely high. And you would probably not be motivated to do a thorough job.

This example illustrates why independent entities that work in tandem with outside agencies, interests, or regulators are a good thing. It's about checks and balances. A house can't be built without numerous experts inspecting it. A law can't be passed by an individual legislator.

The same standard should be expected in the field of financial advice.

While it's true the US government and independent agencies regulate certain aspects of the financial sector (the FDIC makes sure deposits are insured at banks; the SEC regulates the investment profession), there is a lot of gray area that is loosely regulated or up for interpretation. One of those gray areas has to do with independence.

"Independence" in Relation to Financial Advice

It's difficult to pin down a specific definition of *independent financial advice* (and, by extension, *independent advisors*), but I tend to think of it in simple terms: advice that is free of conflicts of interest.

As discussed in chapter 8, conflicts of interest can arise in a variety of ways. If a financial advisor also works as a broker, they may receive bonuses or incentives for selling certain financial products. If a bank or insurance company partners with a financial advisory firm, that firm will likely be incentivized to promote products sold by its bank and insurance company partners. These are clear conflicts of interest, but they can be much more nuanced and difficult to pin down. For example, a broker may receive a kickback for selling certain securities, but that kickback might be built into a transaction fee.

Truly independent financial advisors are not tied to any specific products or product-selling companies. Their focus is on delivering prudent, unbiased advice to their clients since they have no motivation to do otherwise. Dave Butler,* co-CEO of Dimensional Fund Advisors, learned a different way to think about the qualities of a client-centered, independent financial advisor from Dan Wheeler, founder of the financial advisor business at Dimensional. He says that Dan described this type of advisor as sitting "on the same side of the table as their client." Butler goes on to say, "That visual really made

* Dave Butler serves as the co-CEO of Dimensional Fund Advisors LP and is a Dimensional director. He joined the firm in 1995 and was named co-CEO in 2017. Additionally, he serves on the boards of Dimensional's US mutual funds and exchange-traded funds. Dave is a passionate investor advocate.

sense to me, and it was a true 'aha' moment in my career. And nearly three decades later, I believe just as passionately in this model of conflict-free advice that does what's right for investors."*

Another aspect of independence and being conflict-of-interest-free involves maintaining separation between the company and regulators. You'd probably be cautious if you walked into a restaurant that was bribing the local health and safety inspector. And it would be wise to exercise the same kind of caution when working with a financial advisor who has intimate ties with the SEC (as was the case with the infamous Bernie Madoff, whose daughter—who led the firm's compliance staff—was married to a former SEC compliance examiner).

Why Independent Financial Guidance Matters

Let's look at the case of Bernie Madoff to highlight why independent financial guidance is vitally important. Madoff not only acted as a financial advisor for his clients but also as a broker and the investment manager of a proprietary selection of securities. He handled all aspects of his clients' investments as a custodian, broker, banker, and investment manager. There were no checks and balances, no outside money manager, financial planner, or investment advisor to raise a red flag.

With no third party to sound the alarm, Madoff was able to maintain his shady practices for seventeen years.

In an article by CNBC, fraud attorney Andrew Stoltmann notes the importance of investing money with reputable third parties. He says, "Ensuring a financial advisor uses a reputable, third-party custodial firm like Fidelity or Charles Schwab to hold investor money is essential. . . . That makes it much harder for an advisor to steal money or take advantage of a client, since the assets aren't held in-house."†

Another aspect of independence (which I've already touched on) has to do with conflicts of interest. If a financial advisor is incentivized by sales commissions or bonuses, they—and the advice they give—are not truly independent. Their advice may be colored by the pressures

---

* Butler, interview by author, August 30, 2023.

† Iacurci, "Here's How Investors Can Spot the Next Bernie Madoff."

of the financial advisory firm or third-party product providers to sell specific products.

If an investment advisor is also registered as a broker, they are not required to uphold the same fiduciary standards as someone who is solely licensed as a Registered Investment Adviser (RIA). While an RIA is legally required to meet a fiduciary standard, a broker has historically only been required to meet a "suitability standard," which means they may not always be acting in the client's best interests. On June 5, 2019, the Securities and Exchange Commission adopted a package of rulemakings and interpretations that include a new Regulation Best Interest (often referred to as Reg BI) which provides guidance for brokers to act in the best interest of the customer. Reg BI is a new rule that requires brokerage firms to act in the best interest of their retail customers when making recommendations of securities transactions. There are some experts who believe that if the SEC and FINRA were to enforce Reg BI in a meaningful way, that it could significantly enhance the quality of recommendations and reduce conflicts of interest in the broker-dealer business model.

I understand all too well the temptations of financial incentives and bonuses. When I worked as a broker back in the 1980s, I was certainly not immune to them, and neither were my colleagues, despite our best intentions. My eventual rejection of a commission-based system led me to start my own financial advisory firm, Allodium Investment Consultants, in 2005. When I selected the name for my firm, I chose a word that directly relates to independence.

Allodium is defined by the Collins English Dictionary as "lands held in absolute ownership, free from such obligations as rent or services due to an overlord."* Contrast the allodial system of independent land ownership with the feudal system, which required allegiance to an overlord through servitude. The concept of allodium represents the philosophical foundation of Allodium's fiercely independent approach to investment advice, unrestricted by the conflicts of interest that plague Wall Street banks and brokerage firms. As a fee-only firm, we

---

* "allodium," *Collins English Dictionary—Complete & Unabridged 10th Edition*, retrieved August 23, 2024, from Dictionary.com, http://www.dictionary.com/browse/allodium.

provide objective investment advice that is not biased by the sale of commission-based investment products.

How Can You Determine If a Financial Advisory Firm (or Financial Advisor) Is Operating under an Independent Framework?

I suggest following a few basic steps to determine if a financial advisory firm is independent. Keep in mind, it can be exceedingly difficult to pinpoint *all* potential conflicts of interest, but doing some cursory research can set you up for success.

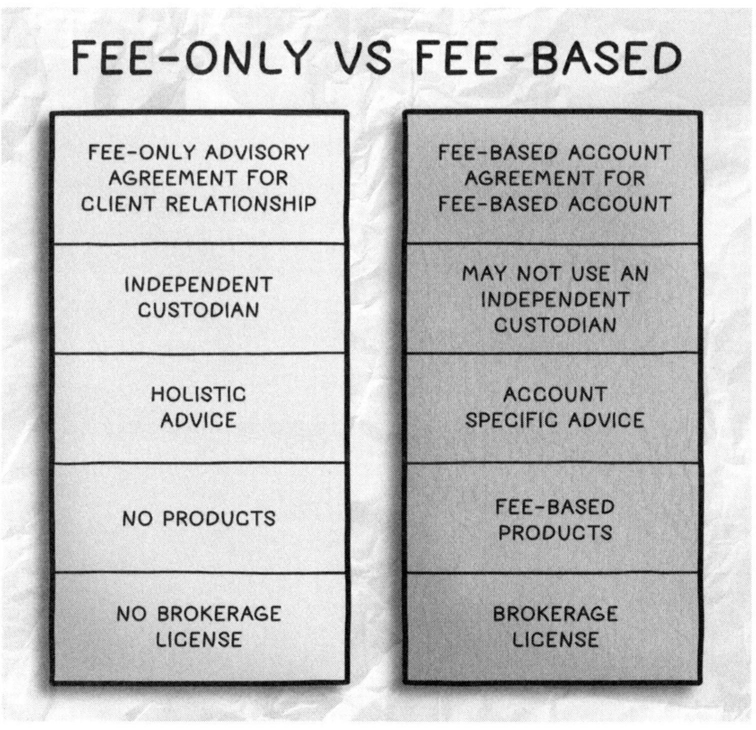

1. Avoid investment securities brokers.

For reasons we've already discussed, investment securities brokers have inherent conflicts of interest and cannot be considered independent. Avoid working with brokers by visiting Financial Industry Regulatory Authority's (FINRA) BrokerCheck website, which allows you to type in the name of an individual financial advisor or institution to determine who is licensed as an investment securities broker and who is registered as an investment advisor. Keep in mind, some investment advisors are also registered as brokers, which means they carry the same conflicts of interest as a typical broker.

2. Choose fee-only financial advisors.

According to the National Association of Personal Financial Advisors (NAPFA), "a Fee-Only financial advisor [is] one who is compensated solely by the client with neither the advisor nor any related party receiving compensation that is contingent on the purchase or sale of a financial product."* Though not *every* fee-only advisor is completely independent, you (as a consumer) will have a much better chance of finding an independent financial advisor if you focus your search on fee-only advisors. To do this, navigate to online matching platforms that pair individual investors with fee-only financial advisors who are part of NAPFA, the largest professional association of fee-only financial advisors in the nation. Reliable online directories and matching platforms include FeeOnlyNetwork, NAPFA's Find an Advisor, and Wealthramp.

3. Look for language about independence.

If a financial advisory firm is committed to providing independent, unbiased advice, it will likely describe that commitment on its website or other literature. Take, for example, this statement from financial advisory firm Steele Capital Management, Inc.:

> Our independence is what makes us different. We have no proprietary interest in any of the securities we recommend. We are not employees of a brokerage firm, bank or mutual fund company. We work only for you.†

Another investment advisory firm called Ellwood Associates (recently acquired by CAPTRUST) released a statement in 2019 called "Why We Think Independence Matters." In that statement, it declares itself a "truly independent, unbiased investment consultant, for

---

* The National Association of Personal Financial Advisors, "Our Standards."

† Steele Capital Management, "Home Page."

which 100% of revenue comes from consulting—not from soft-dollar arrangements or from other product lines and services." It goes on to state that "all of Ellwood's own revenues are derived from our consulting services. We are not a broker/dealer. We do not offer products, research, or services to money managers. We receive no compensation from money managers. We don't revenue share with investment managers or other service providers."*

Clear language about independence is a great sign the financial advisory firm is committed to this value.

4. Look for checks and balances.

An optimal investment structure includes a series of checks and balances. Unlike Madoff's system, the truly independent financial advisor will ideally be acting separately from investment managers, brokerage firms, and custodians. This way, any advice given to the investor will be free from the influence of these other investment service providers.

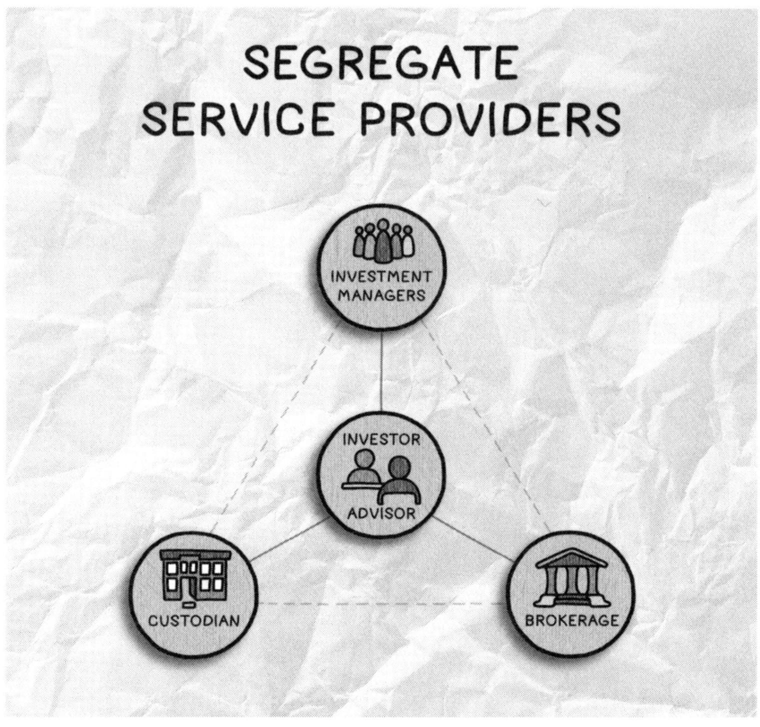

---

* Ellwood Associates, "Ellwood Viewpoint: Why We Think Independence Matters."

Independent financial guidance matters. If a financial advisor is saddled with conflicts of interest, they will constantly deal with that friction and may find it difficult to provide you with unbiased advice. As a consumer, do not underestimate the importance of independence when it comes to seeking a financial advisor.

Chapter 18
Why Maintain a Disciplined Investment Strategy?

You've probably heard the wild success stories—the tales of rogue investors playing the market and making hundreds of thousands in an afternoon. These stories are flashy and glamorous. They tempt even the most logical among us to eschew best practices and take a gamble.

But that's the problem. Attempting to outsmart the stock market *is* a gamble, and it rarely pays off. For every effortless, get-rich-quick story you hear, there are dozens of other stories that ended in loss or, at best, mediocre gains. No one likes to flaunt their losses, so these humiliating endeavors probably remain close to the chest.

The antithesis of reckless risk-taking is discipline. A disciplined investment strategy goes hand in hand with prudence and logic. However, there are many external factors that tempt both investors and financial advisors to throw caution to the wind and make not-so-prudent decisions. Let's talk about what comprises a disciplined investment approach (and how to seek discipline-centered advice), the pressures that tend to erode discipline, and how to put disciplined investment decision-making at the core of your investment strategy (using tools and resources from reliable financial organizations).

What Is Disciplined Investing?

In essence, disciplined investing is data-driven, evidence-based, and process-oriented. It's *not* based on unproven methods or hunches but is, instead, steady and focused. Vice President of the Centre for Fiduciary Excellence (CEFEX) Carlos Panksep* says, "Disciplined investing must employ prudent decision-making at every step. A prudent approach is characterized by documented and structured processes, whether at the individual or institutional level."†

Another characteristic of disciplined investing is the utilization of a *repeatable* quantitative research process. An investment manager should be able to trace back their steps and explain to the investor how each investment decision was made. This isn't like throwing spaghetti against the wall and seeing what sticks. Disciplined investing is planful and deliberate. If you want to make sure you're receiving discipline-centered advice, ask your financial advisor about their investing approach and which factors, statistics, or evidence they use to drive their decisions.

Investment advisors have a variety of tools at their disposal (we'll discuss a few later in this chapter) to help them put together a sensible investment strategy for a client. A prudent financial advisor will stay the course, leverage these tools to their clients' advantage, and not let "hot stocks" or unproven methods cloud their judgment.

One way for financial advisors to approach financial planning for clients is to use Fi360 methodology. Fi360 is an organization that "helps financial intermediaries use prudent fiduciary practices to profitably gather, grow and protect investors' assets."‡ Their recommended steps for developing a disciplined investment strategy are broken down into four main parts:

1. Organize
2. Formalize
3. Implement
4. Monitor

---

* Carlos Panksep is the vice president of the Centre for Fiduciary Excellence (CEFEX) and is a consultant for Broadridge Financial Solutions, Inc. He managed certification operations for ISO Registrar for seven years and has decades of experience in high tech management.

† Panksep, interview by author, July 6, 2022.

‡ Fi360, "What We Do."

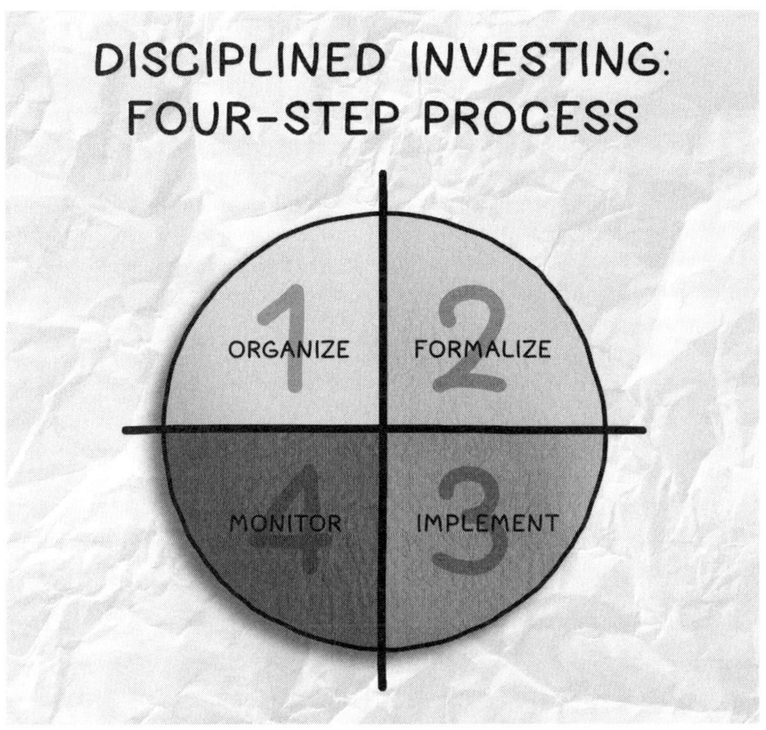

Carlos Panksep explains this four-step structure succinctly. He says, "The first step is to Organize the investment information, whether that be legal or other practical information. Next, one must Formalize the strategy, which can include identifying objectives and constraints, formulating asset allocation and adopting an Investment Policy Statement. The third step is to Implement, or decide on the investments, usually using some form of due diligence. Lastly, the Monitoring step is essential to ensure that objectives and constraints are being met."*

This stalwart approach has been proven to work time and again. When an investment strategy is prudent and disciplined, the consumer wins. The Centre for Fiduciary Excellence, or CEFEX, is an independent certification organization that assesses financial advisory firms and promotes fiduciary best practices. CEFEX describes the benefits of a disciplined approach for the consumer by saying, "Documented, repeatable processes are more likely to generate higher returns over

* Panksep, interview by author, July 6, 2022.

time, because they are not dependent on timing, luck, 'in-fashion' or un-substantiated decisions."* Exactly. This approach may not be flashy, but it works.

When Your Investment Discipline Falters

If a disciplined investment approach is so reliable, why do some investors and financial advisors choose undisciplined, or even risky, investing options? To me, there are two main factors that erode discipline: hope and fear.

Hope *sounds* like a good thing (and it is in everyday life), but prudent investment strategies are not built on hope. A data-centric, evidence-based, proven approach is a much safer route when it comes to investing. You might feel inspired by someone's unconventional investing approach and *hopeful* that you'll have the same luck, but ultimately, smart investing is not emotion-driven. It's not based on gut feelings, hunches, or sudden bursts of inspiration.

On the opposite end of the emotional spectrum is fear. When an investment approach is rooted in fear, people tend to make rash decisions, such as pulling their money out of the market when stock prices dip. Unfortunately, fear is a common tactic used by the news media and social media to get more viewers, listeners, or clicks. Frankly, boring news doesn't sell. It's difficult to turn heads or garner attention when your big headline is "Experts Agree Your Investments Are Fine" or "Stock Market Experiencing Absolutely Normal Fluctuations."

Because *normal* and *steady* are not words that sell newspapers or get website clicks, the media generally glosses over any good news and emphasizes the bad. And when a person is exposed to sensationalized, doom-and-gloom stories again and again, that can have major psychological consequences.

On the brink of the Great Recession in the late 2000s, I was working with a client who was well-educated and seemed perfectly rational. We had established a comprehensive, disciplined investment strategy, and he had no qualms with the direction we were headed . . . until the economy started showing signs of distress.

---

* CEFEX, "How Clients Benefit from Their Advisor's CEFEX Certification."

The housing bubble burst, leading to the subprime mortgage crisis. The stock market crashed. Two Bear Stearns hedge funds collapsed. Joblessness was high and morality low.

My client started to panic. However, despite the market's prolonged slump, I wasn't terribly worried. If history is any indication (and, in truth, it's an *excellent* indication), the economy would eventually recover, and the stock market would bounce back. Sure, a few companies might not weather the storm, but that's hardly an issue if you, as an investor, maintain a properly diversified portfolio.

This client's portfolio *was* diverse. He was invested in an array of companies and asset classes. Yet, his decision-making logic began to steadily give way to blind fear.

He immersed himself in television news programs morning, noon, and night. He listened to the dire economic forecasts and fear mongering. He internalized the message that was repeated over and over: "Pull your money out of the market! We're headed toward another Great Depression!"

I tried to calm and reason with him. I even asked him to bring a trusted friend to our next meeting so he could get a third-party opinion about his current investment strategy. He agreed and asked a banker friend to sit down with us during our next meeting.

At the meeting, I went over the client's investment strategy with the friend and asked him to weigh in. The friend agreed that the strategy seemed sound, and we decided that the best course of action was, really, no action at all. Stay the course, and the market will sort itself out.

The client remained unconvinced.

A week later, he called and said the nation's financial state was giving him so much anxiety, he had to pay a visit to his doctor. He couldn't sleep. He decided to pull his money from the stock market and end his relationship with my firm.

The client's irrational and decidedly undisciplined approach only led to disappointment and loss. In 2009, the stock market bounced back and made one of the most spectacular recoveries in history—and my former client lost out on all that growth. In fact, he did the opposite of what any financial advisor would suggest by selling low and

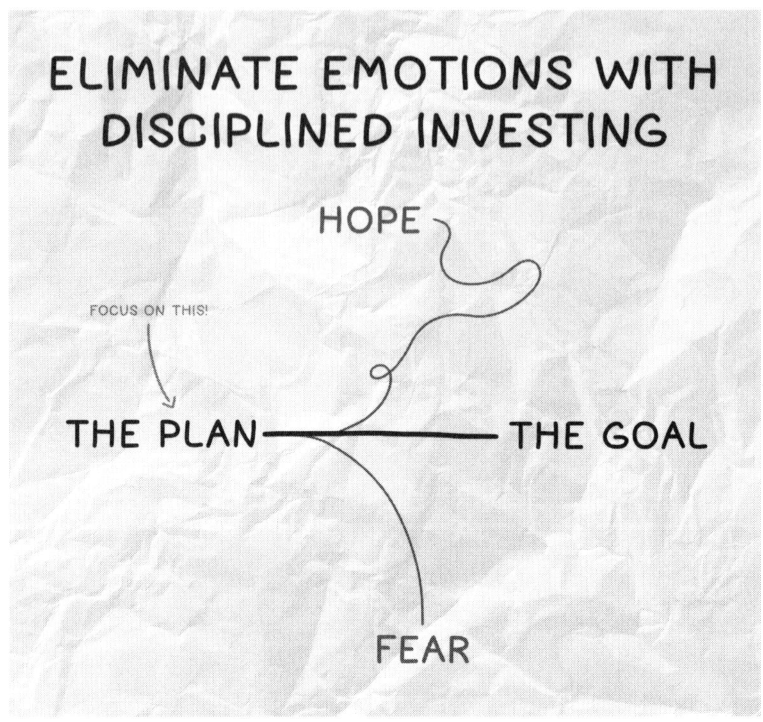

(if and when he re-entered the market) buying high. His fear-based decision to vacate the market was a hard-knocks lesson in the merits of maintaining a disciplined investing approach.

Tools to Develop (and Maintain) a Disciplined Investment Strategy

Developing and maintaining a disciplined investment strategy does not have to be overly difficult. Several tools are available for both investors and investment managers to formulate a prudent, comprehensive, and disciplined strategy. Here are three:

1. Prudent Practices *handbook*

The *Prudent Practices for Investment Advisors* handbook is a powerful tool for both advisors and investors. It provides information and strategic guidelines to develop ethical, client-centric, and prudent investment strategies. The first version of this handbook was released in 2003, and, although it has been updated periodically, the core tenets of the book remain the same, centered around a disciplined, principled investing approach.

Fiduciary consultant and lead AIF® instructor Rich Lynch[*] agrees that using this handbook is an excellent way for investors to ground themselves in a disciplined investment approach. One of his top tips for investors is to "become familiar with and implement as best as possible a prudent investment process as defined in the 'Prudent Practices for Investment Advisors' or 'Prudent Practices for Investment Stewards' handbooks published by Fi360."[†]

2. Fi360 Fiduciary Score

As discussed above, Fi360 is an independent organization that promotes prudent fiduciary practices. This laudable organization has developed an evaluation called the Fi360 Fiduciary Score. Their score "evaluates investments across a spectrum of quantitative data points to determine if the investment meets a minimum fiduciary standard of care."[‡] Some of the factors the score takes into account are regulatory oversight, stability of the organization, and performance of a specific investment relative to its peers.

When working with a financial advisor, be sure to inquire about the Fi360 Fiduciary Score and ask how your investments measure up.

3. CEFEX Fiduciary Assessment

As mentioned earlier in this chapter, CEFEX is an independent certification organization that assesses financial advisory firms and promotes fiduciary best practices. CEFEX will only certify advisory firms who utilize a factual approach that facilitates information-gathering and decision-making based on market data. Discipline is baked into

---

* J. Richard "Rich" Lynch is a retired fiduciary consultant, instructor, and subject matter expert for Fi360. He is also a former member of the CEFEX Registration Committee. As the primary instructor for Fi360 Training, he was instrumental in providing investment education and training programs that award the Accredited Investment Fiduciary® (AIF®) and Accredited Investment Fiduciary Analyst®(AIFA®) professional designations. As a former CEFEX Registration Committee member, he oversaw and approved the assessment and certification of all CEFEX-certified firms.

† Lynch, interview by author, July 20, 2022.

‡ Allodium Investment Consultants, "Manager Screening: Investment Process."

the CEFEX Fiduciary Assessment. Advisors who choose speculation over data and emotion over discipline would not meet CEFEX's rigorous standards.

As a consumer, it's a good idea to search for CEFEX-certified financial advisory firms. If an advisor has earned CEFEX's stamp of approval, you'll likely be in good hands.

When it comes to developing and maintaining a prudent investment strategy, discipline is key. While it's true some investors have made it rich by playing the market, betting on unproven securities, or using unconventional methodologies, these approaches will likely let you down. Decades of data shows us that a prudent and disciplined path is the best, and most reliable, way to build wealth. This is how I handle my own investment planning, and I treat my clients' assets with the same level of discipline and care.

Chapter 19
Financial Advisors, Professionalism, and Being a Smart Consumer

We are a nation of do-it-yourselfers (DIY-ers). YouTube is littered with videos on everything from turning wooden bowls on a lathe to teaching your dog basic commands. Pinterest can provide "recipe hacks" or instructions for building a garden shed. You can take online classes in French, coding, or crocheting. With so many resources available, is it any wonder people believe they can take on financial planning on their own?

Admittedly, this DIY approach *can* make sense, especially if an individual has a straightforward financial situation (no dependents, no estate, very few assets). However, the train can quickly go off the rails when you add in layers of complexity. And the truth is, many people do have a complicated financial situation and would be ill-advised to attempt their own financial planning.

I once worked with a client who insisted on drawing up his own estate planning documents. He was a lawyer (though not an estate planning lawyer) and thought he knew enough to take matters into his own hands. When I pressed him on the issue and asked why he didn't hire one of his colleagues to draft the documents, he replied, "Those guys charge too much."

He saw no irony in his statement. He honestly believed it was not worth it to pay another lawyer to do their job.

Skeptical, I asked if I could review the documents he had produced. Almost immediately, I noticed errors in his approach. As written, his estate would end up incurring an unnecessary tax, and his heirs would lose approximately $300,000.

When we noticed this oversight, I sat down with the thrifty lawyer and his wife and said, "If I were to show you a way to save $300,000, would you do it?"

The man hesitated, but I'm certain he could feel his wife's eyes boring into him.

"Sure," he said.

I then proceeded to explain how he could retitle his assets to avoid the steep estate taxes his heirs were currently set up to incur. The client had to swallow a bit of pride that day and admit that he had been penny-wise and pound-foolish.

I wish I could say this case was unique, but the truth is, many people attempt to take a stab at their own financial planning, no matter how complex their situation. I can think of a dozen clients off the top of my head who decided they could do the work of a professional financial planner but failed utterly. This is mainly because they lacked one crucial attribute: professionalism.

What Is Professionalism?

When it comes to financial planning, we can think about professionalism in two distinct ways. On the one hand, professionalism is defined by behavior—acting in a professional, businesslike manner. This might involve showing up for meetings on time, returning a client's calls and emails, and not sharing sensitive information with anyone who is not privy to it.

The other definition of professionalism has to do with competency and qualifications in relation to a specific profession. Colonel Sean Hannah (Retired) is an experienced senior leader, scholar, and leader development expert. He discusses professions and professionalism in his eloquent article "Toward a Noble Profession." In it, he says, "A business, or a specific field of business, cannot simply declare itself to be a profession. Professions are granted status only when they earn it from the constituents and society they serve." This status is granted based on "the legitimacy and trustworthiness earned by the profession through its actions and practices and the value it provides to constituent parties and society."[*]

In the financial arena, not just anyone can be considered a professional. It takes years of training, experience, exams, and continuing education to become a professional financial advisor. It's not enough to take a two-hour online course or watch a handful of YouTube videos. Although people *think* they can easily learn how to create their own comprehensive financial plan, they often do not understand the nuances involved. As the saying goes, "You don't know what you don't know." There are many complex and less-than-obvious aspects of financial planning that most consumers will not even entertain or consider, simply because they aren't aware such aspects exist. When it comes to receiving quality financial advice, it is prudent to seek counsel from a qualified professional.

Choosing a Professional

If you, as a consumer, decide you need professional guidance to create and maintain a financial plan, where do you turn? As we discussed in past chapters, anyone can call themselves a financial advisor, financial planner, or wealth manager. One way to separate the wheat from the chaff (the qualified and trustworthy financial advisors from the underqualified financial advisors and the charlatans) is to consider certifications and designations.

There is a reason that professional organizations exist. They create a standard of excellence and act as a safeguard for consumers. For financial advisors, one of the most reliable indications of professionalism is the Certified Financial Planner® designation. This designation represents "a high level of competency, ethics and professionalism" and indicates that the financial advisor is held to a fiduciary standard of care.[†]

To earn a CFP® designation, financial planners must go through a rigorous certification process that includes demanding **education,**

---

* Hannah, "Toward a Noble Profession."

† CFP Board, "Personal Financial Planning: A Guide to Starting Your Personal Financial Plan."

examination, experience, and ethical requirements. These standards are called "the four E's," and, collectively, they indicate a high level of professionalism. This person must also take continuing education courses each year and adhere to a fiduciary standard of care. Brian Thorp, founder and CEO of Wealthtender, says, "Most consumers will benefit considerably by narrowing their search to advisors who have earned this gold-standard credential. Consumers choosing to hire a CFP® can feel confident their advisor has completed a rigorous curriculum and gained industry experience with a commitment to place their clients' interests ahead of their own."*

Keep in mind, however, that a CFP® designation does not necessarily guarantee you're working with a flawless financial advisor *or* a financial advisor who is right for you and your circumstances. As Steve Atkinson, former managing director of advisor relations for Buckingham Strategic Partners, LLC, points out, "There are many non-CFP®-holding advisors that do a phenomenal job, and I've met plenty of CFP® title holders that I wouldn't refer anyone to."† Consumer discretion is always advised.

To find a list of CFP® professionals in your area, visit www.plannersearch.org (a database maintained by the Financial Planning Association®, a membership organization for CFP® professionals).

In addition to becoming a certified CFP®, financial advisors may choose to pursue other professional designations. I consider these designations a bonus since they demonstrate a deep commitment to professionalism and involve specialized training and specific areas of expertise. These include:

- **CFA® (Chartered Financial Analyst®):** This highly sought-after designation takes about four years to complete and is considered one of the top finance certifications. The main areas of focus of this finance certification are portfolio management and investment analysis.
- **AIF® (Accredited Investment Fiduciary®):** This designation

---

* Thorp, interview by author, August 12, 2023.

† Atkinson, interview by author, August 10, 2023.

focuses on fiduciary duty and providing a high level of fiduciary care to clients. Earned through Fi360 (an organization focused on fiduciary education), the AIF® designation demonstrates that the financial advisor has the necessary education, competence, and commitment to ethical standards to serve their clients' best interests.

- **CPA (Certified Public Accountant):** A CPA is a licensed provider of professional accounting and financial management services. This often includes performing financial audits or preparing tax documents or other financial statements. To become a CPA, an individual needs to pass a rigorous four-part exam in addition to meeting their state's education requirements.

One Step Further

If you work with a CFP® professional (and/or someone who holds the other three designations I've discussed), you will almost assuredly be working with a competent, qualified individual. That is a great start, but it does not address the problem with Certified Financial Planners® who are dually registered as both an Investment Adviser Representative and a stockbroker.

As we've discussed, this dual registration can be problematic because a dually registered Certified Financial Planner® can act as a financial planner in the morning and a broker in the afternoon. You can never be certain who you're dealing with. A broker is not obligated to uphold a fiduciary standard of care and can (and often does) earn commissions.

To protect yourself, you could interview a financial planner using the Financial Planning Association's® sample questions.* Or, you could take a shortcut to bypass any CFPs® who are also registered brokers. The shortcut is simple: use credible online directories and matching tools which pair investors with qualified fee-only fiduciaries (as a reminder, Wealthramp, FeeOnlyNetwork, and NAPFA's Find an Advisor are among the best for the job).

* Financial Planning Association, "Choosing a CFP® Professional: Questions to Ask."

Essentially, we can encapsulate the advice in this chapter in three steps:

1. Value professionalism.

Instead of attempting to "hack" and DIY your way to a financial plan, acknowledge that you could benefit from the assistance of a professional financial planner. Just as you would trust a medical professional with your health care or a pilot with flying a plane, so, too, is it wise for you to leave comprehensive financial planning to qualified professionals.

2. Seek a CFP®.

When searching for a professional financial planner, it makes sense to look for those who have a Certified Financial Planner® designation. These individuals have had to submit to rigorous education, examination, experience, and ethical requirements. Financial educator Michael Kitces emphasizes this point by saying, "Seeking out a CFP® professional is so important—it's a marker for those who have actually invested into their education to give financial planning advice by completing all the educational requirements and sitting for a (much more rigorous) exam. Simply put, if you're hiring a professional for advice, make sure they've actually gotten training and education for it!"*

3. Seek NAPFA-Registered Financial Advisors.

NAPFA-Registered Financial Advisors are highly trained, fee-only, and adhere to NAPFA's code of ethics. This organization sets a high bar for trustworthiness, competency, and integrity.

BONUS: Other Certifications/Designations

Consider any supplemental certifications or designations your financial advisor might have. The three designations we discussed earlier in the chapter can all be tremendous assets, especially if you are seeking specific guidance or expertise.

Financial planning is more than a hobby; it's a profession that

* Kitces, interview by author, July 24, 2023.

involves rigorous training, a profound depth (and breadth) of knowledge, and continuous education. Since anyone can call themselves a financial advisor or wealth manager, it's imperative for consumers to be wary of charlatans. Do your due diligence and pay attention to financial advisors' professional designations and certifications, which can be excellent indications of competency.

Chapter 20
Fiduciary: A Difficult Term to Define

If I asked a dozen different people to describe ice cream, I would probably receive similar answers. Most would agree that ice cream is traditionally made of frozen milk or cream, sweetened in some way, and flavored with any number of fruits (strawberry, black cherry, peach) or spices (chocolate, vanilla). If I showed this same group of people a collection of pictures, they could probably effortlessly identify the pictures of ice cream. Even if all the pictures depicted desserts, ice cream would likely be distinct.

What if I tried this same exercise using the term *fiduciary*? What if, instead of asking a dozen random people, I asked a dozen subject-matter experts about the meaning of *fiduciary*? Would I come to a similar consensus, as in the ice cream experiment?

I did, in fact, run this exercise recently with members of a prominent group of investment fiduciaries. This distinguished group is far better qualified to define *fiduciary* than anyone else I can think of. Even so, their answers varied greatly. Some focused on the root of the word *fiduciary* (which stems from the Latin word *fidere*, which means "to trust"), while others focused on the legal obligations of a fiduciary and still others articulated the ethical and moral responsibilities of a fiduciary.

Who's right?

They all are. Each definition made sense in its own right and was justified by facts and precedence. And this is precisely why investors are often befuddled by the term *fiduciary*. There is no single agreed-upon definition. It's possible to think about the term on many different levels and from many different perspectives. Instead of defining *ice cream*, we're suddenly trying to define *American cuisine*. If you said "burgers, fries, and apple pie," you'd be correct; if you said "a wide variety of dishes adapted from countries across the world," you'd also be correct. The same is true of *fiduciary*.

The exercise was not futile, however. As I combed through online definitions of *fiduciary* and read the responses of members of the group of investment fiduciaries, I did find several commonalities and general points of agreement, which I will discuss in this chapter. I believe it's important for consumers to develop an understanding of the key attributes of a fiduciary, in addition to learning about a few different ways of defining *fiduciary*. Armed with this knowledge, investors will be better equipped to find knowledgeable, trustworthy financial advisors who are committed to upholding a fiduciary standard of care. And, on the other side of the coin, they will gain a better understanding of who to avoid and how to identify red flags.

In this chapter, I will focus on defining *fiduciary* from several different angles. In the next chapter, I will discuss how investors can use this definition to guide their search for a trustworthy, prudent financial advisor—someone who will provide excellent fiduciary-based advice.

Defining Fiduciary

One of the earliest official attempts to define *fiduciary* came in the aftermath of the Great Depression. With the goal of fighting fraud and improving transparency in the financial industry, the US government passed the Securities Act of 1933, followed by the Investment Advisers Act of 1940. The Investment Advisers Act defines the meaning of *fiduciary* as one who has "a duty of loyalty and duty of care, which means that the advisor must put their client's interests above their own."*

Though the roots of the Investment Advisers Act remain strong, the meaning of *fiduciary* has morphed over the decades. It has been redefined by state governments, legal entities, and independent

* Kagan, "Investment Advisers Act of 1940: Definition, Overview."

organizations (some of which are committed to promoting transparency and integrity in the financial arena). However, aspects of the original definition remain intact.

Today, when searching for different definitions of *fiduciary*, you're likely to come across one term over and over again: ***trust***. Merriam-Webster offers the following definitions:

fiduciary (adjective)—of, relating to, or involved in a confidence or trust

fiduciary (noun)—one that holds a fiduciary relation or acts in a fiduciary capacity[*]

When thinking about *fiduciary* from a legal angle, it's helpful to turn to a legal dictionary, such as the one provided by Farlex, which defines fiduciary as follows (emphasis added):

> "An individual in whom another has placed the utmost **trust** and confidence to manage and protect property or money. The relationship wherein one person has an obligation to act for another's benefit."[†]

Trust was also mentioned in the survey I conducted. CEO of InvestSense James Watkins is an expert on fiduciary law. He says, "A fiduciary is an individual or any entity to whom another individual or entity **entrusts** the management of their affairs. It can be limited to just one issue or a broad range of issues."[‡]

The word *trust* also appears when referring to "trustees." In the state of Minnesota, a fiduciary is legally defined as "an agent, **trustee**, partner, corporate officer or director, or other representative owing a fiduciary duty with respect to an instrument."[§]

Some legal definitions of *fiduciary* deviate somewhat from the core tenet of trust. The state of Delaware, where over half of the nation's Fortune 500 companies are incorporated, has a somewhat different definition of *fiduciary* and fiduciary duties. Delaware corporate law

* Merriam-Webster, "Fiduciary."

† The Free Dictionary by Farlex, "Fiduciary."

‡ Watkins, interview by the author, April 15, 2022.

§ Minnesota Legislature, *Notice of Breach of Fiduciary Duty.*

necessitates corporate directors adhere to a **duty of care** (acting with prudence and being reasonably informed) and a **duty of loyalty** (putting the corporation's and shareholders' interests before the director's personal interests).*

James Watkins defines a fiduciary's duties similarly, saying, "A fiduciary has several duties, the two primary duties being the **duty of loyalty** and the **duty of prudence**."†

Allan Henriques,‡ a CEFEX Analyst, expands the definition of fiduciary duty even further, saying, "Typically, there are three recognized 'fiduciary duties.'" He lists them as **duty of loyalty**, **duty of care** (to act prudently), and **duty to obey** all applicable legal requirements.§

These definitions focus on fiduciaries and fiduciary duty from a legal perspective, but it is possible—and beneficial—to look at these terms through a different lens.

Beyond the Legal Definition

While it is helpful to understand how fiduciary/fiduciary duty is legally defined, these definitions do not necessarily articulate the moral and ethical standards followed by trustworthy fiduciaries. If we expand our definition to consider moral/ethical implications, we introduce a whole new set of terms and expectations. Some of the words that cropped up in my survey were:

- diligence
- continuous improvement
- best interest
- documented processes

---

* Bradshaw Law Group, "Duty of Care and Duty of Loyalty Owed by Directors in Delaware."

† Watkins, "Battle of the Best Interests: Why the Financial Services Industry Opposes a True Fiduciary Standard and Genuine Investor Protection."

‡ Allan Henriques, ESQ, is a Registered Financial Consultant (RFC®) and Accredited Investment Fiduciary Analyst® (AIFA®) who is FEFE® certified. He is a CEFEX Analyst and also a fiduciary consultant for FiduciaryPath.

§ Henriques, interview by author, June 1, 2022.

- understanding
- [free from] conflicts of interest
- full disclosure

Carlos Panksep, vice president of the Centre for Fiduciary Excellence (CEFEX), said, "In order to best serve an investor, an advisor must have **prudent fiduciary practices** in place and work in a culture of **continuous improvement** supported by **documented processes**."*

Marie Pillai,† former chief investment officer and treasurer at General Mills, defined a fiduciary as "one who ALWAYS looks out for **the best interest** of the person/group in helping them satisfy a specific need(s); taking into consideration and **understanding their situation** as fully as possible; **updating the solution** as circumstances evolve, across the arc of time."‡

To me, it is important to include this moral terminology in a standard definition of *fiduciary*. Without it, fiduciaries are held to a lower standard—the bare minimum to be considered legally acceptable.

Groups such as the Committee for the Fiduciary Standard—a cohort of investment professionals and stalwart fiduciaries founded in May 2009—have advocated for a stricter definition of *fiduciary* in the aftermath of the 2008 financial crises. The investment professionals and fiduciary experts in this group want "all investment and financial advice [to] be rendered as fiduciary advice and meet the requirements of the five core fiduciary principles."§ Those five principles are as follows:

1. Put the client's best interests first.

---

* Panksep, interview by author, July 6, 2022.

† Marie Pillai is an accomplished financial professional with thirty-plus years of experience. She is the former vice president and chief investment officer and treasurer at General Mills and the former vice president and chief investment officer at Siemens. She serves as a trustee of the Putnam Funds, and is a senior advisor to Hunter Street Partners.

‡ Pillai, interview by author, March 28, 2022.

§ Committee for the Fiduciary Standard, "Committee Names Kathleen M. McBride Chairman."

2. Act with prudence, that is, with the skill, care, diligence, and good judgment of a professional.
3. Do not mislead clients—provide conspicuous, full, and fair disclosure of all important facts.
4. Avoid conflicts of interest.
5. Fully disclose and fairly manage, in the client's favor, unavoidable conflicts.

Financial advisors and firms that follow these guidelines often adopt a similar fiduciary oath. Kate McBride,* who is the former chair of the Committee for the Fiduciary Standard, emphasizes that the fiduciary oaths developed by the Committee are "available at no cost for anyone who wishes to use them."† My financial firm upholds an oath like the one published by the Committee. In its current form, it reads as follows:

Our firm is proud to commit to the following five fiduciary principles:

1. We will always put your best interests first.
2. We will act with prudence—using the skill, care, diligence, and good judgment of a professional.
3. We will provide full disclosure of all important facts.
4. We will avoid conflicts of interest and strive to provide unbiased advice.
5. We will manage any unavoidable conflicts in your favor.

It is important for consumers to not only understand the legal obligations of fiduciaries but also their moral and ethical responsibilities as well. Ideally, anyone who claims to be a professional fiduciary will adopt a fiduciary oath and commit to upholding it. As of the writing of this chapter, however, this is not the case. Therefore, consumers must act with caution and ask the right questions whenever they are thinking about using the services of a so-called fiduciary.

---

* Kate McBride is an Accredited Investment Fiduciary Analyst® and a CEFEX Analyst with more than forty years of investment industry experience. She is the founder and president of FiduciaryPath and the former chair of the Committee for the Fiduciary Standard. She is an AIFA® designee, fiduciary education trainer, CEFEX Analyst, and fiduciary consultant.

† McBride, interview by author, March 29, 2022.

Chapter 21
How to Identify True Fiduciaries

As we've established, it is difficult to pin down the definition of *fiduciary*. It is possible to think about the term from a purely legal standpoint or to use an impersonal dictionary definition, but, to me (and to many of my colleagues), that isn't enough. The most trustworthy fiduciaries are those who not only comply with the law but also adhere to a strict code of ethics, which is often embedded in a fiduciary oath (see chapter 22 for more).

Keeping this information in mind, let's take the discussion one step further and talk about how you, as a consumer and potential investor, can leverage your knowledge about fiduciaries to identify financial advisors who do or do not hold themselves to a strict moral and ethical standard.

Professional versus Lay Fiduciaries

First of all, it's imperative to note that just about anyone can be considered a fiduciary. James Watkins, CEO of InvestSense, notes that legal precedence demonstrates that "a fiduciary relationship exists when one person is under a duty to act for or to give advice for the benefit of another upon matters within the scope of their relationship. . . . It may be based upon a professional, business, or personal relationship."*

To complicate matters, there are two main categories of fiduciaries: professional fiduciaries and lay fiduciaries. A professional fiduciary provides fiduciary services for a living, while a lay fiduciary generally

* Watkins, interview by author, April 15, 2022.

operates outside the financial industry and usually has little training in financial services. An example of a lay fiduciary might be a co-executor of a will or a member of a nonprofit's board (see financial advisor Kate McBride's excellent article[*] about nonprofit lay fiduciaries, if you'd like to learn more). Incredibly, about 17.5 million people in the US can be classified as lay fiduciaries, while only about four hundred thousand people are considered professional fiduciaries.[†]

If you happen to work with a lay fiduciary, don't expect the same standard of care and expertise that you would get with a professional fiduciary. Guerdon Ely, financial advisor and founder of Ely Prudent Portfolios, explains the difference between the two, stating, "A lay fiduciary, which is also referred to as an amateur, is expected to comply with the same standard of prudence as a professional. However, the expectation of the reasonableness with which they exercise their duties is lower than that of professional fiduciary."[‡]

Fortunately, it's not usually too difficult to tell the difference between a professional and a lay fiduciary. A professional fiduciary will likely work at a financial institution and will have completed advanced training in financial services. It's a good idea to take note of an individual's education, certifications, and accreditations. A professional fiduciary might have certifications/designations such as Accredited Investment Fiduciary® (AIF®), Accredited Investment Fiduciary Analyst® (AIFA®), or Certified Financial Planner® (CFP®), among others.

Once you've determined someone is, indeed, a professional fiduciary, the real digging begins. How do you determine who *really* follows fiduciary best practices and who does not always act in the best interest of the consumer?

Fiduciary Standards

All professional fiduciaries are held to a minimum standard when it comes to client care. The US federal government requires fiduciaries to act in their clients' best interests and to put client interests before

---

* McBride, "Did You Know That There's More Than One Type of Fiduciary?"

† InvestmentNews, "Ever Hear of a 'Lay Fiduciary'? There Are 17.5 Million of Them."

‡ Ely, interview by author, March 28, 2022.

their own. This legal requirement is open to interpretation, and some fiduciaries have chosen to interpret its meaning loosely.

In an effort to tighten regulations around fiduciaries, the Department of Labor attempted to expand the definition of an "investment advice fiduciary" in the mid-2010s. The revised definition "elevated all financial professionals who work with retirement plans or provide retirement planning advice to the level of a fiduciary, bound legally and ethically to meet the standards of that status."*

The expanded definition put brokers, insurance agents, and other product providers who earn a commission for financial services in a panic. The new rules would have likely disrupted their rewards-based compensation systems. So, they fought, and, ultimately, they won. After several delays and court battles, the fiduciary rule was vacated in June 2018.

With government regulations remaining fairly loose, many people who dole out financial advice do not feel obligated to adhere to a fiduciary standard of care (which, in essence, requires them to put their clients' best interest above all else). James Watkins discusses the fiduciary standard of care, saying, "for 'financial advisers,' there is no one standard. A Registered Investment Adviser (RIA) and/or an Investment Adviser Representative (IAR) of an RIA is held to a fiduciary standard. Stockbrokers and other 'financial advisors' will argue that they are held to a much less stringent standard of care than a fiduciary standard."†

Allan Henriques, a CEFEX Analyst, says that stockbrokers and other brokerage firm advisors owe their "highest duty" to their employer or firm and are merely required to provide "suitable advice" to clients. He explains that "the 'suitable' standard would not require the advisor to sell the client an investment product at the lowest available cost."‡

All this is to say: be cautious. You may think you're working with a fiduciary, but that person may be a wolf in sheep's clothing (i.e., a commission-based investment securities broker or insurance agent

---

* Peters, "Everything You Need to Know about the DOL Fiduciary Rule."

† Watkins, interview by author, April 15, 2022.

‡ Henriques, interview by author, June 1, 2022.

who is not legally required to put your interests first). I've talked with investors who think they're working with an investment advisor, only to learn their advisor is, in truth, dually registered as a broker-dealer.

With so many financial advisors motivated by sales and commissions, how can you, the consumer, possibly figure out who is *actually* looking out for your best interests? If you're feeling frustrated, I can't say I blame you. I'm frustrated too! However, there are several tools you can use and precautions you can take to find trustworthy financial advisors who are committed to fiduciary best practices:

1. The AIF® designation

Does your financial advisor have the Accredited Investment Fiduciary® (AIF®) designation? If so, that's another positive signal they are serious about customer care and putting the best interests of their clients above all else. To earn an AIF® designation, financial advisors must complete training, comply with a code of ethics, and pass an examination through Fi360 (an organization affiliated with the Center for Fiduciary Studies).

2. BrokerCheck

As I've discussed in past chapters, a financial advisor could be (and most often is) dually registered as both an Investment Adviser Representative and an investment securities broker. This can be problematic because the individual can act in either capacity. You never know if you're dealing with the broker (who is incentivized by commissions and bonuses) or the investment advisor.

As a rule, I advise against working with anyone who has an active broker license. To find out if a financial advisor is a licensed broker, use FINRA's BrokerCheck tool. Visit the website, type in the name of an individual or organization, and learn more about their licensing and background.

3. Prudent Practices for Investment Advisors *handbook*

When the *Prudent Investment Practices* handbook (now called *Prudent Practices for Investment Advisors*) was introduced in 2003, I was excited. This handbook was cutting-edge at the time, providing information and strategic guidelines to develop a legal, ethical, client-centric fiduciary practice. It was so client-focused, in fact, that the company where I was employed at the time forbade me from sharing the handbook's contents with coworkers, clients, or the general public. They were scared. They saw the handbook as a threat—a way to enlighten clients about some of the company's less savory practices, such as pushing certain products to gain commissions. For me, this was the straw that broke my relationship with that firm.

Today, the *Prudent Practices for Investment Advisors* handbook is still a powerful tool for both advisors and investors. It discusses the role of investment fiduciaries, defines the meaning of fiduciary excellence, and details how to promote a fiduciary culture. I believe this is mandatory reading for anyone who is an investment fiduciary or who is hoping to work with an investment fiduciary. When you're interviewing financial advisors, ask them for their thoughts on the *Prudent Practices for Investment Advisors* handbook. Any trustworthy fiduciary will take your question seriously and articulate their support of the handbook's tenets.

4. CEFEX

The Centre for Fiduciary Excellence, or CEFEX, is an independent assessment and certification organization. If an investment advisory firm is CEFEX certified, it has demonstrated it adheres to fiduciary best practices. CEFEX audits are quite stringent, and firms must meet specific criteria to gain certification. Additionally, these audits take place every year, so firms must be diligent about continuously upholding fiduciary best practices. If a firm is CEFEX certified, that's a good indication it is putting its clients' needs first.

All investors should exercise an abundance of caution when selecting and working with a financial advisor. To ensure your best interests—instead of the financial firm's profits or the financial advisor's compensation—are the priority, do some digging to determine if they are a professional fiduciary *and* uphold fiduciary best practices. Fortunately, many tools exist to assist with the search, and anyone armed with a little background knowledge should be able to identify trustworthy financial advisors who are committed to adhering to a fiduciary standard of care.

Chapter 22

Why Request a Fiduciary Oath?

Getting a commitment in writing marks the seriousness of the agreement or occasion. When you get married, you sign a marriage license. When you buy a house, you sign a purchase agreement. When you download a new version of a Mac operating system, you agree to the written terms and conditions. With written agreements being so commonplace, it's hardly a stretch to ask your financial advisor (or potential financial advisor) to sign a written statement of fiduciary responsibilities, aka a fiduciary oath.

A fiduciary oath refers to a statement signed by a fiduciary which declares the fiduciary's duties and responsibilities in writing. Groups such as the Committee for the Fiduciary Standard, founded in 2009 after the infamous series of financial crises, have emphasized the importance of signing such an oath to clarify the relationship between the fiduciary advisor and the client (and to help clients determine *if* a financial advisor is acting as a fiduciary).

Before we discuss the importance of obtaining a written fiduciary oath, let's rewind and answer one core question:

Why Seek a Fiduciary?

If we condensed the information we've covered in the last two chapters, we see that the merits of working with a fiduciary boil down to a few key points. For one, a professional fiduciary is held to a higher standard of customer care than a broker, insurance salesperson, or bank representative. *True* fiduciaries are legally obligated to put their clients' best interests first and adhere to a fiduciary standard of care, whereas brokers or other product salespeople are only held to a "suitability" standard. The suitability standard does not prevent profit-seeking activities, and invisible costs can pile up (as retirement plan expert Scott Simon eloquently explains in his article "Why I'm a Fiduciary").*

This may seem straightforward, but things easily get muddled because brokers, bankers, and other professionals who deal with product sales can call themselves whatever they wish. Their title might be wealth manager, financial advisor, money manager, or anything of the kind. Titles are not regulated.

To complicate matters even further, some brokers are dually registered as Investment Adviser Representatives, meaning they *do* have a fiduciary duty . . . when acting as an Investment Adviser Representative. However, that duty is nullified when the same person is acting as a broker. This dual registration should make investors wonder who they're interacting with on any given day—the broker or the Investment Adviser Representative?

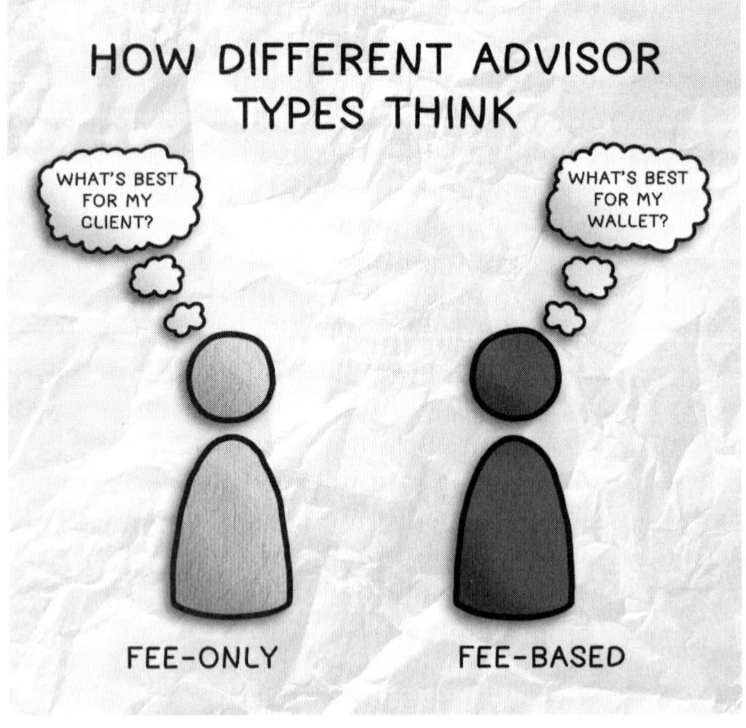

* Simon, "Why I'm a Fiduciary."

Ideally, anyone who provides personalized financial and investment advice should be held to a fiduciary standard. Unfortunately, that is not currently the case, so investors must exercise an abundance of caution when seeking the services of a financial advisor. That's where a fiduciary oath comes into play.

Why Ask for a Fiduciary Oath in Writing?

Working with a professional fiduciary—someone who has the proper training and is committed to upholding a fiduciary standard of care—is a prudent move for investors. However, because of loose regulations, the potential for dual registration, and a general lack of clarity in the financial advising arena, it can be difficult to know if you're *actually* working with a fiduciary or if you're working with someone who *claims* to be a fiduciary.

I could say I'm a golfer, but that doesn't mean I'm a professional (or any good). I might putter around on a mini golf course from time to time and (truthfully) claim to be a golfer. The same is true of those who claim to be fiduciaries. They might be playing fast and loose with that term.

To distinguish the fiduciaries from those masquerading as fiduciaries, it's wise for investors to ask financial advisors to document the meaning of *fiduciary*. What does this term mean, in practice? What are the fiduciary advisor's obligations to the client? These fiduciary responsibilities can be articulated through a fiduciary oath.

Kate McBride, fiduciary consultant and former chair of the Committee for the Fiduciary Standard, says that obtaining a written statement of fiduciary responsibilities is a best practice which drives accountability. "If it's in writing, it is likely that it will happen," McBride says, "and if it doesn't, you can and should find out why. Don't be shy. That's also why it should be in writing—it sets expectations for both the professional fiduciary and the client."*

In addition to setting clear expectations, a fiduciary oath can also offer the client a certain amount of protection. If the financial advisor outlines his or her fiduciary duties in writing and then blatantly

---

* McBride, interview by author, September 6, 2022.

disregards those duties, the client has clear evidence of wrongdoing, which can hopefully be used to help to rectify the situation.

If a financial advisor will not sign a fiduciary oath (like the sample fiduciary oath found on the website for the Committee for the Fiduciary Standard), the investor should find out why. The advisor may have a legitimate reason (e.g., perhaps they have their own fiduciary oath), but it's probable they are either *not* a fiduciary or their company does not allow them to sign such a document.

If I had to guess, I would say 90 percent of financial advisors would run away when presented with a fiduciary oath. These are the brokers, insurance agents, bankers, and other financial advisors whose loyalty lies with their company (and turning a profit) rather than with the investor. These are not true fiduciaries, and signing a fiduciary oath could bring about severe consequences for the employee from their employers.

What Should a Fiduciary Oath Contain?

When my financial advisory firm was putting together its fiduciary oath, we turned to the five core principles outlined by the Committee for the Fiduciary Standard for guidance. These principles are straightforward, easily adaptable, and are not difficult for any true fiduciary advisor to uphold. The Committee's fiduciary oath reads as follows:

I believe in placing your best interests first. Therefore, I am proud to commit to the following five fiduciary principles:

1. I will always put your best interests first.
2. I will act with prudence; that is, with the skill, care, diligence, and good judgment of a professional.
3. I will not mislead you, and I will provide conspicuous, full and fair disclosure of all important facts.
4. I will avoid conflicts of interest.
5. I will fully disclose and fairly manage, in your favor, any unavoidable conflicts.*

* Committee for the Fiduciary Standard, "Fiduciary Oath: Individual."

The financial advisory field can be full of dense language and terminology, but this fiduciary oath is simple and approachable. The average investor can look it over and instantly understand the agreement. While the Committee's version of the oath provides an excellent example, it's certainly not the only one in existence. The fiduciary oath by the National Association of Personal Financial Advisors (NAPFA) is also brief, straightforward, and well-written:

> The advisor shall exercise his/her best efforts to act in good faith and in the best interests of the client. The advisor shall provide written disclosure to the client prior to the engagement of the advisor, and thereafter throughout the term of the engagement, of any conflicts of interest, which will or reasonably may compromise the impartiality or independence of the advisor. The advisor, or any party in which the advisor has a financial interest, does not receive any compensation or other remuneration that is contingent on any client's purchase or sale of a financial product. The advisor does not receive a fee or other compensation from another party based on the referral of a client or the client's business.

Following the NAPFA Fiduciary Oath means I shall:

- Always act in good faith and with candor.
- Be proactive in disclosing any conflicts of interest that may impact a client.
- Not accept any referral fees or compensation contingent upon the purchase or sale of a financial product.*

Though these oaths are a bit different, their core tenets are the same. Both articulate a commitment to act in the client's best interests, disclose any conflicts of interest, and practice integrity.

---

* The National Association of Personal Financial Advisors, "Fiduciary Oath."

What Can Investors Do to Find a True Fiduciary?

1. Research your advisor's background.

Before asking a financial advisor to sign a fiduciary oath, it's a good idea to do a little digging. Comb through the advisor's (or their company's) website to look at their credentials and see if their firm is a Registered Investment Adviser (this doesn't necessarily guarantee the financial advisor will act as a fiduciary, but it's a good first step). You can also search through online databases to find fee-only financial advisors who have been vetted by NAPFA and adhere to its code of ethics.

2. Pay attention to the company's language.

Comb through the website and any literature a financial advisory firm gives you and look for language related to fiduciary duties. Does it appear at all? Is there a fiduciary oath on the company's website? Is the company listed among the firms that signed the Committee for the Fiduciary Standard's oath? If you're having trouble finding language about fiduciary responsibilities (which may be articulated as "putting the clients' best interests first"), that could be a warning sign. But you won't know for certain until you try step three . . .

3. Ask about a fiduciary oath.

When it comes to asking about a fiduciary oath, it's a good idea to be direct with your questioning. You can ask about this over the phone (before you interview a financial advisor) or during an interview. Consider bringing a copy of the Committee for the Fiduciary Standard's oath to your interview meeting and asking the financial advisor to sign it. If they won't sign it, ask why. It's possible they have their own version, but it's more likely they are not a true fiduciary.

As with all important obligations and agreements, it is imperative to obtain a written statement of fiduciary responsibilities before agreeing to work with a financial advisor. If the person you're interviewing is a true fiduciary, they will not be offended if you ask them to sign a fiduciary oath. In fact, they'll probably be pleased that you value a fiduciary's efforts to place the client's interests first.

Part Three

SEARCHING FOR THE RIGHT FINANCIAL ADVISOR

Many of life's queries are answered by a simple online search. Plunk a few words into your search bar and see what comes up. Unfortunately, that methodology is not sufficient when it comes to seeking a competent, qualified financial advisor.

Many financial advisory companies—especially large brokerage companies—shell out plenty of money to populate your online searches. They also have several other pieces of "bait" in their tackle boxes to lure unsuspecting individual investors.

My goal in this section is to help you become the smartest fish in the pond. Instead of falling for the shiny "lures" of brokerage firms, you'll learn several different methods for conducting smart searches for trustworthy financial advisors. On your own terms.

Chapter 23

Five Qualities of a Great Financial Advisor

What if Warren Buffett called you today and offered to be your personal financial advisor? I'm certain very few people would turn him down. Buffett is the sweetheart of the financial world—someone who embodies a rare blend of intelligence and astounding success mixed with humility and personability. He's a grandfather, a Midwesterner, and has owned the same modest family home for six decades . . . but he's also worth over $100 billion, making him the sixth richest person in the world.

If Warren Buffett offers you advice, you take it. He has a proven track record and is not known for underhanded ploys, wild risk-taking, or showmanship (such as some of the theatrics we saw in cryptocurrency during 2022). He might be considered a little "old school," but his methods work, and he certainly wouldn't intentionally lead another investor astray.

Many of Buffett's qualities would make him a competent, trustworthy financial advisor (if he chose to pursue this profession). If we dig in and examine Buffet's attributes, we find that they're not terribly groundbreaking or unusual. Many financial advisors embody these qualities, and it's certainly possible for consumers to sniff them out.

In this chapter, I will define five essential qualities to seek in a financial advisor and how to identify them. First, however, it is essential to establish a few baseline characteristics.

The Essentials

If you've read the prior chapters in this book, you know I urge investors to seek a certain type of financial advisor. My goal is to steer investors toward the most honest, disciplined, and fair financial advisors I can. With that in mind, I generally advise consumers to

- seek fee-only financial advisors;
- avoid investment securities brokers, bankers, and insurance agents for financial planning;
- pay attention to professional designations/qualifications;
- do your research (using sites such as FINRA's BrokerCheck, Wealthramp, FeeOnlyNetwork, NAPFA's Find an Advisor tool, and other resources I've listed in past chapters); and
- look for financial advisors who are committed to a fiduciary standard of care.

To me, these essentials are non-negotiable. They are also distinct from a financial advisor's personal qualities or attributes. Someone could be a perfectly likeable person yet take exorbitant commissions for any sales they make.

I recommend doing your research, establishing whether a financial advisor fits the criteria listed above, and then considering their personal attributes. In my opinion, the following five attributes are among the most important for financial advisors:

1. Authenticity

Have you ever had a conversation with someone who seemed to be hiding their true self at every turn? Maybe they avoided certain topics or gave superficial answers when more depth was expected. Maybe they acted guarded or skittish or overly buoyant. Whatever the case, you might not have been able to put your finger on *exactly* what was wrong, but you sensed that the person across the table was not truly authentic.

Authenticity is a vital trait in financial advisors. If an investor doesn't believe an advisor is being authentic, why would they trust them with big financial decisions (decisions that could impact their life)? If the advisor is hiding aspects of their personality, what else are they hiding?

There isn't a step-by-step handbook on how to determine someone's authenticity; you'll simply have to rely on gut instincts. Fortunately, gut instincts/intuitions are more reliable than you might realize. Our brains are constantly processing information, and we may subconsciously pick up behaviors in other people that make us uneasy or distrustful. An article in *Psychology Today* highlights scientific research behind gut feelings and says, "Intuition is rooted in science. Gut feelings are the result of many channels of information processing and provide a road map that integrates our emotions and physical sensations with a given environment."*

If a financial advisor seems inauthentic, trust your instincts.

2. Curiosity about the customer

Good financial advisors are adept at interviewing. They know which questions to ask to start a meaningful dialogue about the consumer's

* *Psychology Today*, "Intuition."

unique situation, and, most importantly, they will *listen attentively* to the answers they're given. These are signs that the financial advisor genuinely cares about the consumer, wants to develop a deep understanding of their circumstances, and will create a personalized financial plan that caters to the consumer's needs.

On the flip side, a financial advisor that isn't particularly interested in the consumer's unique fact set will railroad them with advice/thoughts/ideas before the consumer has had a chance to share their circumstances and goals.

Wendy Cook, finance content writer and owner of Wendy J. Cook Communications, recommends that consumers pay close attention to the behavior of the financial advisor in the interview process: "If you are a couple, do they include both of you in the conversation, drawing out the individual who is less likely to speak up? Do they ask insightful questions about what you've said? . . . Do they answer your critical questions openly and candidly, or do they instead become vague or defensive?"*

3. Integrity

It's not always possible to determine if a financial advisor is honest, but you can get a sense of their integrity through researching their background and interviewing. Do their statements line up with what you already know about them/their company? Do they say something one minute, then contradict themselves the next? Do their claims seem outlandish (guaranteeing a 10 percent return every year, for instance) or overly ambitious?

If you were to interview someone who invests like Warren Buffett, that person would be realistic about potential outcomes and would exercise a healthy amount of caution. A Bernie Madoff type, on the other hand, would talk about things like "beating the market," "guaranteed returns," or "outperforming index funds." Remember the maxim I stated earlier: if something sounds too good to be true, it probably is.

4. Empathy

If you're an investor who depends on a financial advisor to guide your financial future, you want to make sure that person genuinely cares

* Cook, interview by author, November 14, 2022.

about you and your situation. If you mention your parents recently passed away and you received a large inheritance, do they offer condolences? Or focus on your windfall?

Empathy is related to authenticity and genuine curiosity. It's far better to work with someone who cares and can put themselves in your shoes than someone who only sees their clients as dollar signs or "buying units." The latter will likely be more concerned with pushing products or services (even if they're not an exact match) than getting to know the people they are supposed to be serving.

5. Strategic, disciplined, and process-driven

Andrew Bloomenthal of Investopedia writes that Warren Buffett has a long-held belief that "people should only buy stocks in companies that exhibit solid fundamentals, strong earnings power, and the potential for continued growth."* In other words, he's not a gambler. He believes in the merits of a value-based investing model and doesn't easily stray from his principles.

David Booth, chairman and founder of Dimensional Fund Advisors, suggests steering clear of *stock pickers* and *market timers.* He says, "They're the ones who get into and out of the market, trying to buy the dip and sell at the peak. The problem with these strategies is that it's unlikely any individual will be able to pick the right stock and the right time—especially more than once. Over 50 years of research confirms that people can neither pick stocks nor time markets consistently year after year."†

It's possible to determine if a financial advisor is strategic, disciplined, and process-driven by gleaning information from their website and by talking with them in person. Even before your interview commences, the advisor should show signs of being disciplined and process oriented. How organized are they? Are they punctual when you visit their office? Do they offer you a bottle of water and a parking validation stamp right away? During the interview, do they know which questions to ask to prompt a conversation?

In addition to noticing these clues about the financial advisor's

---

* Bloomenthal, "Warren Buffett's Investing Strategy: An Inside Look."

† Booth, "Trust the Financial Advisor Who Trusts the Market."

personality, you can also ask direct questions about their strategies, investment philosophies, and processes during the interview. Are they committed to evidence-based investing and maintaining a disciplined approach? Or is their investment strategy fairly loose? Do they gravitate toward proven methods, or are they chasing the "latest thing"?

Larry Swedroe, head of financial and economic research at Buckingham Strategic Wealth, says in a recent article, "An advisor's investment recommendations should be based on facts, not personal opinions. A potential wealth manager's advice should be derived from evidence-based, peer reviewed academic periodicals such as *The Journal of Finance.* All suggestions should be easily understandable, transparent and make sense."*

I wholeheartedly agree.

Once you've winnowed down your search for a financial advisor to a few potential candidates, it's wise to interview each of them and pay attention to their personal attributes. Words are important but so are behaviors and body language. If a financial advisor seems anxious, annoyed, closed off, or isn't forthright with information, would you really trust them with your financial planning? If their processes or philosophies skew more toward Bernie Madoff than Warren Buffett, would you entrust them with a large percentage of your hard-earned wealth? When it comes to selecting a financial advisor, personal attributes matter.

---

* Swedroe, "How to Find an Advisor You Can Trust."

Chapter 24
Three Effective Steps to Find a Financial Advisor

Let's say you've decided to hire a financial advisor to help plan for your future. Perhaps your financial circumstances have changed (you've received a large inheritance, earned a significant promotion, had a child, combined households with a new spouse), or maybe you're simply thinking about retirement and wondering how and when to make it happen.

I recently helped a married couple in their late fifties that came to us looking for financial advice. Shannon was the primary breadwinner and financial earner in the family, and she spent most of her days focused on her day job, which required her to be creative to develop innovative new ideas for her company. Her husband Jim was a semiretired firefighter with a lot of free time on his calendar. He was a DIY investor and liked to invest by himself (picking stocks) as a hobby to pass the time. The family did not have a comprehensive financial plan, and this lack of a formal financial plan made Shannon uncomfortable. They were both nearing their retirements, and she felt they were disorganized financially. To appease Shannon and help them find a financial planner, Jim conducted a Google search for fee-only financial advisors and found our firm as a possible solution to help them to get organized and develop a comprehensive financial plan.

A Google search is not my recommended method of finding a trustworthy financial advisor, given all the sponsored content, fake fiduciaries, and insurance salespeople masquerading as financial advisors on the internet. Fortunately, Jim was savvy enough to scroll past any suspicious links until he landed on our financial advisory firm. But many people may not be able to parse the true fiduciaries and fee-only financial advisors from the charlatans.

If you're like most Americans, you don't entirely trust financial advisors, and you want to make sure you pick someone who is honest and transparent. You also need to make sure you choose someone whose expertise aligns with your needs. With over four hundred thousand personal financial advisors in the United States, this can feel like a monumental task.

Fortunately, with the right methodology and some handy tools, it is possible to narrow down this vast pool of candidates to a few viable options.

Paths of Least Resistance

When faced with a difficult decision, it's human nature to take the path of least resistance. We tend to gravitate toward the easiest solutions, the simplest answers. We also tend to seek safety and comfort—a behavior tied to the oldest parts of our brain, such as the amygdala (which governs our "fight or flight" reflex). These tendencies may serve us well in some situations (I see a bear; I run to safety!), but they are a hindrance when it comes to choosing the appropriate financial advisor.

With so many financial advisors to choose from, chances are you won't stumble upon the right one by chance or through a five-minute online search. You're also not likely to align with whatever advisor your uncle Gary recommends. Instead, the best way to find a financial advisor to suit your needs is to plan, understand your criteria, and conduct a logical and curated search.

First, let's talk about the typical "paths of least resistance" people follow when seeking a financial advisor and why these methods are flawed.

Flawed Method 1: Family and Friends' Recommendations

Your comfort-seeking brain probably likes the idea of simply asking your friends and family members for personal recommendations. If they're happy with their financial advisors, why wouldn't you be happy?

Personal recommendations *could* work out, but they are riddled with problems from the get-go. For one, it's difficult to know the full financial situation of a friend or family member. We typically don't get to see what goes on behind the curtain. We're not privy to their tax statements, savings account balance, mortgage statements, or other financial documents. We don't know the balance on their credit cards or about the inheritance their great aunt gave them last year.

In short, your financial situation is unique and should be treated as such. It's best to seek a financial advisor that can work with your personal situation and circumstances—not one who is perfectly suited to uncle Gary.

Additionally, family and friends may not fully understand how their financial advisor operates. They may fail to grasp crucial details, such as how their financial advisor is paid, whether they are committed to a fiduciary standard of care, or if they are dually registered as an investor advisor and a broker. This lack of understanding isn't necessarily the consumer's fault; far too often, compensation for financial advisors is unnecessarily complicated or shrouded in layers of legalese. It's better to do your own research, with clear parameters of what you want from a financial advisor.

Flawed Method 2: Financial Advisors in the Media

Have you ever turned on the TV, flipped to a news program, and watched a segment with a guest financial advisor? Or maybe you've turned on a radio program, and the announcer is interviewing a wealth manager about the stock market. Or perhaps a financial advisor is discussing her new book in a newspaper interview. These "experts" and "guests" appear with some regularity in the media. If they're on a state-wide news program or appearing in the local newspaper, they must be somewhat accomplished and trustworthy, right?

Not necessarily. Oftentimes, when financial advisors appear in the media, they are sponsoring the show/article/segment. Translation: they're paying money to be there. This isn't always the case, but it happens more often than you might realize. Even if the guest financial advisor is reliable and competent, this person may or may not be for you.

If you're thinking about contacting a financial advisor you encountered in the media, proceed with caution. There's no harm in researching this person or their company but understand that they may not necessarily be as astute as they seem on the TV or radio program.

Flawed Method 3: Pamphlets and Promises

It's not uncommon for people purporting to be financial advisors to send out mass marketing campaigns that involve attractive incentives. In exchange for your time (just a quick, one-hour meeting!), they might entice you with a free steak dinner, complimentary tickets to a concert or basketball game, or a six-month wine club membership. On the surface, these seem like great perks, and, hey, you just might get a new financial advisor out of the deal!

I advise you to run (don't walk) away from these so-called deals. It's likely this meeting would take place with a professional sales representative—someone trained to sell financial services (or connect you with a financial advisor within their company). This is their job, and they're damn good at it. They've perfected their pitch so this sounds like an opportunity you can't miss, when they may be representing a company that is, at the very least, based on a system of product sales commissions, or, at worst, incompetent and purely profit-driven. When it comes to searching for a financial advisor, *you* should set the terms and reach out to potential candidates, not the other way around.

Flawed Method 4: Internet Search

It may seem logical to pull up Google, type in "best financial advisors nearby," and see what comes up. After all, this is how we conduct most of our searches, whether we want to know the local weather, the capital of Nicaragua, or the best backpacks for a three-day hiking trip.

However, this approach is problematic when searching for a financial advisor. You'll have to sift through a lot of paid advertising and sponsored content before financial advisors organically crop up, and even then, these advisors may not be suited to your needs. The financial advisors and companies at the top of the search pile will inevitably be those with the largest budgets—companies like Ameriprise, Merrill Lynch, Morgan Stanley, Bank of America, and UBS Financial.

Occasionally, you might see a list of "top advisors" or "five-star advisors." This may be a legitimate list . . . or it may be even more sponsored content. As a financial advisor, I regularly receive invitations to purchase fake awards or buy advertising space on lists. I suggest viewing these lists with a skeptical eye, keeping in mind that the individual financial advisors listed may simply have money, not merit.

A Better Approach

By now, you might be wondering how, exactly, to begin your search for a financial advisor. How can you possibly avoid these numerous pitfalls and dubious advertising schemes? Fortunately, it's not as difficult as you might fear. Consumers now have access to several reliable databases which list very specific types of advisors (and do not deal with sponsored content). I advise taking the following three steps:

1. Determine what you need.

Before diving into your search, it's essential to determine what type of financial guidance or support you need. Are you only looking for financial planning, or are you also interested in investment management? Do you need help with estate planning? Retirement planning? Tax planning?

In chapter 25, we will discuss how to pinpoint and articulate your financial needs, but for now, keep in mind that it's important to have a good understanding of what type of financial guidance you're seeking.

2. Determine your criteria for a financial advisor.

Someone may call themselves a financial advisor, wealth manager, investment advisor, or something similar, but, as we've established, those terms have little meaning. Instead of emphasizing titles, I recommend focusing on the financial advisor's background, credentials, and compensation structure.

The ideal financial advisor for many people is a qualified professional, operates independently (their advice isn't tainted by outside influences), upholds a fiduciary standard of care, and operates under a fee-only compensation structure.

You may choose to seek *individuals* with these qualifications, or you might decide to look for *firms* which promote these principles. Either way, you can find suitable matches by conducting searches with trustworthy databases, which brings us to step three.

3. Use smart/trustworthy databases.

Unlike a broad internet search, using specific, curated databases can help you find qualified financial advisors, without all the sponsored content. Several databases exist that are independent, reliable, and unbiased.

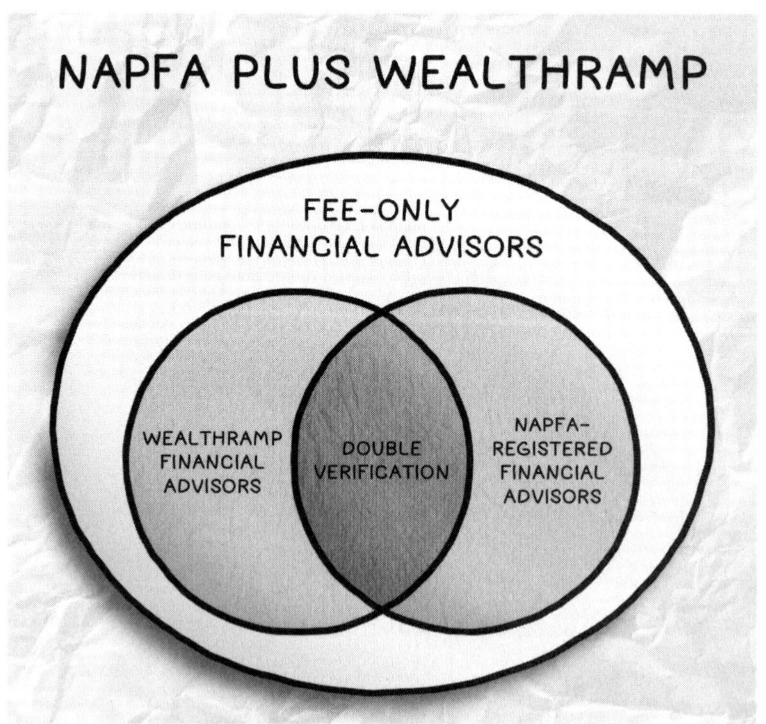

To search for a financial advisory ***firm***, consider using the following online resources, listed in order of priority:

1. Wealthramp*

Wealthramp personally vets each financial advisory firm it includes on its list. The firms must be solely fee-only, never earning money from sales or commissions. Other criteria Wealthramp considers include credentials, experience, responsiveness, client retention, specializations, and more.

2. FeeOnlyNetwork†

According to their website, "gaining a listing on FeeOnlyNetwork.com is exclusive to fee-only advisors and firms that have been vetted by at least one of our association partners."

3. NAPFA‡

Use NAPFA's Find an Advisor online search tool to find local, fee-only financial planning firms.

4. CEFEX§

CEFEX provides a registered company list of certified investment advisory firms.

5. Fi360¶

Use Fi360's fiduciary-centered online search tool to find investment firms registered with CEFEX.

6. The Committee for the Fiduciary Standard**

The Committee lists investment advisory firms that are willing to acknowledge a fiduciary relationship with the investor.

---

* https://wealthramp.com/

† https://www.feeonlynetwork.com/

‡ https://www.napfa.org/find-an-advisor

§ https://www.cefex.org/RegisteredCompanyList/

¶ https://www.fi360.com/app/designee/search

** http://www.thefiduciarystandard.org/fiduciary-oath/

7. Institute for the Fiduciary Standard[*]

The IFS is a list of firms that adhere to a fiduciary standard of care for the investor. This organization has a Real Fiduciary™ Practices Advisor Registry of firms that agree to adhere to the high standards of the (Real Fiduciary™) Practices and publicly state to federal and state regulators they do so.

8. Dimensional Fund Advisors[†]

Dimensional's Find an Advisor online tool identifies local firms with an evidence-based investment philosophy.

9. US SIF (The Forum for Sustainable and Responsible Investment)[‡]

Use the US SIF's membership directory to find investment firms who help investors with socially responsible investing.

10. Charles Schwab[§]

The Find Your Independent Advisor online search tool, created by Charles Schwab, locates independent investment advisory firms that use Schwab as a custodian.

To search for an ***individual*** financial advisor, consider using the following online resources, listed in order of priority:

1. Wealthramp[¶]

The financial advisors on Wealthramp's list are fee-only fiduciaries who represent fee-only, customer-focused companies which have been thoroughly vetted. Individual investors are matched with financial advisors who best fit their unique needs and circumstances.

---

* https://thefiduciaryinstitute.org/real-fiduciary-advisors/

† https://www.dimensional.com/us-en/individual/how-to-invest

‡ https://www.ussif.org/AF_MemberDirectory.asp

§ https://www.findyourindependentadvisor.com/FindAdvisor

¶ https://wealthramp.com/

2. FeeOnlyNetwork*

The FeeOnlyNetwork allows individual investors to easily search for fee-only advisors who never receive commissions or kickbacks from brokerage firms.

3.CFP Board†

The Find a CFP® Professional online search tool finds local Certified Financial Planners® (CFP®).

4. Financial Planning Association®‡

Use the FPA® PlannerSearch® online search tool to find local Certified Financial Planners® (CFP®).

5. Fi360§

Use Fi360's fiduciary-centered online search tool to find a local Accredited Investment Fiduciary® (AIF®).

6. National Green Pages¶

Use the Find Green Businesses online search tool to find an individual financial advisor or financial planner to help with socially responsible investing.

Your search for a financial advisor does not have to be overly complicated or hindered by biased perspectives or search results. Fortunately, many useful tools exist today to help consumers navigate the path to a competent, suitable, and trustworthy financial advisor or firm. Before diving into these searches, make sure you have a clear vision of what you expect from a financial advisor and how this individual can assist you with your unique financial situation. This is a major decision, and a simple Google search or a recommendation from your golfing buddy probably won't lead to the results you want. Invest your time and effort in your search for a financial advisor, and you can expect to reap the rewards of a trusted relationship with a good financial advisor for years to come.

---

* https://www.feeonlynetwork.com/

† https://www.letsmakeaplan.org/

‡ https://www.plannersearch.org/

§ https://www.fi360.com/app/designee/search

¶ https://www.greenamerica.org/all-business-listings?field_category_target_id=204

Chapter 25
Define Your Objectives to Choose the Right Financial Advisor

In the late '90s, my wife and I began hunting for a new house. We loved our little home near the south end of Lake Harriet in Minneapolis, but it was quickly becoming too cramped for our family of five. There was always a toy underfoot, and it constantly felt like we were tripping over each other.

At the time, the housing market was very tight. There wasn't much on the market, and houses tended to be snapped up quickly. Because of housing market conditions, we kept our criteria minimal, only telling our realtor that we wanted a place near Lake Harriet. That's it.

I'm sure I toured at least thirty houses over six or seven weekends. Every time we stepped through the door of a new place, my wife and I felt hopeful, but our optimism was usually quashed immediately. Nothing was quite right—too small, too big, too rundown, not enough space in the kitchen or living room, not enough bedrooms, a cramped yard, a busy street. We were striking out left and right.

Then, we decided to take a different approach. Instead of being loose with our criteria, I made a spreadsheet that detailed exactly what we wanted—our needs, wants, and "nice-to-haves." My wife and I put a lot of thought into our chart, making sure to list all the factors that were important to us. We knew we needed (among many other considerations) five bedrooms and two bathrooms, a house that was in good repair, and, of course, someplace located close to

Lake Harriet. In the "wants" column, we listed items such as garage and big yard, because they were not absolute necessities for us. In the "nice-to-have" column, we listed features such as swimming pool and sauna.

After defining our list, we brought it to our realtor. I worried he might think we were seeking a unicorn, but instead he surprised us by saying, "I think I have the perfect house for you. It's not yet on the market, but I think I can convince the owner to let you take a look."

Once we had permission to tour the house, my wife and I paid it a visit. As soon as we stepped through the door, we knew it was the one. It ticked all the boxes on our "needs" list, fit most of the criteria on the "wants" list, and had a few of the "nice-to-haves." It even had a sauna!

Today, we've lived in that house for twenty-five years. It's where our three kids grew up; where we've hosted friends and family; where we've worked, relaxed, and made memories.

I learned through this experience that it is incredibly valuable to dial in your needs, wants, and nice-to-haves when making a major decision. This applies to buying a house or car, choosing a new doctor, or (and maybe you saw this coming!) choosing a financial advisor.

Why Set Defining Objectives When Choosing a Financial Advisor?

As a financial advisor, it is always a relief when a prospective client knows what they ***want***. If someone can tell me what kind of help they are seeking, what type of advisor they would like to work with, and their vision of an ideal financial advisory firm, I can usually tell whether or not we'll be a match (and if we're not, I can easily refer them to someone who *is* a match).

When you know what you ***need***, your search for the right financial advisor is much easier. Defining objectives gives you clarity, keeps you focused on the qualities that are most important to you, and makes it easier for you to find an advisor who is qualified to serve you.

It also allows you to weed out advisors who don't match your needs. For example, if you are looking for a financial planner who specializes in estate planning, you can easily avoid advisors who don't offer such services and, instead, focus on those who do. This helps you avoid wasting time and energy on advisors who might not be the right fit. Once you have narrowed down your list of prospective advisors, you can begin making phone calls and arranging in-person meetings.

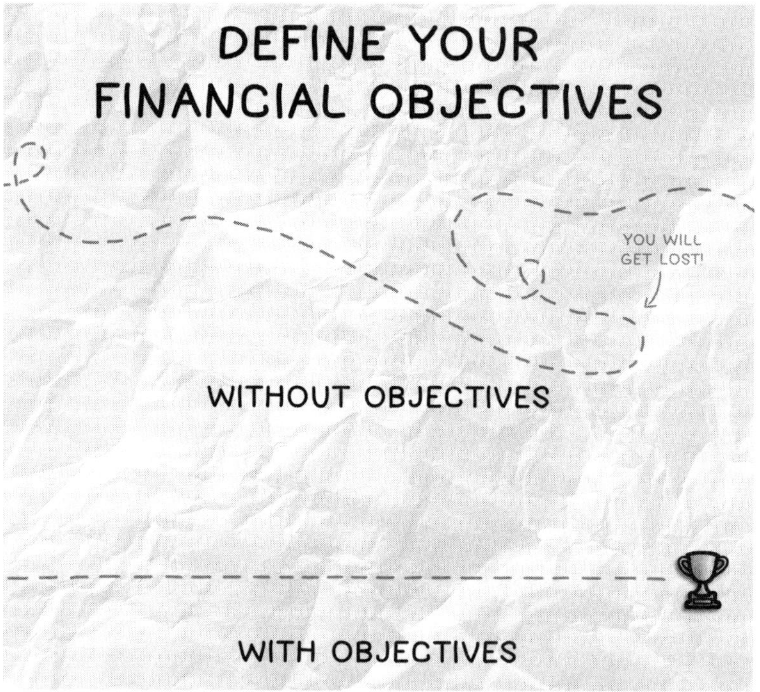

Setting Defining Objectives

When it comes to choosing a financial advisor, there are several key factors to consider. For one, you need to determine what kind of help you need. Are you looking for someone to manage your investments, help you navigate estate planning, provide advice on retirement planning, or all the above? You'll also need to think about whether you would prefer to work with an individual advisor or a larger financial firm.

Next, you need to consider what your ideal advisor looks like. Are they a fiduciary? What does their fee structure look like? What certifications and other credentials do they have? Are they part of a larger financial institution? Are they conveniently located and/or easy to contact? Answering these questions before you start your search can help you identify the right financial advisor much faster.

Make a list of your needs and make sure you discuss those items with a prospective financial advisor. At times, potential clients will fail to mention crucial items on their needs list, which can waste a lot of time for both parties. In one case, I collaborated with my team to put together a comprehensive financial plan for a woman who was hoping to retain our financial advisory firm. We presented her the plan, and she was very happy with what we had put together. Then, she dropped a bombshell: "I'll need to run all this by my kids."

We were caught off guard because this potential client hadn't mentioned her kids until that moment.

She went on to say that she wanted the financial plan to cover her kids' accounts as well. The kids—who were all in their thirties—would be part of the package.

Things . . . derailed from there. The kids did not want to change financial advisors, and the prospective client refused to work independently from her children. Our hands were tied, so we had to part ways.

If we had known from the start that the prospective client's children would be part of the relationship, we would have approached things differently, and the kids would have been part of the decision-making process from the beginning. Instead, we all squandered a good deal of time and energy.

Which Defining Objectives to Consider

Setting your defining objectives—those needs, wants, and nice-to-haves—can seem overwhelming to many people. Where do you begin? What areas do you need to consider? I suggest following these four steps:

1. Identify your purpose.

Something drove you to consider working with a financial advisor. What was it? Are you thinking about retirement planning? Did you inherit some money? Are you concerned about funding your children's college education? Alternatively, are you fed up with your current financial advisor and need a change?

Whatever the case, it's important to reflect on the main reason you're searching for a financial advisor. Keep that purpose in mind as you begin to list your needs, wants, and nice-to-haves. If you're not certain how to answer this question, the financial planning goals information sheet, found below, can help you pinpoint your purpose.

Financial Planning Goals

The secret of wealth is to spend less than you earn and invest the difference.

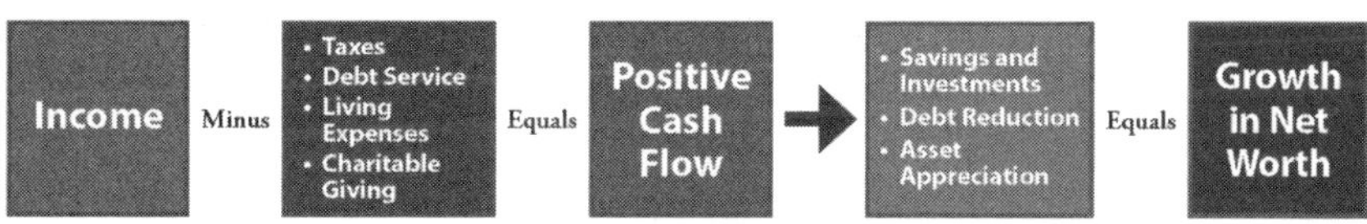

Comprehensive Financial Planning

Financial Position

- Personal Financial Statement
- Cash Flow Management
- Debt Reduction Strategies
- Identity Theft Protection

Asset & Income Protection

- Life Insurance
- P & C Insurance
- Health Insurance
- Disability Insurance
- Long-Term Care Insurance

Income Tax Planning

- Income Tax Strategy
- Asset Placement Strategy
- Tax-Advantaged Investments

Investment Planning

- Asset Allocation
- Due Diligence Research
- Selecting Managers
- Monitor Investments

Estate Planning

- Asset Titling
- Wealth Transfer
- Family Education
- Trust Management
- Charitable Planning

Retirement Planning

- Short- & Long-Term Goals
- Retirement Income Projection

The role of the Financial Planner is to find ways to help you increase your net worth and to help you to accomplish all of your financial objectives.

Define the purpose of your money: what is the purpose of your wealth?

☐ Attain Financial Security
☐ Provide Retirement Income
☐ Reduce or Eliminate Debt
☐ Fund College Expenses
☐ Fulfill Lifestyle Desires
☐ Start a New Business
☐ Establish Financial Independence
☐ Support a Charitable Giving Plan
☐ Wealth Transfer to Family
☐ Other Purpose(s):

Notes:

www.allodium.com

2. Ask the big questions first.

Start by asking yourself big-picture questions first. These are some of the questions that you might want to address:

- What are my main financial goals? (See above.)
- What type of financial help do I need? Do I require financial planning, wealth management, or a combination of the two? (The informational sheet below can help you determine which route is right for you.)
- What type of financial advisor am I seeking (individual versus team, fee-only versus commission-based or fee-based, qualifications and professional certifications, etc.)?
- Do I require any special services (income tax planning, charitable giving advice, help with international tax laws, etc.)?

Wealth Management Services

Wealth management combines investment management, financial planning and specialized financial services, which can include personal retail banking services, estate planning, legal and tax advice. A CERTIFIED FINANCIAL PLANNER® professional can provide you with a personalized, written financial plan based on the major financial planning subject areas published by the CFP Board of Standards.

Financial Planning Services

1. Financial Position Analysis
2. Investment Planning
3. Retirement Planning
4. Financial Goal Setting and Prioritization
5. Income Tax Planning
6. Asset & Income Protection
7. Estate Planning & Wealth Transfer

In addition to traditional financial planning services, wealth management services may also include:

Wealth Management Services

1. ***Maintaining your comprehensive financial plan with an annual review:***
   - Creating and maintaining an action plan with reminders when appropriate
   - Introducing you to outside professionals (accountants, attorneys, etc.)
   - Reviewing proposals for health, life and property and casualty insurance
   - Reviewing your social security to maximize your benefits
   - Reviewing your insurance policies (life, disability, health, etc.)
   - Reviewing your income tax returns and estate plan documents
2. ***Integrating your financial plan with your investment portfolio:***
   - Implementing a recommended investment portfolio(s)
   - Rebalancing your investment portfolio back to target when appropriate
   - Harvesting capital losses for income tax benefits when appropriate
3. ***Introducing tax advantaged investment strategies:***
   - Establishing tax advantaged accounts (HSA & 529 plans) when appropriate
   - Establishing qualified retirement plans (IRA, Roth IRA, etc.) when appropriate
   - Analyzing the opportunities to convert IRA accounts to Roth IRA accounts
4. ***Integrating your financial plan and estate plan with related entities:***
   - Coordinating with your company retirement plan accounts, charitable trusts, etc.
   - Identifying your beneficiaries and updating your documents
5. ***Educating your family members:***
   - Helping your children to learn about investing and personal finance
   - Helping fiduciary decision-makers learn about fiduciary investment management
6. ***Collaborating with other professional advisors:***
   - Meeting with your professional advisors such as accountants, attorneys, etc.

3. Think about key financial planning areas.

If you're interested in financial planning assistance, it can be helpful to consider the main areas that a financial planner can address (see the financial planning explanatory sheet below to help):

- financial statement preparation and analysis
- investment planning and risk management
- employee benefits
- investment planning
- income tax planning
- retirement planning
- estate planning

Financial Planning

"Financial planning is a collaborative process that helps maximize a client's potential for meeting life goals through financial advice that integrates relevant elements of the client's personal and financial circumstances."

Certified Financial Planner Board of Standards, Inc. (CFP Board)

A CERTIFIED FINANCIAL PLANNER® professional can provide you with a personalized, written financial plan based on the major financial planning subject areas published by the CFP Board of Standards.

Financial Statement Preparation and Analysis

Develop a summary of your current financial position including net worth statement, cash flow summary, and debt review. Includes cash flow analysis/planning and budgeting.

Insurance Planning and Risk Management

Provide a risk management analysis to protect your assets and your income, which may include life insurance, medical insurance, disability, long-term care, property and casualty, liability, and identity theft.

Employee Benefits Planning

Review employer retirement plans, business group benefits, executive benefits, and other employer-provided benefits.

Investment Planning

Establish a formal investment policy, asset allocation recommendations, and investment selection and monitoring.

Income Tax Planning

Identify tax-deferred and tax-efficient investing strategies to optimize your financial position. This may include a review of retirement benefits available to you.

Retirement Planning

Prepare financial projections and assist you in developing a savings and/or withdrawal plan incorporating other financial goals as applicable.

Estate Planning

Review your estate plan, your wealth transfer plan, and the coordination of your estate plan with asset titling and beneficiary designations.

www.allodium.com

4. Utilize resources.

If you're unsure of how to begin defining your financial objectives, you can always utilize resources that are available through financial institutions or from various educational websites. Look at the service menu worksheet below that was developed to help individual investors get started. This worksheet asks the investor to identify their primary needs and wants in the areas of investment management, comprehensive performance reporting, financial planning services, and investor education. Other worksheets can be found online through financial websites. Just be wary of any checklists or worksheets that require you to give away your personal information to view them.

Service Menu Worksheet

Purposeful individual investors are proactive in selecting the specific services that truly add value. Use this worksheet to identify the specific investment advisory services that will help you to accomplish your financial goals.

INVESTMENT MANAGEMENT	NEED	WANT	PASS
Comprehensive cash flow assessment.	✓		
Comprehensive goal clarification.			
Comprehensive financial risk assessment.			
Strategic asset allocation policy to manage investment risk.			
Portfolio construction analysis and written investment plan.			
Due diligence research on investment managers.			
Negotiation with custodians and investment managers to minimize fees.			
Full disclosure of all fees and compensation paid to investment advisors and money managers.			
Implementation of the recommended investment portfolio.			
Periodic rebalancing of investment portfolio.			
COMPREHENSIVE PERFORMANCE REPORTING	**NEED**	**WANT**	**PASS**
Comprehensive quarterly portfolio performance evaluation reports.			
Comprehensive monthly portfolio performance evaluation reports.			
Comprehensive tax reports on investment portfolio holdings.			
Quarterly meetings to review your investment portfolio.			
Quarterly conference calls to review your investment portfolio.			
Comprehensive annual investment review meeting to review your investment strategy and policy.			
Online access to portfolio holdings with daily valuation, gain/loss data and year to date performance.			
FINANCIAL PLANNING SERVICES	**NEED**	**WANT**	**PASS**
Personal Financial Statement (Net Worth Statement).			
Cash flow analysis and budget planning.			
Retirement income planning.			
Income tax planning.			
Asset and income protection planning.			
Estate planning.			
Philanthropic planning.			
Annual Review Meeting.			
Annual Review Booklet with Letter of Understanding and updated Personal Financial Statement.			
Collaboration with your other advisors (accountant, attorney, banker, insurance agent, etc.) as needed.			
Coordination with related entities and related portfolios.			
INVESTOR EDUCATION	**NEED**	**WANT**	**PASS**
Educational presentations on wealth management for individual investors.			
Educational presentations on personal finance for children and young adults.			
Educational presentations on fiduciary investment management for foundations, endowments, and trusts.			
Optimal investment structure for the efficient governance of your investment portfolios.			

Setting clear objectives when choosing a financial advisor is essential to a successful search. Know what kind of help you need, define what your ideal advisor looks like, and make sure you communicate your needs and wants clearly to any prospective advisors. This will not only save you time and energy, but it also ensures that you'll find a financial advisor who is qualified to serve you. Just as my wife and I found the perfect house by narrowly defining our search criteria, so, too, is it a good idea to know exactly what you want from a financial advisor.

See appendix 2 for related AdvisorSmart® educational resources including a Sample Selection Criteria "needs, wants, and nice-to-haves" list. Visit the AdvisorSmart® website for additional up-to-date, free educational resources at www.AdvisorSmart.com/Resources.

Chapter 26
Should You Work with a Solo Financial Advisor or a Team?

Let's say you want to hire a personal chef to cater a party. You find someone who is competent, trustworthy, and has great reviews. But when you tell the chef you'd like to feature Thai cuisine on the menu, they balk. They specialize in American and European (specifically, Italian) cuisine. They *could* stretch their skill set somewhat and prepare a basic Thai meal, but they know they are not well-suited for the job.

Instead, the chef recommends a colleague who specializes in Thai cuisine for your upcoming party, and the chef then asks that you keep them in mind for any future events that you plan featuring Italian cuisine.

This scenario can also be applied to financial advisors. Though many advisors can offer advice in a wide range of areas, they cannot be experts in *everything.* They might feel comfortable with estate planning but not income tax planning. Or they may frequently engage in retirement planning for US residents but do not usually work with clients who retire abroad.

Because of these (and other) limitations, it can be immensely helpful for financial advisors to work alongside a team. When an ensemble of financial advisors has different areas of expertise, they can draw on each other's unique skills and better serve their clients. In my own experience, I have had clients remark on how it is comforting to have a "deep bench" of financial advisors to work with, in addition to their primary financial advisor.

That said, a solo financial advisor can be a suitable option as well, especially if the investor is seeking guidance that is relatively common or straightforward.

Let's discuss some of the advantages and disadvantages of financial advisory teams versus solo advisors and how to identify a competent and collaborative team.

Solo versus Team

One of the most basic financial advisory relationships available is between a solo practitioner and a client. A solo financial advisor does not work with anyone else when creating a financial plan for their client; they simply rely on their own expertise. For some, this type of relationship is perfect. They appreciate the simplicity and straightforward nature of the advisor-client arrangement.

When working with a solo advisor, the client often has direct access to that person. The client can ask questions and, ideally, receive a response from their advisor quickly.

Additionally, many fee-only advisors choose to become solo practitioners, which, as we've discussed, is beneficial for the client. They are removed from the temptations and incentives offered by large financial institutions, such as sales commissions, contests, and bonuses. Solo advisors may still charge hidden fees, so practice caution and do your research no matter what!

It may be appealing to work with a solo advisor, but this setup quickly falls short when deeper knowledge, more resources, or specialized guidance is required. Eric Hutchens,* president and chief investment officer at Allodium Investment Consultants, says, "The truth is, no one can be an expert in everything. With a team approach, we can be generalists in everything, and each advisor serves as an expert in one or more areas, such as estate planning, tax planning, or responsible investing. That allows [the advisor] to concentrate on that area,

---

* **Eric Hutchens is the president and chief investment officer at Allodium Investment Consultants, specializing in investment strategies and comprehensive financial planning for high-net-worth individuals and families. He is a Certified Financial Planner® (CFP®) and Accredited Investment Fiduciary® (AIF®).**

keep the team updated on important changes, and be available when their deeper expertise is needed with a client."*

A solo financial advisor generally won't have the depth of experience and specialization in certain areas that a team of multiple advisors may have. This can be an impediment when it comes to more complicated financial situations and personal financial goals that require sophisticated solutions.

Additionally, if the solo advisor becomes ill or needs to take a break, the client runs the risk of going without advice for an extended period. Eric Hutchens underscores the advantages of working with a team by saying, "If the primary advisor is on vacation, is hit by a bus, or retires, the secondary advisor and service team can step up to help the client with little disruption." He goes on to describe clients who urgently needed to speak with their solo advisor . . . only to discover that person was unavailable. "It can be very unsettling to be in the midst of a market crisis and have no one to talk to."†

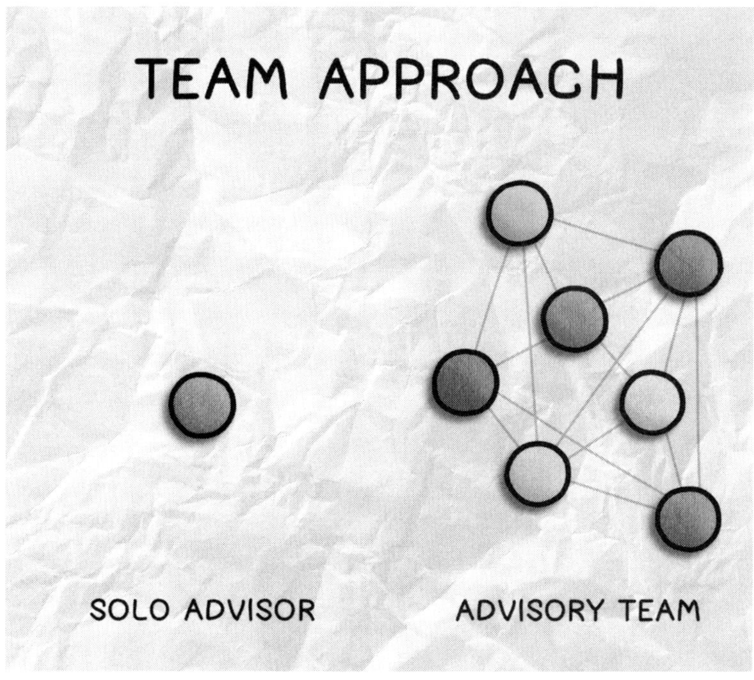

* Hutchens, interview by author, December 22, 2022.

† Ibid.

Furthermore, having a team of financial advisors can provide the client with a sense of security and continuity. If a financial advisor is planning on retiring or leaving the company, the client can rest assured that another trusted advisor from the same team can step in and become their primary advisor with relative ease.

Avoid Ineffective Teams

It is important to note that not all teams are created equal. Some clash, collaborate ineffectively, or do not collaborate at all. Just because a financial advisory firm employs dozens (or even hundreds) of people, it doesn't mean they form a unified team or strive to work together toward the same goals. It's important to look out for teams like this, as they are more likely to provide subpar advice or not work in the best interests of the client.

At the beginning of my career, I worked for a large financial advisory firm that rewarded its financial advisors with sales incentives and bonuses. Even though the firm employed fifty other advisors in my office (and thousands across the nation), I never collaborated *with* any of them. In fact, I was mostly working *against* them to acquire clients and make as many sales as I could. We did not collaborate with each other in any sense.

In this investment product sales environment, financial advisors were free to carve their own path. If someone wanted to focus mainly on selling stocks, they could. If someone else wanted to specialize in bonds or mutual funds, they could. It was a very entrepreneurial atmosphere, but it didn't much benefit the client. How could the client know, for example, that their financial advisor was mainly focused on selling a limited selection of financial products rather than exploring a wide range of options that may be better suited to their needs? How could the client know that competition among the salespeople was far more important than collaboration?

To determine whether (or not) a team is effective, knowledgeable, and collaborative, I suggest taking a few steps to become a savvier consumer.

Identifying Effective Teams

Conducting adequate research is essential for identifying a team that is knowledgeable, experienced, and committed to working together for the benefit of the client. Here are a few tips for finding an effective and collaborative team of financial advisors:

1. Start with fee-only financial advisory firms.

To avoid cutthroat competitive financial product sales environments, like the one I experienced early in my career, it's smart to begin your search by seeking fee-only advisory firms. At this point in the book, this piece of advice should not come as a surprise! The advantage of working with a fee-only firm is that financial advisors have no incentives to make financial product sales. They are therefore more likely to make solid investment recommendations and focus their attention on the client's best interests.

Find fee-only financial planning firms by using databases that connect individual investors with fee-only fiduciaries.

2. Research the team.

Once you have identified a few fee-only financial planning firms, investigate the backgrounds and qualifications of their financial advisors. This is a great way to learn if the team is knowledgeable and experienced, with a variety of specialties that complement one another. Hutchens says, "Having multiple Certified Financial Planners® (CFP®) should be a minimum starting point. Beyond that, certifications such as AIF® (Accredited Investment Fiduciary®) and CFA® (Chartered Financial Analyst®) on staff are helpful."*

3. Ask about collaboration.

When you interview a potential financial advisor, request an overview of their team. Ask about their knowledge and specialties, as well as about their team's collaborative practices. Do the advisors regularly request insights from each other? Does the advisory firm have committees that address different subjects? Do certain people specialize in specific areas? Are there any major differences of opinion within the

---

* Hutchens, interview by author, December 22, 2022.

team? Additionally, it's a good idea to find out what kind of internal policies the team has in place to ensure all members work together in the best interests of the client.

A successful financial advisory team will have the right combination of skills, knowledge, and an emphasis on collaboration. That should come across during your interview.

When it comes to financial advisors, it is important to recognize the advantages of working with a team. Teams can offer a more comprehensive and tailored approach to financial planning. While a solo financial advisor may be a good fit for certain situations, teams can be especially helpful for those who need more specialized advice. It is important to choose a financial advisory team that works together in a transparent and collaborative way. It is also important to ensure that the team's advisor-client relationships will remain transparent and free of any potential conflicts of interest. By conducting thorough research and asking the right questions, you can identify an effective financial advisory team that will work in your best interest.

Chapter 27

Directories and Matching Platforms: Use with Caution

Let's say it's time to purchase a new car, and you'd like to find a new vehicle that's a bit different than the one you own now. What do you do first? Probably, you hop online and begin to research. You might search for something like "SUVs with best gas mileage" or "4-door sedans that perform well in winter." From there, you'll find guidance from several major websites—Kelley Blue Book, CarGurus, Edmunds—and the guidance will probably be sound. These websites aren't trying to sell a specific make and model of vehicle. They primarily exist to provide information.

Researching cars online isn't entirely foolproof, of course. You may come across articles sponsored by specific car manufacturers or encounter biased consumer reviews. However, if someone is making a wildly untrue claim about a vehicle ("The Dodge Ram 1500 truck gets fifty miles to the gallon!"), you can easily double-check this statistic on the manufacturer's website.

Unfortunately, researching potential financial advisors is often not so straightforward.

First of all, many investors are not exactly sure what type of financial advisor they need. They also may not understand the subtle distinctions between financial advisors, such as "fee-based" versus "fee-only." This is hardly the fault of the consumer, since financial acumen is not often taught in school, and only about half of the US population is financially literate.

And even if someone has a decent understanding of the financial planning and investment management industry, they may still be bamboozled by opaque terminology, confusing websites, and misleading language. Investor advocate and educator Pam Krueger says, "Let's focus on 'Mr. and Mrs. Smith,' the consumers who are almost retired and have every reason to be confused about who to turn to for the most important financial advice of their lives. For them, asking for advice is like a black box. As an industry, we've done nothing but try to confuse people with jargon, sales pitches, and expenses and fees that are never openly explained." Krueger goes on to explain that much of this confusion stems from those not legally held to the fiduciary standard—the brokers, bankers, and insurance agents masquerading as fiduciaries. As Series 7 brokerage representatives, they've been allowed to call themselves "financial advisors"; at the same time, the SEC (or state) doesn't even oversee brokers unless they are currently registered as investment advisors.*

Second, even if the consumer has a rough idea of what they're looking for, a Google search may not yield great results. For example, if you search for "best estate planning financial advisors in Minneapolis," the top results will likely be sponsored ads—organizations that paid to be at the top of the pile. Fortunately, reputable companies such as FeeOnlyNetwork (which we'll discuss later in this chapter) are working to appear at the top of the search results, but it's difficult to compete against big-budget brokerage firms.

When searching online for a financial advisor, consumers will likely see three main types of results: directories, matching platforms, and specific financial advisory firms. In this chapter, we're going to focus on directories and matching platforms.

What Is a Financial Advisor Directory?

Think of an online financial advisor directory like a telephone book (if you're old enough to remember those!) or an index. The main goal of a directory is to compile relevant information in one spot so someone can easily search through that information to find what they need. Whether you're searching for a local ice cream shop, a dentist

---

* Krueger, interview by author, August 7, 2023.

that accepts your insurance, or a specific bird in the *Birds of North America* book, a directory can cut through irrelevant information and point you in the right direction. The same is true of financial advisor directories.

Allan Slider, founder and president of FeeOnlyNetwork, says it is important to understand the difference between a directory and a matching platform. "A matching site," he says, "will commonly require contact or situational information before showing advisor profiles. A directory, on the other hand, allows the consumer to look up profiles without being 'matched.'"*

A directory may sound like a neutral source of information (like a bird book or a telephone book), but not all directories adhere to the same standards. Most directories of financial advisors will list whoever pays the requisite fee. These financial advisors *could* be fee-only fiduciaries, but most directories are packed with fee-based financial advisors, brokers, and even insurance agents and bankers who allegedly offer financial planning (chapters 10–12 address why working with these individuals could be problematic).

An example of an exclusively fee-only financial advisor directory is FeeOnlyNetwork, founded in 2011 by digital marketer turned consumer advocate Allan Slider. Slider recognized the need to help fee-only advisors stand out among brokers and non-fiduciaries. He says, "We want every consumer to ask their current or potential financial advisor one simple question, 'Are you fee-only?' If their answer is anything other than a resounding 'YES!', then you may be working with a salesperson focused on making a commission. I believe that an educated investor chooses a fee-only advisor nearly every time."† FeeOnlyNetwork gives vetted, fee-only fiduciaries a platform to grow their online visibility and showcase their expertise while educating consumers on the importance of working with an advisor focused on true financial planning.

Other organizations also feature fee-only advisor directories, such as NAPFA, XY Planning Network, Alliance of Comprehensive Planners, Garrett Planning Network, and more. These directories

---

*** Slider, interview by author, August 30, 2023.**

† Ibid.

make their intentions to promote fee-only advisors clear through their websites' language ("fixed/flat charges," "fee-for-service financial advisors," "fee-only advisors"). If a directory does not include words or phrases such as these, I encourage you to proceed with caution.

A directory can be highly valuable, but some consumers prefer the convenience of a matching platform. Although many matching platforms participate in dubious practices, they're not *all* bad. I do recommend, however, approaching them with caution.

What Are Matching Platforms?

Matching platforms are websites that attempt to pair potential investors with "ideal" financial advisors. They promise to streamline the process of finding an advisor by pinpointing the consumer's financial needs and matching them with someone who specializes in those specific areas. After a consumer answers a few questions about their financial goals and circumstances, they're given the contact information of a few local financial advisors. While directories are like phone books, matching platforms resemble online dating sites or apps that match people with similar beliefs, political leanings, hobbies, and other criteria. Sounds like a great system, right?

Unfortunately, due to the abundant conflicts of interest of some (not all) matching platforms, you could end up with a less-than-ideal advisor. For starters, these platforms often receive referral fees from the advisors they recommend to customers. They may also only feature certain advisors in their search results, due to financial incentives. This means that the most qualified advisors may not be featured, even if they are the ideal fit for a consumer's specific needs. As a result, investors may end up with a financial advisor who doesn't understand their needs.

Can you imagine how annoyed you would be if a dating app matched you with someone, you decided to go on a date, and then you discovered you have nothing in common? What a waste of time! Since many matching sites favor financial advisors (and financial advisory firms) with the biggest budgets, this disregard of criteria is probably quite common. The real problem, however, is that most consumers likely won't realize they've been given a rotten match. Through no fault of their own, they may choose to establish a relationship with the financial advisor (and their firm) without realizing the "set up" wasn't a true match.

An additional problem with matching platforms is their propensity to collect private data from consumers. This means they might sell your private information to other companies without your knowledge. This could potentially expose private information like your financial goals or household income to identity thieves. Or it might mean you'll receive nonstop calls from companies trying to win your business.

As a consumer, it's important to keep in mind that nothing is free. Companies have to make money somehow, and often that money comes from you. If an online service offers to match you with a financial advisor, it's possible they're making money by selling your information to third parties, including other advisors you may not have selected. Pam Krueger, founder and CEO of Wealthramp, an online matching platform featuring exclusively fee-only financial advisors, says, "Lead generation is a big business in America. You must read the privacy policies of each website where you're entering all your information. It's called 'lead gen' for a reason, and it's for them, not you, the consumer. Not every advisor-matching website operates this way. Wealthramp is designed to make sure the consumer's privacy is respected and is the only advisor matching service that doesn't share personal information. This way, the individual has the power to choose how and when to initiate contact with an advisor to whom they're matched."*

How Can You Identify Inferior Directories and Matching Platforms?

Though unscrupulous directories and matching platforms can be tricky to avoid, it's important to be aware of them when looking for a financial advisor. In general, you should be wary of any platform that pulls from a large pool of financial advisors that includes

* Krueger, interview by author, August 7, 2023.

brokers and hybrid advisors. It's also a good idea to question the platform's methodologies. How, exactly, are financial advisors vetted? And, for matching platforms, how is the consumer paired with a given financial advisor or advisors? Do the survey questions make sense and provide the platform with enough depth to make a decent recommendation?

Although some reputable directories and matching platforms exist (FeeOnlyNetwork and Wealthramp among them), most of these platforms are more interested in making money than connecting consumers with reputable financial advisors. Directories such as Investor.com and AdvisorFinder include people who may call themselves financial planners, wealth managers, and financial advisors, but they are more than likely interested in sales than evidence-based financial planning.

Matching services go a step farther than directories by collecting consumer data before pairing them with a few financial advisor "matches." I've encountered matching services through companies such as SmartAsset, Paladin Registry, WiserAdvisor (which recently acquired IndyFin), and Zoe Financial, which are representative of the typical look and feel of a matching platform (type each company's name into your search engine followed by "match with advisor" to access their matching platforms).

If you're unsure if you're dealing with an ethical matching platform, try asking yourself these three questions:

1. Does the platform explain exactly how its matching process works?
2. Are the search results logical (instead of random sponsored results?)
3. Does the platform have a privacy policy in place to protect your data?

If the answers to any of these questions are "no," it's probably best to steer clear. Comb through the fine print (tedious as it may be!) to figure out how a matching platform gathers and disseminates data and how it pairs consumers with financial advisors.

For example, if you decide to use the matching platform designed by SmartAsset, an online financial technology company that provides financial planning advice, you'll immediately see a disclaimer that says the survey will "match you with up to 3 vetted fiduciary financial advisors," and the matches are selected based on location and asset amount. The disclaimer goes on to state, "We also consider each advisor's advertising budget, therefore advisors with larger budgets are more likely to appear in the results page."*

The most obvious red flag in this disclaimer is the statement relating to "advisors with larger budgets." Financial advisors and financial advisory firms can essentially buy their way into the results, which means the matching platforms will find you financial advisors with financial firms with large advertising budgets, as opposed to the most qualified financial planners.

Reputable directories and matching platforms will not favor one financial advisor over the other due to their "larger budget." FeeOnlyNetwork makes its stance very clear on its website, saying, "We do not aspire to become a 'Match.com' or 'Yelp.com' for financial advisors. These business models create a bias toward firms willing or able to pay more for promoting their advisors (buying leads) or focusing their resources on a sophisticated sales process. In fact, we recommend you avoid 'advisor matching' sites that collect and sell your information in your quest to find a financial advisor."† (It is worth noting that FeeOnlyNetwork *does* recommend working with the matching platform Wealthramp and has recently partnered with this service. This partnership makes sense since the values of the two companies are aligned).

The second part of SmartAsset's disclaimer says it matches consumers with "vetted fiduciary financial advisors." That may sound appealing, but it doesn't tell the full story. As we've discussed in past chapters, financial advisors may be dually registered as both investment advisors and brokers. They may act as fiduciaries in the morning and brokers in the afternoon. Or they may "switch hats" partway through a meeting. In short, if you're working with a dually registered

---

* SmartAsset, "Find a Financial Planner."

† "FeeOnlyNetwork.com Is Different by Design." FeeOnlyNetwork. https://www.feeonlynetwork.com/about-fee-only-network/

financial advisor, you can never be quite certain who you're working with on any given day—the investment advisor or the broker.

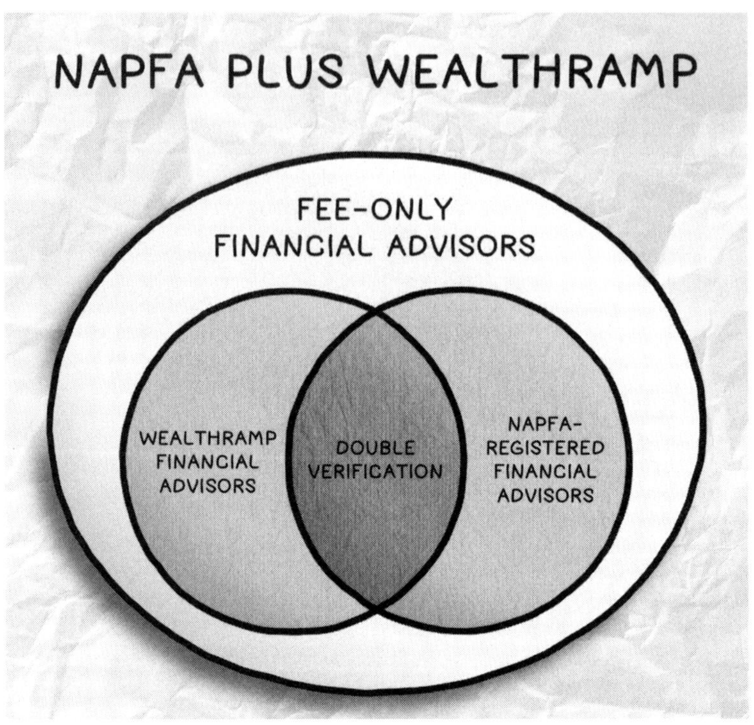

A Better Approach to Directories and Matching Platforms

If you want to find a trusted financial advisor, it's best to dodge directories and matching platforms that are more concerned about profit than the consumer's well-being. To do that, I encourage you to use smart, trustworthy databases.

Unlike a broad internet search, using specific, curated databases can help you find qualified financial advisors, without all the sponsored content. Several databases exist that are independent, reliable, and unbiased. See chapter 24 for a list of my top recommendations (such as CEFEX and Fi360's websites) for searching for both financial advisory firms and individual financial advisors.

If I had to boil that list down to one key recommendation, it would be to utilize the online tools I've described in previous chapters that

FIND AN ADVISOR

CATEGORIES		EXAMPLES
ONLINE MATCHING SERVICES	LEAD GENERATION PLATFORMS (SELL DATA)	SMARTASSET
	CLIENT INTRODUCTION PLATFORMS (DO NOT SELL DATA)	WEALTHRAMP
ONLINE MEMBERSHIPS		FEEONLYNETWORK
ONLINE DIRECTORIES		NAPFA'S FIND AN ADVISOR

introduce individual investors to qualified fee-only financial advisors. Wealthramp, FeeOnlyNetwork, and NAPFA's Find an Advisor are my top picks.

Ultimately, it's important to use your best judgement when considering a directory or matching platform. By doing your research and using the resources outlined in this chapter and others, you can make an informed decision about who is best suited to help you manage your finances. A reputable and ethical online platform is one tool that can help you find a trustworthy advisor, but it's a tool that should be used with caution. If you don't have a good grasp of your financial goals and needs, you'll end up playing "financial advisor roulette" with directories and matching platforms. Instead, take the time to pin down your requirements and only seek databases that will connect you with ethical, knowledgeable, and professional fee-only fiduciaries.

Chapter 28

Identify and Avoid Slick Marketing Tactics Used by Financial Advisors

Let's say you've decided the time is right to enlist the expertise of a financial advisor. You're considering your options and just beginning to dive into your research. Any piece of news, or radio ad, or flyer related to financial guidance will inevitably snag your attention. You're trying to learn as much as you can before making a decision.

So, when you receive a mailer offering an evening of "free financial advice" *and* a complimentary steak dinner, you're immediately interested. "How serendipitous!" you think. "Why not attend the dinner and see what these financial advisors have to say?"

What you don't realize is that you're essentially a little fish stepping into a pool of savvy, often ruthless sharks.

As a financial planner, I'm highly cognizant of the slick marketing tactics many so-called financial advisors use to reel in clients. While some strategies may be more ethical (like offering a free financial review to those with minimal assets), other tactics are simply meant to lure in unsuspecting clients to sign up for services they may or may not need.

Let's talk about the different types of sales tactics you might encounter and how to identify and avoid them. Among the many questionable marketing approaches I've come across are the following four types:

1. Sales presentations with freebies

Who doesn't like getting something for free? The problem is many financial advisors use freebies to incentivize sales. This could mean offering a free gourmet dinner or tickets to a sporting event. Sure, these freebies can be nice, but remember it's ultimately a sales pitch, presented by an experienced salesperson. The presenter may start off their pitch with purely educational material but shift over to a high-pressure sales ask or a "limited-time offer." This is a classic setup that has proven to be effective time and again (the same types of high-pressure sales are used to pitch time-shares or sell used cars).

And don't be fooled by the presenter's credentials. Just because someone is a Registered Investment Adviser doesn't mean they aren't dually registered as a broker.

2. Sales disguised as educational classes

You may come across an offering for a course titled "The Fundamentals of Investing," or "Maximizing Your Social Security," or "Retirement Planning 101." In my experience, many of these course offerings will land right in your mailbox in the form of an attractive pamphlet or flyer.

An educational course seems harmless enough (and *some* may be legitimate), but far too often they devolve into little more than a sales pitch. Be wary of courses that have any sort of tangible reward involved, like a free lunch, a goodie bag, or a free one-hundred-page book. If a pamphlet or mailer conveys a sense of urgency or seems to be pressuring you into attending, chances are this isn't purely an education course but a wolf in sheep's clothing (a salesperson masquerading as an educator). For example, I've received invitations to educational courses in the mail that say, "Seating is limited! Reserve your spot today!" and "You cannot afford to miss this educational workshop!"

The best way to distinguish a legitimate course from an outright sales pitch is to ask for details about the instructor, the specific topics that will be discussed, and the types of materials that will be provided. You could also look online for testimonials about the class or ask around to see if any friends or family members have attended. When in doubt, steer clear.

3. Sales embedded in the media

Have you ever watched a news segment or listened to a radio program where the host invites an "expert" guest speaker to discuss a financial topic? Some of these experts are legitimate and provide bias-free information, but others are only on the program to gain name recognition for themselves or their company. The advice is secondary to advertising their brand.

Some financial advisors even pay to appear on some of these programs. They might choose to "sponsor" a segment, in which they give a few words of advice and establish themselves as an expert. As a comprehensive article by Thinkbox says, "Many TV programmes are themselves powerful brands. Their prestige, popularity and perceived values can rub off on those brands that associate with them through successful sponsorship."* In short, the financial advisors build up their credibility simply by being associated with a trustworthy TV program.

The same tactic—sometimes referred to as native advertising—can be used on the radio, in magazines, or even in newspapers. Pay attention and be on the lookout for anything called "sponsored content." Sponsored content can be well disguised as information, but if the news segment or program seems to be promoting a specific product or

---

*** Thinkbox, "Introduction to TV Sponsorship."**

name-dropping a certain brand, be wary. Some segments may even include a disclaimer at the beginning or end (often rushed through or written in fine print).

4. Bogus awards

You may look up a financial advisor and see that he or she has a "five-star rating." On the surface, that might sound impressive, but what does it *actually* mean, and how does one obtain this perfect rating?

Unfortunately, several companies are known for giving out bogus awards to financial advisors. In my experience, a company might contact the financial advisor and say something along the lines of, "Congrats! We've determined you're a five-star financial advisor. You now can purchase a quarter-page, half-page, or full-page advertisement in our upcoming top wealth advisor issue of our monthly magazine. To advertise this prestigious award, pay us the low price of $______, and we'll make sure to put it in front of potential clients."

Essentially, the award is useless for the consumer to differentiate financial advisors. Everyone earns five stars, and everyone can advertise their "accolades" online. If you see an award next to a financial advisor's name, take it with a grain of salt and do a little digging to find out if the award is legitimate. To me, it's better to look at an advisor's experience (their background, credentials, and any customer testimonials you can find) than to trust third-party awards.

Tips for Avoiding Slick Marketing Tactics

Though some marketing tactics can be tricky to identify, others are relatively straightforward. To avoid being taken in by a sales-based financial advisor, I recommend taking a few basic precautions:

1. Read the fine print.

Many marketing materials or offers will contain a disclaimer at the bottom of the page. Take the time to read it, since this may reveal whether (or not) the offer is actually a sales pitch. For example, I received a mailer recently advertising a "complimentary lunch presentation" that centers on financial planning for retirement. On the surface, it seemed like a decent opportunity, but at the bottom of the mailer the small print read, "By contacting [name of financial advisor], you may be offered information regarding the purchase of insurance products, including fixed index annuities and life." A clear sign that this program is really about sales!

2. Look out for pressure.

Financial advisors should never pressure you into signing up for anything. If you feel rushed or pushed in any way, it's a red flag. As I mentioned before, you should be extremely cautious if an advisor is offering "special deals" or claims to have access to "limited-time-only" investments.

3. Do your homework.

Read reviews and testimonials, look for customer complaints, and contact the state securities department or use FINRA's BrokerCheck tool to check an advisor's credentials. Learning about a financial advisor's background will help you understand if they are commission-driven and, thus, using "educational courses" or presentations as a vehicle to make a sale.

4. Follow your gut.

If an offer or a class seems too good to be true, there's a good chance it is. Be wary of offers that come with large rewards attached, like a free dinner, complimentary concert tickets, or free seats at sporting events. It's always best to trust your instincts.

It's important to be aware of marketing tactics used by financial advisors. By understanding the strategies that advisors may use to try to influence you, you'll be better equipped to distinguish between legitimate advice and slick sales tactics. Don't be taken in by offers that sound too good to be true. By exercising caution and doing your due diligence, you'll be able to avoid charlatans who are far more interested in their bottom line than doing right by the customer.

Part Four

SELECT AND HIRE A FINANCIAL ADVISOR (AND FIRM)

You've adjusted your compass toward trustworthy financial advisors, you've identified the direction you'd like to go, and you've put in the legwork to search for financial planners (and financial advisory firms) that will fit your needs. But you're not out of the woods yet.

After whittling down your search for a financial advisor to a few select candidates, the second part of your efforts begin—the part that involves interviewing, reading legal documents, doing extra research, and going on tours. Many individual investors have no idea how to approach this last leg of the journey, which is why, in part 4, I've put together a road map of how to select, hire, and compensate a financial advisor (and financial advisory firm).

I've also included a few bonus chapters that provide helpful insights to kick off your new investing journey.

Chapter 29
How to Select a Financial Advisory Firm That Fits Your Needs

Far too often, individual investors pick out a financial advisor before selecting a financial advisory firm. They might receive a recommendation for a financial advisor from their brother-in-law, or they might know their daughter's soccer coach is a financial advisor, and, heck, they like the guy, so why not?

This approach is cavalier, reckless, and could lead to some hefty financial consequences. What if the person your brother-in-law recommended works for a company that does not adhere to a fiduciary standard of care? What if the "likeable" soccer coach works for one of the huge national financial companies that is far more concerned with sales than doing right by its investors?

Even if the individual financial advisor is likeable and seems trustworthy, the firm they represent may not have your best interests in mind. To me, picking out a financial advisor *before* selecting a financial advisory firm is akin to picking out furniture for a new home before you've purchased the home.

Take my black leather reading chair, for instance.

After buying our dream house in the late '90s, my wife and I began to think about how to outfit a reading area. We knew the dimensions of the room we wanted to furnish, as well as the look and feel we wanted to achieve. So, it didn't take long to decide on a furniture set for the space—a black leather reading chair with a matching ottoman and loveseat. Buying these items before purchasing our home would not have made sense, even if we liked the items or found them on sale. The house we purchased directed our furniture choices.

Not only that, but furniture is also relatively easy to swap out—much easier than purchasing a brand-new home. If my doctor informs me that I have developed a leather allergy, I could (sadly) replace my leather chair with a cotton-covered one. Similarly, if your financial advisor can no longer work with you (due to retirement, death, a relocation, or some other reason), you can remain with the same financial advisory firm, knowing you're aligned with its values and vision.

So, how can you find your ideal financial advisory firm *first* and a suitable advisor second (find the house first, followed by the furniture)? Let's discuss how to approach the selection process logically and intelligently.

Before the Interview

The selection process can really be broken down into two parts: pre-interviewing and interviewing. You can do plenty of independent research on your own before you even pick up the phone or set foot in the company's office.

First, make sure you know what you're seeking in a financial advisory firm (your "needs, wants, and nice-to-haves" list), and narrow down your list of prospective firms accordingly. I recommend (no surprise!) looking for independent Registered Investment Adviser (RIA) firms that use a fee-only compensation model, adhere to a fiduciary standard of care, and are professionally qualified.

To search for a financial advisory firm, consider using the following online resources, listed in order of priority:

1. Wealthramp

Use Wealthramp to find financial advisory firms that solely employ fee-only financial advisors.

2. FeeOnlyNetwork

FeeOnlyNetwork is a directory that allows individual investors to search for vetted, fee-only financial advisory firms.

3. NAPFA

Use NAPFA's Find an Advisor online search tool to find local fee-only financial planning firms.

4. CEFEX

CEFEX provides a registered company list of certified investment advisory firms.

5. Fi360

Use Fi360's fiduciary-centered online search tool to find investment firms registered with CEFEX.

6. The Committee for the Fiduciary Standard*

The Committee lists investment advisory firms that are willing to acknowledge a fiduciary relationship with the investor.

7. Institute for the Fiduciary Standard†

The IFS is a list of firms that adhere to a fiduciary standard of care for the investor. This organization has a Real Fiduciary™ Practices Advisor Registry of firms that agree to adhere to the high standards of the (Real Fiduciary™) Practices and publicly state to federal and state regulators they do so.

Once you have your list of prospective firms, you can visit their websites to learn some more particulars. What qualifications, designations, and education do their financial advisors have? Does a fiduciary oath (or equivalent) appear somewhere on the website? Is the company's Form ADV and/or CRS Form on its website? If not, the SEC has its own searchable database of public ADVs. (We will discuss Form ADV and the CRS Form in chapter 30.)

Only pick up the phone to learn more about a company or to schedule an interview once you've narrowed down your list to a handful of viable candidates. A financial advisory firm's sales process begins as soon as a prospective client calls or emails. While many independent,

* http://www.thefiduciarystandard.org/fiduciary-oath/

† https://thefiduciaryinstitute.org/real-fiduciary-advisors/

fee-only firms (in my experience) are not aggressive with sales, large, commission-reliant companies tend to lean heavily into sales. They have a script they use to get a prospective client through the door and into a meeting with a financial advisor/broker/insurance agent/banker. On the other hand, if I receive a call from an investor who is clearly not a good fit, I usually end the call swiftly by recommending a more suitable financial advisory firm. But that doesn't mean I don't want as many potential clients as possible walking through the door—of course I do. I may not know if someone is a good fit until well into our intake process, which is why it's great for potential clients to "weed themselves out" if they know they're not a good fit.

Before setting up an interview with a financial advisory firm, it's a good idea to request and review documents that outline its services, operations, and compensation model. If you can't find a company's Form ADV on its website, I recommend requesting it and looking it over before moving forward with an in-person visit/interview.

In short, the pre-interview steps can be described as follows:

1. Develop your "needs, wants, and nice-to-haves list."
2. Conduct internet research.
3. Make an initial inquiry by phone.
4. Request relevant documents.

Interviewing a Financial Advisory Firm

My firm has a system it follows for onboarding new clients. After we've talked on the phone and determined we could be a fit, we kick off a series of four meetings (*if* the investor seems to be a good fit; if, however, we determine we're not aligned, we cut our losses and part ways). These meetings are in-depth and result in a proposal for the prospective client(s). The proposals are so long that some have even likened them to a storybook.

These four meetings are as follows:

1. Values meeting

The purpose of this meeting is to determine if we might be a good match with the investor. During this meeting, we try to gain a big-picture perspective of the client's wants, needs, and circumstances. We learn what is important to the investor and why they are seeking an advisor at this time.

The investor, on the other hand, will learn about our investment philosophy, how we're compensated, and other big-picture details. If the meeting goes well and we seem aligned, we set up a second meeting:

2. Diagnostic meeting

A diagnostic meeting tends to be about two hours long, and for good reason! We ask detailed questions about the client's goals, background, financial situation, work, family, and much more. The purpose of gathering (and then analyzing) all this data is to help our financial planning team design a logical, comprehensive financial plan.

3. Proposal meeting

After the diagnostic meeting, we put together an investment proposal for the prospective client. This is usually a highly detailed document that presents investment and financial planning recommendations and opportunities. This comprehensive financial plan is always personalized to meet the client's needs and goals, based on the information we learned in the diagnostic meeting.

At this point, the prospective client can request modifications to the proposal or ask any questions they might have (including questions about compensation). I usually have a good idea of whether the investor wants to work with us *before* this point, but this meeting solidifies that hunch.

4. Implementation meeting

If the client is happy with the comprehensive financial plan and feels comfortable with the company and financial advisors, we move to the implementation phase. The purpose of the implementation meeting is to align and initiate the client's personalized investment strategy. We confirm and clarify how we'll be moving forward with the client, and we sign implementation paperwork to seal the agreement. At this

New Client Intake Process

1	2	3	4
VALUES MEETING **OUR PURPOSE:** Determine if we may be a match	**DIAGNOSTIC MEETING** **OUR PURPOSE:** Understand you and your financial goals	**PROPOSAL MEETING** **OUR PURPOSE:** Share the investment proposal with you	**IMPLEMENTATION MEETING** **OUR PURPOSE:** Align and initiate your investment strategy
WHAT WE DO: • We learn what's important to you • We learn why you are seeking an advisor	**WHAT WE DO:** • We ask questions to learn your story (background, goals, family, work, etc.) • We assess your risk profile	**WHAT WE DO:** • We present your investment proposal and financial planning opportunities • We explain fees and any tax implications	**WHAT WE DO:** • We clarify any investment strategy modifications • We gather your communications preferences
WHAT YOU DO: • You learn about our investment philosophy • You learn how we are compensated	**WHAT YOU DO:** • You provide your financial documents • You share your financial goals	**WHAT YOU DO:** • You ask questions • You are able to request modifications to the proposal	**WHAT YOU DO:** • You confirm your investment plan • You sign implementation paperwork
MEETING DETAILS: • Meet with chief investment officer • Meeting Length: 1 hour	**MEETING DETAILS:** • Meet with chief investment officer and investment consultants • Meeting Length: 2 hours	**MEETING DETAILS:** • Meet with chief investment officer and investment consultants • Meeting Length: 2 hours	**MEETING DETAILS:** • Meet with investment consultants • Meeting Length: 2 hours

www.allodium.com

point, the client should be crystal clear on how their finances will be handled and what their financial advisor's role will be (and, if not, they can ask any lingering questions they might have). We then begin working together to implement the client's financial plan.

The reason I've explained my financial advisory firm's intake process is because I want you, as an individual investor, to have an example of how a financial advisory firm vets *you*, the investor. This gives you an inside glimpse into how the sausage is made and can help you understand what to (potentially) expect when going through the interviewing/intake process with a firm.

Once you understand this process, you can become an active participant. When you decide to reach out to a firm to begin the interviewing process, you can directly ask about these steps. Ask something to the effect of, "What is your intake process like for prospective clients?" or "How many meetings can I expect to attend before we agree to work with each other, and what will each meeting entail?"

Once you understand what's ahead, you can begin planning. This involves solidifying your "needs, wants, and nice-to-haves" list (with your significant other, if relevant) and determining which questions you'd like to ask during the interview(s). See appendix 2 for related AdvisorSmart® educational resources including a Sample Selection Criteria "needs, wants, and nice-to-haves" list. Visit the AdvisorSmart® website for additional up-to-date, free educational resources at www.AdvisorSmart.com/Resources.

It is crucial to ask smart, well-defined interview questions to determine if the financial advisory firm is, indeed, a good fit. We will cover these interview questions in upcoming chapters (chapter 32 will focus on questions related to financial advisory firms, while chapter 33 will focus on questions related to individual financial advisors).

The process of seeking and selecting a financial advisory firm may seem overwhelming, but it becomes manageable when you break it down into smaller steps. Approach your search like you would house hunting—define your goals and needs/wants/nice-to-haves, do your research, and then make an in-person visit. After my wife and I went through this process to find our dream home, I was then able to purchase my dream reading chair, just as a prospective client can find a great financial advisor after identifying the right financial advisory firm. I can now enjoy my morning coffee, or do a bit of reading, while sitting in my comfortable chair. But that wouldn't have happened if we hadn't found our dream house first.

Select your firm first, and then your financial advisor.

Chapter 30

Using Form ADV to Guide Your Search for a Financial Advisory Firm

I always think it's remarkable that so many people put such little thought into choosing a financial advisory firm—a decision that can be crucial for one's future livelihood and financial stability. Many people spend more time researching vacation spots than they do financial advisors or advisory firms. Sure, vacation planning might be more fun, but it's not nearly as impactful as researching potential financial advisors and/or wealth managers.

The research you put into finding a trustworthy financial advisor can (metaphorically *and* literally) pay dividends. Because of the high stakes of this decision, it's essential to understand how a financial advisory firm (and the people it employs) operates before agreeing to work with that firm.

But how can you fully understand the firm's operations? Are you supposed to simply take its financial advisors at their word?

I do believe most financial advisors do not outright *lie* to prospective clients, but some may omit certain details that could make the arrangement seem less appealing or more costly (in terms of fees). As we've discussed in past chapters, the vast majority of financial advisors are *not* fee-only fiduciaries, meaning they may occasionally (or regularly) take commissions or receive sales bonuses.

Caution is the name of the game. If you want to make sure a financial advisor—and the firm they represent—is disclosing all the information they should, it's a good idea to do your research. To help with this process, I recommend reading the company's Form ADV.

What Is a Form ADV?

The official name for a Form ADV is the *Uniform Application for Investment Adviser Registration and Report by Exempt Reporting Adviser.* That's a mouthful, so let's stick with ADV! The SEC requires investment advisors to submit this form, which discloses information about the company and how it is operated. Form ADV is usually quite long (Allodium's form is twenty-two pages long, but large firms can have upwards of one hundred pages) and contains essential information about the firm—services, fee structures, commissions (if applicable), investment strategies, types of clients served, any conflicts of interest, and more.

ADVs are essentially the "public face" that financial advisors and their firms present to investors. They provide investors with a comprehensive disclosure of the firm's business. The SEC requires ADVs to be updated annually and made available to the public. Though this may seem like a lot of regulatory paperwork, it is necessary and immensely beneficial to the client. Tyler Chapman,* the COO and CCO at Allodium Investment Consultants, says that the company doesn't find drafting and maintaining the Form ADV and other disclosures as "a reason to grumble." Rather, "we embrace the opportunity to be transparent and take pride in how our responses can differentiate us. These documents help educate investors about us and where we fit in the industry, and we like working with educated investors."†

Why Do ADVs Matter?

In short, ADVs matter because they give a detailed, honest (by law!), and comprehensive description of financial advisory firms. They are an excellent way to learn about a firm before even setting foot in the door.

Doing your due diligence and reviewing a Form ADV before meeting with an advisor is essential. Even though the language can be dense, ADVs should be viewed as a must-read before you decide to

---

* Tyler Chapman serves as chief operating officer and chief compliance officer at Allodium Investment Consultants. He also chairs the Executive Committee, leads Allodium's company meetings, and serves on the Employee Committee. He received a BA from Amherst College and an MBA from the University of Minnesota.

† Chapman, interview by author, March 12, 2023.

engage with a financial advisor or wealth manager. Believe me, I understand the temptation to skip reading them entirely. It's like reading over the service agreement for your smartphone or the fine print of a store's return policy. Who wants to do that?

But bear in mind this is a major life decision that really does require your time and attention, even if that means reading over a couple dozen pages (or more) of text. Tyler Chapman says that "putting on your 'regulator glasses' could be helpful when parsing through ADV content." When searching for any red flags, he recommends looking for "anything 'different' and determining whether it's a good or bad kind of different. This will give you helpful context, pointed questions, and perhaps some healthy skepticism when you meet with the advisor in person."*

And, when in doubt, seek outside help. If you're a high-net-worth individual, it's not a bad idea to run a firm's ADV past your attorney

* Ibid.

or trusted CPA. And if you're not a high-net-worth individual? It's still worth it to go through the form, highlight areas you don't understand, and ask for clarification from a knowledgeable friend, relative, or even the advisor who gave you the form.

Finding a Form ADV

A Form ADV is required and must be made available to the public, but how do you actually find an ADV?

The simplest way is to contact the financial advisor directly. Most advisors I know are happy to oblige when asked for a copy of their Form ADV. If the advisor is with a larger firm, it should already be available on the firm's website.

The SEC has its own searchable database of public ADVs. It may take a few steps to find a form, but the database can provide useful information. It's also the best way to double-check the information.

At my financial advisory firm, we provide an electronic copy of our Form ADV to every prospective client before our initial meeting. Once the client agrees to work with us, we provide them with an additional paper copy of our ADV.

An Alternative to ADVs: CRS Forms

A cousin to the ADV is the CRS Form (or Customer Relationship Summary). This is essentially a simplified version of a Form ADV, with the same type of information (like services provided and fees) but presented in a much shorter, more user-friendly format. One of the main advantages of CRS Forms is that they are shorter (only two pages long). They make it easy to quickly compare fees and services of different financial advisors.

Though a CRS Form can provide a useful snapshot of an organization, it does not offer the kind of depth an ADV does. Chapman says CRS Forms can be useful to narrow down an investor's list of potential financial firms, but he "personally would not feel comfortable making a final selection without a more comprehensive review of all available disclosures and some transparent conversations. Hiring an advisor is a big commitment."*

The Form ADV (and, to some extent, CRS Forms) are important tools for any investor looking for a financial advisor. ADVs offer an in-depth look at the company, services offered, fees, and any other relevant information that should be considered before making a decision. CRS Forms are a useful way to quickly compare the services and fees of different firms. The bottom line is that doing your research and understanding what you're signing up for is essential before engaging with any financial advisor or institution. You probably wouldn't go on an overseas trip without doing your research first, so why skimp on research when it comes to initiating an important (potentially decades-long) professional relationship?

---

* Ibid.

Chapter 31
Prepping to Interview (Financial Advisory Firms and Advisors)

During my thirty-five-plus years as a financial advisor, I've interviewed *hundreds* of potential clients. Some of these interviews have gone well, and both parties gained the information needed to make a decision about whether or not to work together. Other interviews have flopped.

An interview could flop for many reasons. Someone might come in and ask for a guaranteed return—something I can never promise with absolute certainty (if a financial advisor *does* promise a guaranteed annual return, that's an instant red flag). Or the investor might focus on "beating the market." Or the investor may want free financial services. The list goes on.

Sometimes, customers ask questions I'm unable to immediately answer. For example, an interview should not begin with the question, "How much is this going to cost?" That's like calling up a Honda dealership and saying, "I want a car. How much will that be?"

When it comes to car shopping, there are dozens of variables. Do you want a sedan or an SUV? Do you want to upgrade to leather seats? How about a heated steering wheel or a backup camera? Do you want to add rustproofing? Extended warranty?

There are also many variables to consider when it comes to financial planning. A financial advisor's fee will be determined by dozens of different factors, which can be gleaned through an informational interview. That's why interviewing is so vital and why it's necessary to get it "right."

Before the Interview

If you're ready to begin the interviewing process, that means you've done your due diligence and logically whittled down your list of potential advisors to three or four individuals or firms. Several chapters in this book guide you on how to do that.

Let's recap. Generally, I advise consumers to

- seek fee-only financial advisors,
- avoid investment securities brokers, bankers, and insurance agents for financial planning,
- pay attention to professional designations/qualifications,
- do your research (using sites such as FINRA's BrokerCheck, Wealthramp, FeeOnlyNetwork, NAPFA's Find an Advisor tool, and other resources I've listed in past chapters), and
- look for financial advisors who are committed to a fiduciary standard of care.

Once you've identified a handful of financial advisors/advisory firms that fit your criteria, it's time to set up interviews. To make this process run smoothly, I suggest adhering to the following six guidelines. (Please note, I do not provide many specific questions for you to ask a financial advisor in this particular chapter. That will be covered in chapter 33.)

1. Prepare to discuss your unique situation.

I usually refer to my initial interview with a potential client as a "values meeting." As we talk, the consumer's priorities and values will become apparent, and I will develop an understanding of their unique situation (and how to fine-tune a financial plan to fit that situation).

As a consumer, it's essential to have a good handle on your personal circumstances. What are your most important goals? What do your current financial circumstances look like? What type of financial guidance do you need, in particular? Do you have any special circumstances (a large inheritance, a child with special needs, recurring health issues)?

Be clear and specific. The more relevant information you can provide, the better the financial advisor's understanding will be of your situation, which helps the advisor put together a financial plan that is precisely suited to your needs.

2. Be candid.

Any good relationship with a financial advisor is built on trust. Since that's the case, honesty and candidness should be expected from both sides: the financial advisor should be forthcoming with information, and the investor should be a tad vulnerable and willing to open up about their financial circumstances.

Finance writer Wendy J. Cook passed along a great quote about candid advice from Seth Godin: "Good advice is priceless. Not what you want to hear, but what you need to hear. Not imaginary, but practical. Not based on fear, but on possibility. Not designed to make you feel better, designed to make you better. Seek it out and embrace the true friends that care enough to risk sharing it. I'm not sure what takes more guts—giving it or getting it."*

3. Notice their interviewing style.

As you're engaging in an interview with a financial advisor, pay attention to *how* the interview is conducted. Any good financial advisor should demonstrate genuine curiosity about the customer. They should ask insightful questions, listen attentively, and provide straightforward answers to any of your questions.

Keep the essential attributes of financial advisors, which we covered in chapter 23, in mind.

4. Determine suitability.

If a financial advisor has several years of experience under their belt, it's probably safe to assume they have encountered many different customer circumstances and have put together a variety of financial plans. However, the advisor might not have come across your specific situation, or they might not be an expert in a specific area that requires guidance. Are they experienced in estate planning, for

---

* Godin, "Good Advice . . ."

instance, but not tax planning? Have they worked with hundreds of people who have retired domestically but have only worked with one or two people who retired abroad?

To make sure a financial advisor has experience working with clients whose circumstances resemble your own, it's a good idea to ask specific, pointed questions. If you need to set up a trust fund for a child with special needs, you might ask if the financial advisor has done this before and, if so, how often. If the financial advisor is relatively inexperienced with this type of planning, you might ask if they know of anyone else who does. It's possible that someone in the same firm has the requisite experience and will be better suited to develop a financial plan that fits your circumstances.

5. Understand what you'll get (and for how much).

Before signing on the dotted line, it's crucial to understand the logistics of your potential relationship with a financial advisor and what they charge for their services. Ask about the advisor's process and how they make decisions (reactivity to the market's ups and downs is a big red flag). Ask what your role will be in all of this. (Will you meet regularly? Will a lot of the initial work fall on the consumer, or will the financial advisor take care of it? Is this purely an advising relationship, or will the financial advisor also personally handle transactions?)

After pinning down the logistics of the relationship, you'll want to understand the financial advisor's fee structure. Do they charge a flat hourly rate? A fee based on assets under management? Are there any transaction costs? Hidden costs? If you ask about hidden costs and the advisor starts to squirm, you probably want to look elsewhere! (Turn to chapter 35 for more information about paying financial advisors.)

When you receive an advisor's legal disclosures, read them carefully. Wendy Cook says that these disclosures may be difficult to decipher, but "it's worth becoming familiar enough with the lingo to spot red flags when you see them, such as above-average fees, service offerings that don't match up with your needs, and/or disclosures about past complaints. If you read enough of them, patterns and trouble spots start to emerge."*

When in doubt, consult a lawyer who specializes in the financial industry.

6. Do an integrity check.

Before entering an interview, it's wise to conduct a background check on the financial advisor/advisory firm. Have they been sued for anything? Do they have any public complaints or bad reviews? Any other black marks on their record?

Once you're interviewing them, make sure they are consistent with their statements and not contradicting themselves. Trust your gut when it comes to integrity. Your subconscious brain is great at picking up on expressions and mannerisms that indicate untrustworthiness.

As a final integrity check, I suggest asking for a signed fiduciary oath (assuming the person you're interviewing claims to be a fiduciary). Most true fiduciaries will not hesitate to put their fiduciary obligations in writing. If the financial advisor hesitates or resists, do some digging to find out why.

It doesn't pay to haphazardly interview a potential financial advisor. Hiring an advisor is a major decision that could have an enormous impact (either positive or negative) on your life. Take time to thoroughly prepare, be attentive during the interview, and trust your instincts. And if you need the advisor to clarify anything, do not hesitate to ask. Any good financial advisor will do their best to be aboveboard and clear about their services.

---

* Cook, interview by author, November 14, 2022.

Chapter 32
Interview Questions to Select the Right Financial Advisory Firm

Let's say you're an individual investor who is searching for a financial advisory firm. You've identified a few that seem trustworthy and are also aligned with your needs and several of your wants. After talking with a representative of one of the firms, you show up for a scheduled interview and are led into a conference room with a few financial advisors. Then . . . your brain freezes, and you can't figure out what to say.

You *know* you have questions, but you're not sure which ones to ask or *how* to ask them. You're also worried you won't use the proper terminology or convey exactly what you mean to say. So, you fumble around and, ultimately, let the financial advisors take the lead. You cover a lot of ground during the meeting and learn a lot about the company, but you're not certain if all the critical questions have been answered. And you also don't know if the firm is simply telling you what they think you want to hear, given they took charge of the meeting.

How can you avoid this situation and become better prepared for interviewing potential financial advisory firms?

Let's talk about crucial question categories to address when you're on the hunt for a financial advisory firm (*and* some specific questions that fall into each category). Keep in mind, these questions are focused on **financial advisory firms** and are not questions you would necessarily ask when selecting an **individual financial advisor** (that's a topic for the next chapter!). As I pointed out in chapter 29, there is wisdom in hunting for the *firm* before the *advisor*. When a firm ticks all the boxes, it will inevitably employ financial advisors who reflect its investment philosophy, ethics, and standards.

So, what do you ask when attempting to find a financial advisory firm that's right for you? Start with these nine question categories. It may make sense to ask some of these questions during your initial phone conversation(s) with the firm (e.g., basic questions about the firm's setup), while other questions can be asked during the interviewing process.

The following is a sample of some basic questions that fall into nine categories (for a more comprehensive list of questions, go to the AdvisorSmart® educational resources website page at www.AdvisorSmart.com/Resources to download a free copy of the "AdvisorSmart Questions for an Individual Investor to Ask about a Financial Advisory Firm."

The Firm's Setup

It's a good idea to start with questions that capture the overarching picture of the financial advisory firm. With that in mind, you could choose to start the interview by asking about the overall nature of the firm or how it's set up. The goal is to understand the firm's big-picture—how it operates, who owns it, and whether (or not) they consider themselves fee-only fiduciaries (more on those two specific aspects in the Compensation and Fiduciary question categories).

Specific questions relating to a firm's overall setup include:

- Who owns your firm? (Is your firm privately held? Publicly held? Is your firm owned by a parent company? Employee owned?)
- Is your firm registered to provide financial advice in the state where I reside?
- Is your firm affiliated with an investment securities brokerage firm or broker dealer?
- Is your firm a member of the National Association of Personal Financial Advisors (NAPFA)?

- Are your financial advisors fee-only financial advisors?
- Do you have a minimum portfolio account size? What is your average (median) portfolio account size?
- How many client relationships does your firm have? What is your firm's ideal client-to-advisor ratio? What is its current client-to-advisor ratio?
- Will you work with professionals outside of your firm? If yes, can you provide me with a list of their names, roles, and qualifications?
- Does your firm have any arrangements with brokerage firms under which your firm (or a related company) will benefit if investment managers place trades for their clients with such brokerage firms?

Services

It is imperative to understand what services a financial advisory firm provides and if these services meet your needs and wants. Ideally, the company's website will describe its services, but it may not go into the level of detail you require. To learn more about a company's services, first ask a few basic questions:

- What services do you offer?
- Are you wealth managers? Financial planners? Financial advisors? Investment managers?
- What services do you specialize in?
- What types of financial advisory services do you NOT offer?
- What financial planning services does your firm provide?
- What investment services does your firm provide?

Then, ask some specific questions related to services. Examples include:

- What exactly is the job you will be doing for me?
- What is the scope of the services you will be providing to me?
- What types of decisions can you help me make?
- Can you provide me with a financial plan? How does your firm develop a financial plan for a client?
- Will you provide advice in areas other than investing?

Legal

Questions of a legal nature can clarify certain aspects of the firm right away. They can help you determine how a firm is legally registered, whether any legal problems have arisen, or what a firm's legal obligations are to you, the client.

This is a broad category, and some sample questions include:

- Is your firm a Registered Investment Adviser (RIA)?
- Is your firm registered with the Securities and Exchange Commission (SEC)? (If yes, can you provide me with the disclosures required under the law, such as a copy of your SEC Form ADV Part 1 and Part 2, Form CRS, and code of ethics?)
- Is your firm registered with the Financial Industry Regulatory Authority (FINRA)?
- Is your firm a dually registered "hybrid" firm with both the Financial Industry Regulatory Authority (FINRA) and the Securities and Exchange Commission (SEC)?
- Does your firm have a legal or disciplinary history? (If so, for what type of conduct?)
- Do any of your financial advisors have a legal or disciplinary history? (If so, for what type of conduct?)

- Can you share with me a copy of your firm's standard client agreement?
- What are the potential conflicts of interest that you will have with me?

Fiduciary Obligations

As I have noted in past chapters, it is immensely beneficial to the investor if their financial advisor is a fiduciary who upholds a fiduciary standard of care. The same is true of financial advisory firms. If a firm is committed to fiduciary standards, it should take pride in that commitment and either post a fiduciary oath on its website or be willing to sign a fiduciary oath presented by a client.

Questions to ask about a firm's fiduciary obligations include:

- Is your firm a fiduciary? What is your firm's definition of a fiduciary?
- Is your firm obligated to always act as a fiduciary to your clients?
- Do you have a fiduciary duty to your clients, including myself?
- Does your firm offer a fiduciary standard of care to all your clients? All the time?
- Will you commit to me, in writing, that you will have a fiduciary duty to me?

Qualifications

Just because a firm dispenses financial advice doesn't mean it is necessarily qualified to do so. Keep in mind, anyone can call themselves a financial advisor, wealth manager, or investment manager—there is no law preventing them from doing so. Your neighbor who prepares his mother's taxes every year, or your daughter's hockey coach who likes to short sell stocks, could fancy themselves financial advisors, and no one can prevent them from making this claim (the legal trouble begins once they start playing with other people's money). Even though many financial advisors in many firms *are* qualified to provide financial advice, it's a good idea to ask a few pointed questions to make sure your prospective firm has the proper training and knowledge to provide the guidance you need.

Questions about qualifications include:

- Are all of your financial advisors Certified Financial Planner® (CFP®) professionals?
- What are your firm's qualifications?
- What experience does your team have? How deep is their financial planning experience?
- What are your team members' credentials?
- What professional certifications do your team members have?
- Does your firm have special expertise serving any specific type of investor?

Advice

Anyone can dole out advice, but is it *good* advice? This may be difficult to determine, but you can ask a few specific questions to see just how independent, comprehensive, and objective a company's advice is. Trust your gut on this one; if the person across the table hesitates a bit too long or waffles when you ask one of these questions, that could be a sign they are not being completely forthright about the quality of their advice.

Questions about advice include:

- Is your firm an independent firm? Do you offer independent advice (at all times)?
- Is your financial advice comprehensive? (And how do you define comprehensive financial advice?)

- Is your advice objective? (And how do you define objective financial advice?)

Compensation

How is the financial advisory firm compensated? Even if you *think* you understand a firm's compensation model, it's a good idea to dig deeper. You never know what hidden or undisclosed fees you might uncover once you start asking the right questions. And keep in mind: a fee-based firm is much different than a fee-only firm (see chapter 14 on the topic to understand the difference).

Compensation-centered questions could include:

- The National Association of Personal Financial Advisors (NAPFA) defines a fee-only financial advisor as one who is compensated solely by the client with neither the advisor nor any related party receiving compensation that is contingent on the purchase or sale of a financial product. Is your firm a fee-only financial advisory firm?
- Does your firm receive commissions on the sale of investment products?
- Is any part of the compensation of your financial advisor contingent on the purchase or sale of a financial product?
- How does your firm compensate your financial advisors? (Hourly wage, salary, commission, salary and commission, awards, bonuses, prizes? All the above? A combination of two or more of the above?)
- What is your fee structure?
- What is your fee schedule?
- Fee-based: Is your firm a fee-based financial advisory firm?
- Commission-based: Is your firm a commission-based financial advisory firm?

- Does your firm receive any third-party compensation for recommending a particular investment or group of investments?
- Help me understand how these fees and costs might affect my investments. If I give you $10,000 to invest, how much will go to fees and costs, and how much will be invested for me? What are my all-in costs?

Logistics

Logistics have to do with the firm's general operations or the way they relate to their clients. You might wonder, for instance, how a firm will implement your financial plan, how often you'll meet with your financial advisor, how the firm prefers to communicate, or any number of logistical concerns. Hopefully, the financial advisory firm will provide much of this information up front, but it doesn't hurt to ask about anything you're wondering about.

A few questions about logistics include:

- Who is responsible for investment decisions at your firm? Does your firm have an investment research department?
- Which independent custodians do you use? (And who is your primary custodian relationship?)
- Where will my cash and funds be held?
- Where will my investment portfolio assets be held?
- Who will be sending me my monthly brokerage statements?
- How does your firm monitor investments?
- How will we communicate (in-person meetings, telephone, email)? How often?
- How often do you meet with your clients to review their situation?

- How can I track my financial accounts? Can I access my financial account information online?
- How does your firm safeguard my information?
- What is the process for me to come on board as a new client of your firm?

Investment Philosophy

Last, but certainly not least, it is crucial to ask about a financial advisory firm's investment philosophy. It's important to know if the firm's general philosophy is sound, puts the client first, *and* meets your personal requirements and expectations. If a firm claims it can "beat the market" or offers a "guaranteed return," run the other way!

Questions about a firm's investment philosophy include:

- What can you tell me about your investment philosophy?
- Who are some of the firm's investment role models? Investment heroes?
- What is your investment approach?
- How are your personal assets managed?
- What information do you use to make investment decisions?
- Do you think that you can
  - beat the market?
  - consistently beat the market?
  - pick winning stocks?
  - forecast interest rates?
  - forecast stock market fluctuations?
  - time the market?
- Is your investment approach evidence-based? Which evidence?
- Who is your ideal client?

- What is your firm's corporate culture?
  - What is your vision?
  - What is your mission?
  - What are your core values?

Before choosing a financial advisory firm, it's important to ask key questions during the interview process related to its qualifications, fiduciary obligations, compensation, investment philosophy, and other areas. These questions will help you determine if the firm is trustworthy and if its approach aligns with your financial goals and values. Preparation is key! Use this list as a springboard to come up with relevant questions to help clarify how a firm operates and serves its clients. Doing so can help you determine which firm aligns with your financial goals and values.

You want to select the financial advisory firm that meets your needs.

Chapter 33
Key Questions to Find the Right Financial Advisor

In prior chapters, I have emphasized the importance of aligning with a financial advisory firm. It's critical to be on the same page as the firm you hire since this is a relationship that could potentially endure for decades. Not only that, if you agree with a firm's values, practices, and investment philosophy, it should be relatively easy to switch over to a new financial advisor if the need arises (if someone retires, falls ill, moves, etc.).

While it's imperative to work with a financial advisory firm that can meet your goals, needs, and vision, it's equally important to like, feel comfortable with, and ultimately trust your financial advisor. It's also imperative that the financial advisor meets a basic set of criteria.

How can you determine if you and a financial advisor are well aligned? I suggest exploring basic criteria first and then digging deeper.

Basic Criteria

You might hit it off with a financial advisor and like him or her as a person, but that connection and camaraderie doesn't do much good if they are unqualified for the job, or if their investment strategies or philosophies do not serve you adequately. Therefore, it's essential to learn a few basic facts about a financial advisor to determine if that person has the proper qualifications, is compensated fairly, is a fiduciary, and offers the appropriate services to fit your needs. You'll also want to make sure the financial advisor's investment approach aligns with your expectations. Hopefully, most of these criteria were covered when researching the firm that employs the financial advisor, but it's a good idea to investigate individual financial advisors as well.

To determine if a financial advisor meets these basic criteria, it's useful to ask the critical questions outlined by the CFP Board. Some of these questions could be answered by reviewing the biographies of the individual financial advisors on a company's website; others will have to be asked during the interview process. The CFP Board of Standards' website outlines ten useful questions to ask:

1. What are your qualifications and credentials?
2. What services do you offer?
3. Will you have a fiduciary duty to me?
4. What is your approach to financial planning?
5. What types of clients do you typically work with?
6. Will you be the only advisor working with me?

7. How will I pay for your services?
8. How much do you typically charge?
9. Do others stand to gain from the financial advice you give me?
10. Have you ever been publicly disciplined for any unlawful or unethical actions in your career?

For a more detailed explanation of each question, visit the website for CFP Board of Standards.*

These questions are a great starting point, but you may want to ask about the financial advisor's qualifications in more detail. I suggest asking the following questions about an individual's professional training:

- Do you have any professional training?
- Do you have any professional designations?
- Do you have any professional certifications?
- Do you have any professional credentials?

You may also want to ask additional questions about client relationship management logistics, such as:

- How will we work together?
- How do you typically communicate with clients? How often?
- How accessible are you (typical working hours, typical time to answer an email, etc.)?
- How do you usually send documents to clients?
- Do you work in a team when making certain decisions for your clients?

Beyond the Basics

While it's important for a financial advisor to meet your basic criteria, it's equally important to like and trust the person. This can be a

* CFP Board, "10 Questions to Ask Your Financial Advisor."

highly personal and vulnerable relationship in which you may need to entrust your financial advisor with sensitive information, private life details, or personal plans/goals/dreams.

How likely are you to divulge sensitive financial information to an advisor you don't trust? How likely are you to call your advisor with a question if you don't particularly enjoy talking with them?

In my experience, good financial advisors share many of the same traits. They are personable and easy to talk to, they are good teachers (willing and eager to educate their clients on any financial topic the client doesn't fully understand), and they are transparent (talking in plain English, when possible, avoiding industry jargon, and being forthright with any relevant information).

It is vital to establish an amicable relationship with your financial advisor that is built on mutual trust and respect. And here's the thing: authentic financial advisors want the same thing! They want to work with clients who are friendly, trustworthy, and with whom they share some kind of common ground.

Discovering Commonalities

Do not underestimate the importance of finding commonalities between you and a financial advisor. These common traits or backgrounds can help build trust and create a positive overall experience. If your high school football team was a rival of my high school's team, that's common ground that we can talk and maybe joke about. I suggest reviewing individual financial advisor biographies on the firm's website to look for potential commonalities. When an individual investor looks at our website and requests to work with a specific financial advisor, we almost always will grant the investor's request.

I also recommend asking questions to try to find areas of similarity or commonality which will naturally develop a sense of trust with an individual financial advisor. You likely won't have to ask more than a few questions to find this common ground, and if you struggle to find it, that's a sign that it could be difficult to establish a trusting relationship with that financial advisor. Choose the advisor who you can trust.

Commonalities could be as simple as sharing the same alma mater or having children that are about the same age. Or, they may be more complex and personal, delving into areas of religion or politics. Here are some of my questions for an individual investor to ask a financial advisor about themselves to start building a trust relationship with that individual financial advisor. For a more detailed list (including questions you would ask about the financial advisory firm in general), go to the AdvisorSmart® educational resources website page at www.AdvisorSmart.com/Resources to download a free copy of the thirty-four-page AdvisorSmart Questions for an Individual Investor to Ask about a Financial Advisory Firm.

1. Education
   - Where did you go to college?
   - Any graduate studies?
   - Where did you go to high school?

2. Family
   - What is your hometown?
   - Where were you born?
   - Where do your parents live?
   - Do you have any siblings?
   - Are you married? (What is your spouse's/partner's name? How long have you been married? When is your wedding anniversary?)
   - Do you have any children? (Where do your children go to school? What are your children's interests? Do your children play any sports?)

3. Shared Interests
   - What are your special interests?
   - What are your hobbies?
   - What is your favorite sport to play?
   - What is your favorite sport to watch?
   - What is your favorite sports team?
   - Are you a member of any golf clubs?
   - Are you a member of any social clubs?

4. Previous Employers
    - How long have you worked at this firm?
    - What is your prior work history?
    - Why are you a financial advisor?
5. Sensitive Questions
    - What is your age?
    - What is your birth date?
    - What is your gender?
    - What is your nationality?
    - What are your favorite charities?
    - What is your political persuasion?
    - Are you politically active?
    - What is your religion?
    - What is your religious affiliation?
    - What is your place of worship?

Keep in mind, you likely won't need to ask more than a few questions from this list before figuring out if the person across the table is a good fit. Pick the easy-to-ask questions that resonate with you most and ask those first.

Finding the right financial advisor requires more than just basic qualifications and credentials. It's important to establish a personal bond and trust with your advisor. Common interests and backgrounds can help build this trust and make it easier to communicate effectively. To ask the right questions about a financial advisor's personal and professional background, select the ones from the above list (or others you think of) that are most meaningful to you. Remember, you're not *just* looking for someone to manage your money—you're also looking for someone with whom you can build a long-term, effective relationship.

Chapter 34
What to Look for During a Tour of a Financial Advisory Firm

Let's say you're interested in working with a financial advisory firm, and they have invited you to visit their offices. When you walk in, you notice the furniture is shabby and falling apart, and there are stains on the walls and scuffs on the floor. You're rushed into a dimly lit conference room with scarcely a greeting, and no one offers you water or any other refreshment. The advisor with whom you meet is a little standoffish, dressed in a Hawaiian shirt, and doesn't seem overly interested in you or your background. When you leave, you pay the $15 parking fee and go on your way.

Clearly, this firm wouldn't leave a positive impression on most people. The average investor would question their expertise and professionalism and would not feel appreciated as a potential client.

In this scenario, let's say you cross that firm off your list and move on to another firm.

The next firm on your list has offices in a swanky part of the city. A valet parks your car, and you walk into an entryway bedecked with gold-plated accents and a crystal chandelier. Off to one side, an LED ticker board scrolls through the day's stock numbers. A barista hands you a custom cappuccino, and you're escorted to a posh conference room. There, a financial advisor greets you with a big smile and begins asking questions. However, the advisor does not ask follow-up questions—or personalize the questions at all—and is constantly steering the conversation toward the company's products. It all feels very scripted and insincere.

The first place was a definite strike, but this place doesn't feel right either. The garish environment and the overly salesy/canned pitch simply do not feel right.

Both examples may be exaggerated extremes, but they illustrate a crucial point: the atmosphere of a financial advisory firm can speak volumes about the firm itself and can leave a definite impression.

In most cases, you'll encounter firms that land somewhere in the middle of these two examples. Because the impressions you gain are usually fairly subtle, let's talk about some of the factors to consider when walking into a financial advisory firm. Your experiences may point to certain characteristics or qualities of the company (good or bad), whether you realize it or not.

The Office Itself

The look and feel of an office can indicate the level of professionalism of the firm, how the financial advisors work as a team, and what the company values. How is the office laid out? Are there common rooms where financial advisors can gather for discussions? Do these rooms have whiteboards, notebooks, or other ways to communicate ideas? These are all indications of open communication and collaboration.

The state of the office—whether it is clean, well-organized, logical, and well-maintained—speaks to the level of professionalism of the financial team. Would you trust a financial organization that keeps a sloven, chaotic office? How might they handle your personal information and documents?

An office in disrepair may indicate underlying trouble in the organization. On the other hand, an office that is over-the-top with its décor and decorum may indicate that the financial advisory firm is into flashiness and showmanship—two traits that I would never associate with rational, evidence-based financial planning.

Another feature of a financial advisory firm's office is what it contains. What is hanging on the walls? What is displayed on the sideboards or conference tables? These choices are usually intentional and can tell a lot to a prospective client. Do you notice professional certifications or designations? Awards? Statements related to the company's investment philosophy? If you visit a financial advisor's office, do you see pictures of their family or financial heroes, images related to their faith or values, or professional achievements? Do you see any signs of philanthropy or community service? A financial advisory firm (and its advisors) should be proud of their accomplishments, values, and investment philosophy! What they choose to display (or not display) can tell that story.

The Office's Atmosphere

During a visit to a financial advisory firm, take note of the office's atmosphere. Does it seem calm and quiet (which could indicate that the team is planful)? Is it busy and active (which may show the team is transactional or productive)? Both atmospheres have merit, but what you *don't* want to see is sheer chaos, people running around, tension or brusqueness between colleagues, or carelessness.

If you meet with multiple financial advisors, notice how they interact with each other. Do they seem collaborative, polite, and helpful to one another? Or are they competitive, rude, or disinterested? These interactions can clearly show how well a team collaborates . . . or doesn't.

The Tour

Before you even set foot in a company's office, you can begin to develop impressions of the operation. A professional financial planning firm should send you clear driving directions to its office, parking directions, instructions on what to do when you arrive, guidance on what to bring, and a bit about what to expect during your meeting/tour.

When you arrive, a professional (and personable) firm will make sure you are greeted (genuinely and warmly), offered a bottle of water, coffee, or other refreshments, and guided to wherever you need to be. A firm that does not exhibit this level of professionalism may be brusque, insincere, or unclear about where to go or what to do.

During your meeting or tour, you should be given some time to talk a bit about yourself and ask any questions you might have. Be wary of financial advisory teams that talk over you too much, constantly steer the conversation toward sales of investment products, or avoid answering your questions altogether.

After the tour/meeting, you should leave with some relevant literature, a business card or two, and (if relevant) a validated parking slip. You should also leave with a good impression and a positive feeling about the firm—don't underestimate your gut feelings! Trust your intuition. If you are uneasy or put off by a financial advisory firm, there is likely a good reason for those feelings.

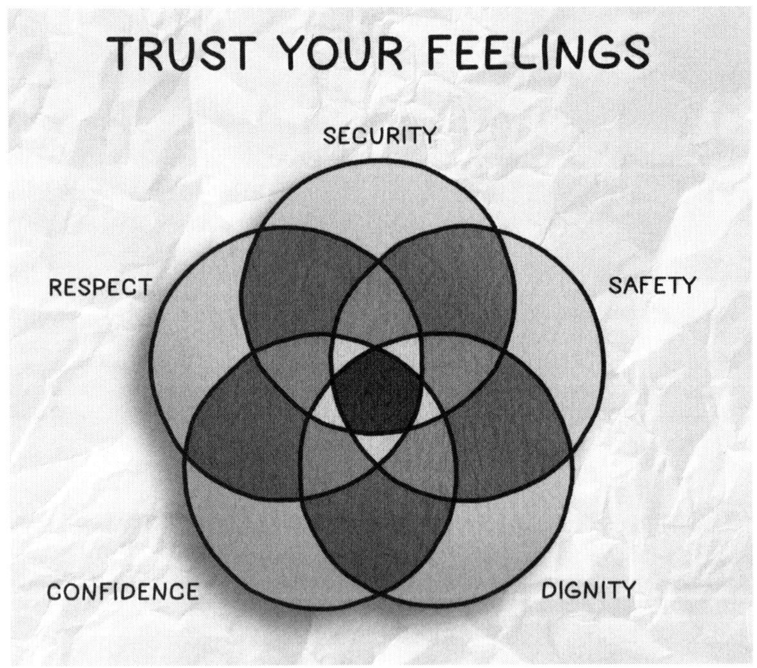

Impressions

Speaking of emotional reactions, while you're visiting a financial advisory firm's office, it's a good idea to pay attention to how you're feeling every step of the way. A professional, intentional, planful, and trustworthy firm should give you feelings of:

1. Security
2. Safety
3. Respect
4. Dignity
5. Confidence

If you do not get these impressions (or are feeling the opposite way), that's not a great sign. Every investor deserves to work with a firm that makes them feel safe and secure, respected, and confident in the firm's abilities and integrity.

In addition to these emotional reactions, it's also a good idea to note your impression of the office as a whole and its employees. Do your observations lead you to believe that this organization embodies or focuses on the following?

1. Integrity
2. Professionalism
3. Organization and order
4. Personal relationships
5. Service

An organization's impressions aren't *everything*, of course. Before setting foot in a financial advisory firm's office, it is important to do your due diligence and research the firm to the best of your ability. However, paying attention to these impressions can help you make better judgments and, ultimately, select a financial advisory firm that will be a good fit for your financial goals and values.

A visit to a financial advisory firm's office can provide valuable insights into the organization's professionalism, communication, collaboration, and atmosphere. Paying attention to details such as the level of organization, the interactions between colleagues, and the overall atmosphere can help investors determine if the firm aligns with their financial goals and values. Additionally, your emotional reactions such as feelings of security, respect, and confidence can also provide valuable guidance. While a visit to the office is just one aspect of an investor's search for the "perfect" financial advisory firm, it is an important one that should not be overlooked.

Chapter 35
Decoding Financial Advisor Compensation Models

Fee-only versus fee-based. Project fees, asset-based fees, and hourly fees. For the average consumer, the compensation models of financial advisors can feel opaque or downright confusing. Few other industries have so much variation when it comes to paying a professional. When you hire an auto mechanic, you pay for parts and hours of labor. When you hire a piano teacher, you pay per lesson or for a set period. For a lawyer, you might put money into a retainer.

All these methods are straightforward and easy to understand. Unfortunately, the financial advisory world is a different ball game. Payment models vary from firm to firm and sometimes from client to client (depending on client needs, services rendered, net worth, etc.).

Since payment models for financial advisors are not always straightforward, misinformation abounds. Consumers might be taken in by "special offers" or "guaranteed returns." Or they might believe they are entitled to free financial planning because large brokerage terms do this for "free." This way of thinking is problematic because a) there's no such thing as a free lunch—those big firms are making their dollars *somehow* and b) answering ten to twenty questions that will be analyzed by a robo-advisor is NOT financial planning. True financial planning is comprehensive, multilayered, and involved. For most people, quality financial planning is worth the price tag.

But how can clients determine if a pricing model is fair? And how will they know if a certain pricing model is right for them?

To clarify the confusion, let's talk about different ways a financial advisor could be compensated AND which methods make sense for certain types of consumers.

Two Compensation Models to Avoid

There are several legitimate, ethical compensation models for financial advisors. However, before we talk about those, I want to briefly recap two models to avoid: **commission-based** and **fee-based**.

When a financial advisor is paid a commission or is incentivized by bonuses or prizes, that will inevitably shape their financial advice. Commission-based advisors are pressured to recommend products or services that make them the most money, instead of making

COMPENSATION MODELS

COMMISSION-BASED	PRODUCT SALES COMMISSIONS
FEE-BASED	PRODUCT SALES COMMISSIONS + FEES
FEE-ONLY	HOURLY PLANNING FEES FLAT "PROJECT" FEE (FOR A PLAN) RETAINER FEE FOR AN ONGOING PLANNING RELATIONSHIP PERCENTAGE OF ASSETS MANAGED

recommendations that wholly benefit the consumer. We discussed this model in more depth in chapter 10 on why to avoid brokers.

Similarly, some financial advisors may be compensated by both fees *and* commissions. Fee-based advisors may charge a flat fee—perhaps an hourly rate or a percentage of assets under management—but they can also charge commissions on top of that. Some of these commissions are fairly well hidden, so consumers may not always realize a commission is being earned. In short, if a financial advisor claims to be fee-based, know that sales will likely make up part of their compensation. To learn more about the difference between fee-only and fee-based advisors, turn to chapter 14.

It's best to avoid commission-based and fee-based models and opt for one of the following **fee-only models**, which I discuss in the chart on the previous page.

Hourly Rate for Financial Planning Advice

Perhaps the most straightforward and easy-to-understand compensation model is the pay-by-the-hour model. In this case, a financial advisor charges for time spent on client services. The hourly rate will vary depending upon the advisor's experience, geographic region, and expertise. You can expect to pay anywhere from $150 to $300 per hour for the services of a qualified financial planner, and sometimes much higher.

For some people, an hourly rate makes sense. Consumers with straightforward financial planning needs, or those who have a one-off financial query, would likely benefit from an hourly compensation model. In these cases, the consumer may briefly meet with a financial advisor, gain some insights, and then part ways.

However, most consumers' circumstances are too involved and intricate to be thoroughly addressed during one or two meetings. And those hours can add up quickly! For many consumers, it makes sense to opt for a different pay model—one that is more comprehensive and all-encompassing.

Project Fee for a Formal Financial Plan

Not long ago, a young investor approached me after she'd had a bad experience working with a commission-based financial advisor. While working with this advisor, it soon became clear they were trying to sell her products rather than provide bias-free advice. She decided to part ways with this financial advisor and seek fee-only guidance through my financial advisory firm instead.

After I learned about the investor's situation, I proposed that we put together a comprehensive, evidence-based plan for her.

But when she heard my proposal, she hesitated. "I already have a financial plan," she said. "My prior financial advisor put it together for me."

"That may be," I countered, "but do you think that plan was truly unbiased and comprehensive?"

The simple truth is that when commission-based financial advisors are incentivized to push or promote certain products, they'll probably do it. Because of that, it's difficult to fully trust any financial guidance they deliver, including "customized" financial plans that are prepared for the sole purpose of selling financial products.

In this scenario, it made sense for the young client to pay a project fee for a personalized financial plan. She didn't have a large enough portfolio to justify money management, but she would certainly benefit from holistic, comprehensive financial guidance.

For comprehensive financial planning firms, that involves a diagnostic meeting (which can be upwards of two hours) in which a team of financial planners interview the investor. Then, using the information gathered, a personalized plan is created, which often involves multiple financial advisors with various backgrounds and specialties working together. After that, the plan (or multiple plans) is presented to the investor, and the financial advisor addresses any follow-up questions or concerns. For such in-depth and involved work, it absolutely makes sense for the client to pay a project fee rather than an hourly fee.

This is just one example of how project-based compensation might work, but it is certainly one of the most common examples. Other project examples might include a focus on estate planning, tax advice, financial coaching, and more.

Asset-Based Fee for Investment Management

A third common compensation model involves a financial advisor charging a percentage of assets under management (AUM). With this method, the investor pays a certain percentage of the value of their investment portfolio each year. The rate, or percentage, may vary depending upon the type of asset (stocks, bonds, real estate, etc.), the complexity of the portfolio, and the total AUM.

In my experience, an asset-based fee makes sense for those with a high net worth who are seeking ongoing money management services (hopefully in tandem with comprehensive financial planning guidance). It can be difficult to track, manage, and rebalance one's assets if they are wide-ranging and diverse. That's where an investment manager comes in (sometimes called a money manager or wealth manager).

For ongoing investment management, it has become industry standard to charge an asset-based fee. This model was introduced when mutual funds were first introduced in the early twentieth century, and it hasn't changed much since then. Because, frankly, it works. When the market is doing well and a client's wealth increases, the fee will increase accordingly. If the market is in a prolonged slump, the client's fee will also go down.

Retainer Fee for Ongoing Financial Planning Relationships

A less-common advisory fee model is the retainer. If the client wants to pay a flat fee that isn't tied to market performance, they may have the option to do so. A retainer-based structure usually involves ongoing fixed fees that may be charged monthly, quarterly, or annually.

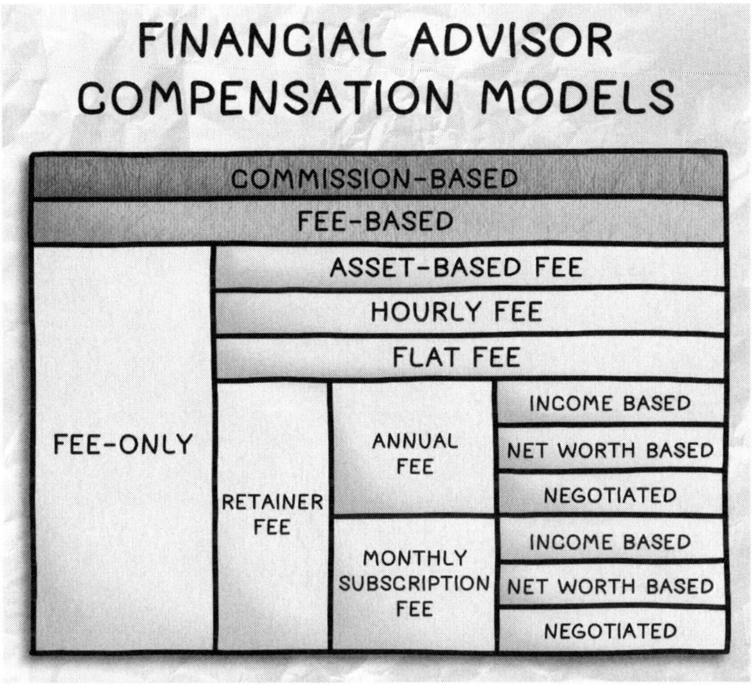

FINANCIAL ADVISOR COMPENSATION MODELS

COMMISSION-BASED
FEE-BASED
FEE-ONLY
ASSET-BASED FEE
HOURLY FEE
FLAT FEE
RETAINER FEE
ANNUAL FEE
INCOME BASED
NET WORTH BASED
NEGOTIATED
MONTHLY SUBSCRIPTION FEE
INCOME BASED
NET WORTH BASED
NEGOTIATED

The fee is often based on the complexity of the client's portfolio and/or complexity of the required services.

In my experience, this option could make sense for high-net-worth individuals who do not want their fees tied to market performance. Not every financial advisory firm offers this option, but many will consider it for individuals whose assets meet a certain minimum threshold.

Today, many financial advisors are beginning to offer some degree of flexibility in their fee structures. They might offer a couple of different approaches or models for their client to choose from, based on the client's circumstances. As an individual investor, I encourage you to ask financial advisors about fee diversity or fee flexibility. You might frame your questions as follows:

"Is there any flexibility in your fee model? Or do you only charge based on ____________?" (The blank in the second question might be AUM, an hourly rate, a flat fee, a retainer fee, or whatever model the financial advisor has presented.)

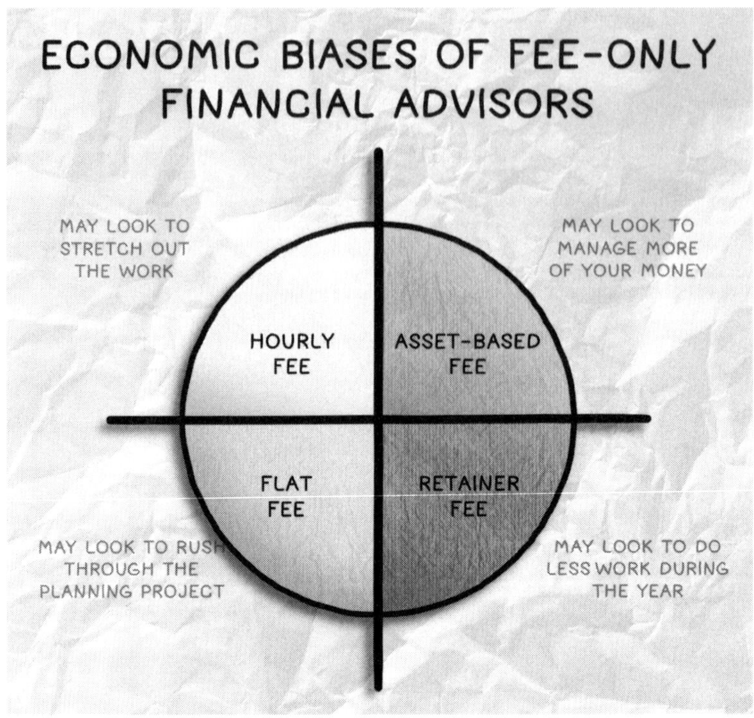

It is important for clients to think about which compensation model best suits their personal needs and circumstances and will be most cost-effective. In the end, the best fee model for a client will depend on the complexity of their individual situation and the services they require. In some cases, a combination of different fee structures may be most appropriate. With the help of a qualified financial advisor, a consumer can evaluate the various fee models and come to the best decision for their individual circumstances.

Chapter 36

Why to Combine Finances and Collaborate on Financial Decisions

Talking about debt, budgeting, or investment strategies typically isn't great first-date material. It isn't romantic to ask a potential partner about their 401(k) contributions or to grill them about their debt tolerance. These are conversations for a later date when the relationship is well established and you're becoming more and more enmeshed in each other's lives.

But what if those conversations never happen?

What if you end up marrying this person, sharing a household together, having children, and filing jointly on tax returns every year . . . but you've never taken the time to sit down and discuss your finances in any depth?

Believe me, this happens far more frequently than you might realize. People can live together for thirty or forty years without ever discussing their investment philosophies or their debt tolerance. They can live alongside a person for decades and never truly know their thoughts on money management or their financial goals.

This is why having honest, open conversations about finances and then collaborating on financial decisions is so critical. Even if you're not married, or you haven't yet tied the knot, it's important to start talking about money. This is vital for building trust and understanding between two people and paving the way for a strong and healthy relationship. Money is the backbone of many major decisions you'll make together (sending your kids to college, buying that lake house, planning vacations, strategizing for retirement), so having a shared understanding will help you plan for those eventualities and make decisions that best suit you both.

Let's talk about *why* and *how* to share financial information, make unified financial decisions, and combine finances with your significant other. Failing to do so could be incredibly costly.

Starting Small

It's a good idea to start discussing money and financial considerations early in a relationship. If you'll be sharing a living space, it's essential to discuss items such as the electric bill, paying for groceries, or how often it makes sense to splurge on food delivery services or nice restaurants. Who will pay the rent each month? Who will manage the bills? Does it make sense to split things fifty-fifty, or is someone making significantly more money and is, therefore, willing to contribute a bit more each month?

Though it may be uncomfortable at first, at some point you will also want to begin talking about your financial goals. Are you both saving for retirement? When it comes to investing, who owns what stocks and mutual funds? What is each person's retirement plan?

It's very possible that one or both of you do not have a plan at all. This is certainly not out of the ordinary, and it's nothing to be ashamed of. What it does mean, however, is that it's imperative for one or both of you to build your financial literacy (there are plenty of books and websites that can help with this) and, potentially, seek guidance from a trustworthy financial advisor sooner rather than later (more on this below).

Keep in mind, these conversations about finances don't have to be adversarial or contentious. In fact, it's best to treat these conversations as opportunities to learn more about each other and to understand each other's perspectives. Your joint financial journey will be much smoother if both of you are on the same page.

Sharing Financial Information

When you reach the point of creating a shared financial plan, it's important to ensure both of you have the same access to financial information. This means sharing bank account particulars, credit card balances, retirement account data, and other financial information that is relevant to your shared life.

Sharing these sensitive details involves a good deal of trust and can be a true relationship test. What if you discover your significant other is deeply in debt? Or that their spending habits or retirement goals do not align with your own?

I say, it's important to take a leap of faith. You're going to discover these details one way or another, so why not discuss them early on?

For example, I once worked with a husband and wife who had very different ideas about spending. The wife was relatively frugal and put a lot of thought into her financial decisions. The husband, on the other hand, was more of a spendthrift. He enjoyed nice clothing and thought nothing about dropping $1,000 on (another) new suit. His spending habits caused quite a bit of tension in the relationship, and it was apparent that this couple had never bothered to sit down and plan a monthly budget that worked for both of them.

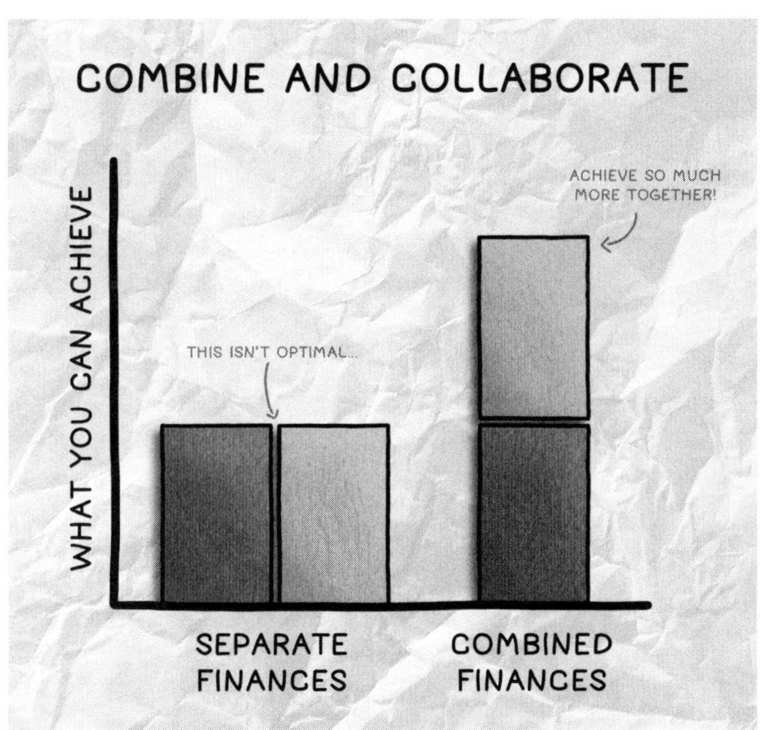

Another source of tension is debt. When you marry someone, you also take on their debt, whether in the form of student loans, car payments, or credit card debt. When you share debt, you also need to share a plan to eventually pay off that debt. That's where open, candid conversations come into play. If you don't talk about these things with your significant other, they will inevitably become buried.

How Combining/Collaborating Saves Money

I've talked with many couples who have taken the "silo" approach to finances during their entire relationship. They have each tended to their own assets, conducted their own planning, and not bothered to check in to see what the other person was doing.

This kind of independent planning can be inefficient and costly. It's often less expensive and more productive to work together. For example, can you make strategic charitable contributions that will come with tax benefits? Can you engage in joint estate planning? Or make income tax-planning decisions that will benefit you both? (See appendix 1 for Allodium resources relating to charitable contributions, estate planning, and income tax planning.)

It can also make sense to combine assets—shared bank accounts, investment funds, or owning a home together—to save on taxes and other costs. For example, when both partners are saving for retirement, they can often benefit from so-called "economies of scale." A couple's assets can be combined, which often results in reduced fees. Furthermore, a financial advisor can often provide more comprehensive planning and advice when working with both of you.

Another reason to work together? Creating a *balanced* and strategic financial plan. If both people in a relationship have made high-risk investment choices, that doesn't create balance (and it certainly doesn't create much of a safety net). If both people had put the bulk of their assets in FTX, the cryptocurrency company that went belly-up in November 2022, they would be in a world of trouble right now. There's no guarantee that the folks who invested in FTX will be getting all or any of their money back.

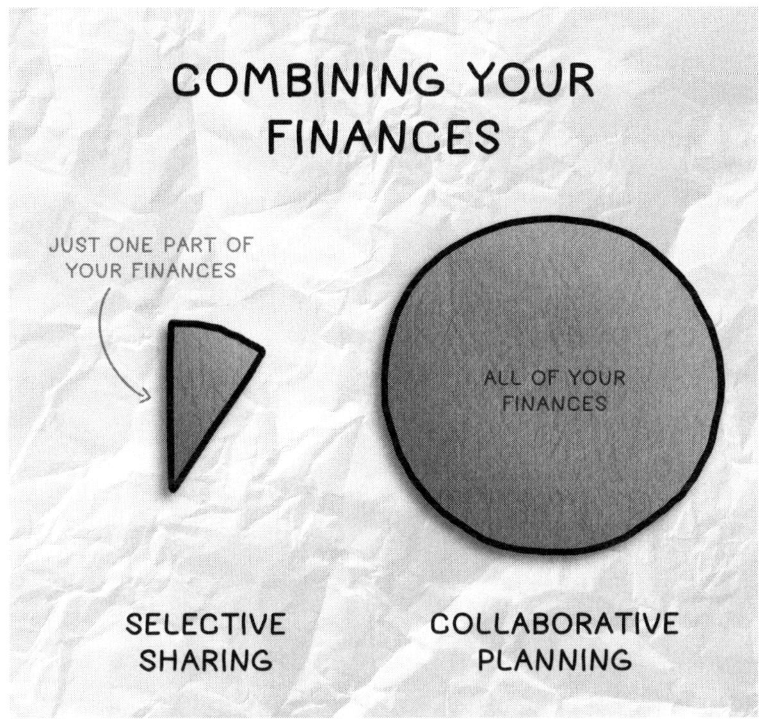

A Few Tips

The essence of my advice boils down to a few simple steps:

1. Be communicative about finances.

It's beneficial for couples to communicate openly and often about their financial situation and their goals. If either or both people do not have a clear idea of their financial picture or don't know how to define their financial future, it's a good idea to seek counsel from a trusted, fee-only financial advisor right away.

2. Combine planning and assets.

A silo approach to financial planning can be inefficient or even harmful. Whenever possible, engage in joint planning. In some cases, it also makes sense to combine assets (talk to a financial advisor to understand when combining finances makes sense).

3. Regularly check in.

Financial situations and goals can change over time, so it's wise to regularly check in with your loved one about these topics. Even though I work as a financial advisor, my wife and I schedule an annual meeting with *our* financial advisor to discuss financial circumstances, plans, and aspirations. When someone else is asking the questions, it's amazing what can bubble up to the surface. I might think we agreed to buy a retirement home in Florida, for example, when my wife has the impression that this is just a passing fancy. Sitting down with a financial advisor can help you and your partner to clarify your goals and dreams.

4. Work with a trusted financial advisor.

Finally, I can't emphasize enough how important it is to find a financial advisor whom you both trust. At its core, joint financial planning is a relationship. It should be a dialogue that helps each of you understand your partner's financial situation and needs, as well as your joint goals and dreams. A financial advisor can be an invaluable partner in this process, so make sure you choose someone who understands the importance of communication, trust, and collaboration.

Sharing financial information with your significant other can seem intimidating, but it doesn't have to be. Take a leap of faith and have open and honest conversations about finances, while also defining your goals. If you align your financial visions, you'll be more likely to achieve your dreams. Additionally, combining planning and assets can make sense and save you money in the long run. Work with a financial advisor to get the best advice and support, and make sure you regularly check in on each other's financial situation. Collaboration is the name of the game.

Chapter 37
Receiving Comprehensive Financial Advice from a Team

It may sound odd to admit, but I go out of my way to hire financial advisors who are smarter than me (or, at least, smarter than me in certain areas). If you run an investment management consulting firm, as I do, there's no place for hubris. You won't always be the smartest person in the room, and that's okay! In fact, it's *more* than okay; it's preferable.

When a financial advisory team consists of brilliant individuals with different backgrounds and areas of expertise, the client benefits. That's because no single financial advisor can be an expert in *everything.* For the client to truly receive comprehensive advice, it's best to tap into the knowledge of a team of financial advisors, all of whom specialize in different areas.

If you've read chapter 16, you already know comprehensive advice is important. Let's take that basic principle a step farther and discuss how to find comprehensive advice, how to ensure it *is* comprehensive, and how to avoid sources of advice that are likely NOT comprehensive.

CFP® Expectations

One common aspiration for financial advisors is becoming a Certified Financial Planner® (CFP®) professional. A CFP® is a credentialed expert in the field of financial planning. Keith Loveland,* a consultant

* Keith Loveland is an acclaimed and nationally recognized consultant, author, and attorney. From 1983 to 2001, Loveland served as a subject matter expert to the New York Stock Exchange Qualification Committee. He is the author of *The End of the Empire*.

and author says, "The CFP® designation is rightly regarded as the gold standard in the financial planning profession. Candidates must demonstrate competence of subject matter which is comprehensive, and which also requires expertise in the actions, communication skills, contexts, and practice of holistic personal financial planning."*

For a financial advisor to earn this credential, they must meet certain educational, experience, and examination requirements that demonstrate extensive knowledge in the field. As of last year, CFP® hopefuls were expected to be fluent in seventy principal knowledge topics that fall under the following eight principal knowledge domains:

1. Professional conduct and regulations
2. General financial planning principles
3. Risk management and insurance planning
4. Investment planning
5. Tax planning
6. Retirement savings and income planning
7. Estate planning
8. Psychology of financial planning†

With so much to learn in so many different areas, a CFP®'s knowledge might be classified as "a mile wide and an inch deep." Any given CFP® may know about each of the seventy principal knowledge topics, in theory, but their knowledge may be limited in many areas.

However, in my experience, people tend to take a "deep dive" into topics that interest them. Someone might be passionate about estate planning, for example, or have a deep interest in tax laws. Or maybe they have a background in law or were a former social worker—experiences that could inform or influence their areas of expertise.

Because of this tendency to specialize, CFPs® will inevitably be more knowledgeable about certain topics, despite having taken the same test (covering seventy topic areas) as their peers. That's why it's often beneficial for investors to work with a team of financial planners. When a team has members with different backgrounds, experiences, and interests, the resulting comprehensive advice can be exceptional.

---

* Loveland, interview by author, August 16, 2023.

† CFP Board, "CFP® Certification 2021 Principal Knowledge Topics."

Finding Comprehensive Advice

I recommend starting your search for comprehensive advice by looking into financial advisory teams. When you're vetting a potential team, look for indications that team members are specialized in different areas. Ask about their backgrounds and inquire about their strengths and the topics each member specializes in. A financial advisory team should be able to provide you with an overview of their team's collective skill set.

You can also sometimes discern a financial advisor's area of expertise by looking at their various designations and certifications. A Chartered Financial Analyst® (CFA®), for example, is someone with a deep knowledge of investments and portfolio management. CFAs® have a strong background in statistics, economics, and probability theory, and, in my experience, they tend to be very quantitative. Someone with this designation could help you solve complicated investment strategies or assist with risk management.

The most comprehensive teams will have members that specialize in a wide range of topics. Although you'll likely work with a primary financial advisor, the rest of the team should be available to offer specific advice and guidance. Maybe you're in a position where you need help with estate planning, or perhaps you're hoping to improve your tax planning before retirement. Whatever the case, one financial advisor might be more qualified to help you than another.

However, not all teams are created equal. Some teams fail to work well together, do not communicate effectively, or clash. I discuss how to avoid this type of team in chapter 26, which addresses the pros and cons of working with solo financial advisors and teams.

Signs You're Not Receiving Comprehensive Advice

I have worked with clients in the past who *think* they've received comprehensive advice from a financial advisor, but when we examine the advice together, we find that isn't the case. A large company might, in theory, have access to all types of financial advisors with various expertise and backgrounds . . . but they work in silos, independently from each other, or, worse, compete with one another (for bonuses or to win sales competitions). That means financial advisors generate financial plans on their own, and it's up to their discretion to determine what kind of "plan" the client actually receives.

This is problematic because it means the client might be receiving recommendations that directly benefit the individual financial advisor. If, for example, the advisor receives a large commission whenever they sell life insurance products, those products will likely feature heavily in the overall financial plan.

This is not some theoretical scenario. I've seen this play out again and again, with clients showing me financial plans that were put together by someone more incentivized to sell products than practice a fiduciary duty. We then have to start from scratch so I can gather the necessary facts and collaborate with my team of financial planners to create a strategy that is cohesive and holistic.

I recently met an individual investor who showed me his financial plan from a large name-brand financial institution. The "financial plan" was focused on investment planning and excluded many

of the other essential aspects of comprehensive financial planning. Curiously, this "financial plan" recommended that the investor implement the investment strategy using a list of the financial firm's proprietary mutual funds. This investor was pleasantly surprised when we took him through a thorough diagnostic meeting (with thoughtful planning questions) to help him to develop a comprehensive financial plan for his family.

Making Sure You Receive Comprehensive Advice

How do you make sure you're not receiving biased advice that skews heavily toward a certain product or service? Or advice that only considers certain aspects of your financial situation? How do you avoid financial advisors who fail to collaborate with others to ensure your financial planning needs are met?

Here are five signs you *will* be set up to receive comprehensive financial advice:

1. You're working with a cohesive team.

A successful financial advisory team communicates frequently and emphasizes collaboration. When interviewing potential financial advisors, ask about their team's collaborative practices. Do the advisors regularly request insights from each other? Does the advisory firm have committees that address different subjects? Do certain people specialize in specific areas? Are there any major differences of opinion within the team? Financial advisors who work cohesively with their team should be able to answer these questions easily.

2. You're working with a knowledgeable team.

To avoid receiving advice that is a mile wide and an inch deep, it's important to work with financial advisors with various backgrounds and areas of expertise.

3. A diagnostic meeting is conducted.

Before a financial advisor draws up a personalized financial plan, it is crucial for them to conduct a diagnostic meeting with the client. This entails sitting down (often for an hour or more), asking questions to understand the client's financial picture, and uncovering the areas where advice is most pertinent. This process of gathering (and then analyzing) data is imperative for creating a comprehensive financial plan.

4. You're not just getting a plan—you're getting a strategy.

Plans are important, and the planning document should lay out the steps an investor is taking to reach their financial goals. But a comprehensive financial strategy should include more than just a plan. The strategy should also consider cash flow, risk management, tax planning, estate planning, and more. Ask the financial advisors you interview what kind of strategies they implement and how these strategies are integrated. If a financial advisor is not taking these other financial planning topics into consideration on an ongoing basis, it's not comprehensive advice.

5. Your financial advisor is fee-only and committed to a fiduciary standard of care.

As we've established, fiduciary advisors that work on a fee-only basis are committed to the client above all else. They are less likely to be driven by the potential for sales commissions or other bonuses and, therefore, more likely to put their client's financial well-being first. Search reliable online directories and matching platforms (NAPFA's Find an Advisor tool, Wealthramp, FeeOnlyNetwork) to find fee-only financial advisors.

Making sure you receive comprehensive financial advice is essential to achieving your long-term goals. To ensure you receive the advice and support you need, it's important to work with a team of financial advisors who emphasize collaboration, possess a wide range of knowledge and expertise, conduct diagnostic meetings, provide strategies, and adhere to a fiduciary standard of care. Doing so will give you the best chance of success in your financial planning journey.

Chapter 38
Establishing a Trusted Relationship with Your Financial Advisor

It's difficult to go through life without trusting others. We extend trust to doctors and surgeons to tend to our health needs. We trust firefighters to show up and put out the blaze. We rely on tradespeople to rewire our houses, fix plumbing issues, and accurately install gas lines. It's impossible to become an expert in *everything*, and even if you have a working knowledge of, say, a car engine, would you really want to attempt a major repair when you can simply hand your vehicle over to an experienced mechanic?

Trust is also imperative in the financial arena. An investor must extend a certain amount of trust to their financial advisor to make the right decisions and act with integrity.

Unfortunately, trust is severely lacking in this area. Investors have long been wary of stockbrokers and money managers, and that trepidation has only increased since the spate of scandals that took place in the mid-2000s (from the Enron scandal to Bernie Madoff's notorious Ponzi scheme).

A recent survey by Morning Consult found that only 36 percent of respondents trust investment and wealth management firms and advisors (compared to 61 percent who trusted banks/bankers).* That's pitiful, but I understand why financial advisors rank so low. Too many advisors are consumed by "making their numbers" or earning commissions. When the focus is on factors other than the customer's best interests, that makes trust difficult to attain.

---

* Browning, "Advisors Have a Serious Trust Problem with Consumers, Research Shows. Here's Why and What to Do."

Despite widespread distrust, I believe financial advisors have the power to turn their negative image around. It starts with building trust.

Why Extend Trust to a Financial Advisor?

First, it's worth discussing why trust is an important pillar of the financial advisor/client relationship and why investors should bother extending trust to a financial advisor in the first place. Why not opt out entirely and manage your own finances?

Sure, that's a possibility for some—especially those who are just starting to build wealth—but most people do not understand the intricacies of asset management. Many people have made grave errors when they *thought* they could handle their own finances. In truth, many investors' financial situations are complex and multifaceted, and there's little chance an untrained individual can capture all the nuances of a well-crafted, comprehensive financial plan.

Hence, the need to extend trust. Most people wouldn't tinker with their car engine, and, similarly, most investors would be wise to trust the experts with financial planning (if those experts are deemed trustworthy—more on this later in the chapter).

Trust between clients and financial advisors is especially salient when the client is experiencing some kind of crisis and must make a quick finance-related decision (or several). Years ago, one of my clients was given a grim prognosis: she was terminally ill and had only a matter of months left to live—no more than six. Being the practical and caring person that she was, she immediately thought of her family and their future. She wanted to make sure to get her financial affairs in order so they would be sufficiently cared for and would not have to deal with any loose ends. When she approached me and informed me of her situation, I knew we had a lot of work to do.

We moved quickly and put together a plan that suited her situation. She had many considerations—from estate planning to tax planning—and worked hard to make sure all aspects were covered. When I presented her with the plan, she admitted that she did not understand everything (completely normal for an untrained investor), but she trusted me. She had faith in my integrity and judgement and knew I was acting in her best interest. She gave me the green light, and the plan moved ahead.

If our relationship had not been rooted in trust, my client would have been hesitant or nervous about moving forward so quickly. Fortunately, trust had already been established, and she was confident in the financial plan I had put together.

And here's the thing about trust: it does not exist unless some kind of risk is involved. The higher the risk, the greater the need for trust. Herman Brodie*—a specialist in behavioral economics, international speaker, and founder of the consultancy firm Prospecta—describes this phenomenon in his book, *The Trust Mandate,* saying that trust is "inseparable from risk or vulnerability. There is no need for trust in the absence of risk. The greater the vulnerability, the greater the potential for trust."†

Certainly, some risk is involved when you decide to hire a financial advisor, but that risk can be somewhat mitigated by educating yourself on your options.

Educated Trust

In past chapters, we have discussed ways to use the process-of-elimination method to find a financial advisor who will likely act in your best interest. This is a great starting point on the road to a trusting relationship. If the financial advisor is not motivated by commissions or other incentives, and if they are committed to upholding fiduciary duty and NAPFA's code of ethics, those are excellent indications that you can trust the financial advisor. I always recommend opting for a fee-only, NAPFA-Registered Financial Advisor to give you the best chance of receiving objective, comprehensive advice.

In addition to identifying fee-only, NAPFA-Registered Financial Advisors, it's a good idea to look at the advisor's other credentials and designations (as we discussed in chapter 19 on professionalism).

---

* Herman Brodie is a specialist in behavioral economics, author, educator, and founder of Prospecta, a United Kingdom–based consultancy firm that advises businesses on the use of behavioral sciences research. He is the coauthor of *The Trust Mandate*.

† Brodie and Harnack, *The Trust Mandate*.

This part of the search is relatively straightforward, but what about other considerations? It's a good idea to like your financial advisor and have some kind of rapport with them. It's difficult to trust someone who makes you uncomfortable or with whom you simply do not gel.

Herman Brodie calls these trust-building attributes "warmth" signals. When we detect "warmth" from another person, we believe that they have (in his words) "benevolent intentions toward us, our best interest at heart."

Oftentimes, we make snap judgments about others when we're seeking this "warmth." Brodie calls this a "product of our evolutionary history. We trust our families and are wary of non-family. So, anything that suggests a family resemblance will be a positive warmth signal. There is no right or wrong. These are just our perceptions."*

We tend to look for commonalities in others—similar backgrounds, physical features, values, social circles, and more. While I'm not suggesting you seek out a financial advisor who is exactly like you, I *do* think it's valuable to be aware of these unconscious biases. If you have a "good feeling" about someone, ask yourself why that might be. If you're aware of your biases, you might become more open and accepting of financial advisors who look different than you or hail from a different background.

And pay attention to the "warmth" signals you receive. You might develop warmth toward someone if they seem kind, are paying attention to what you say, or seem authentic and/or vulnerable—all valuable traits in a financial advisor.

A caring financial advisor *should* exhibit some warmth. If they truly want to put you and your best interests first, they will ask plenty of questions and practice active listening (asking clarifying questions, playing back what you've said, etc.). They will hopefully also care about you as a person (and will demonstrate that by asking about you, your family, or your well-being). Trust your instincts on this. You can usually tell when someone is truly listening and sincerely wants to provide the best care possible.

---

* Ibid.

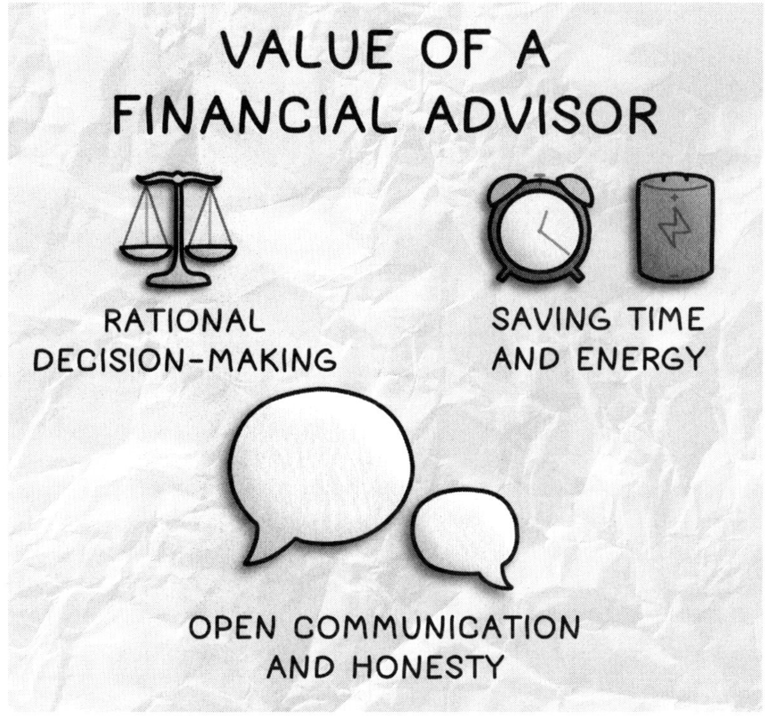

When Trust Is Established

Trusting your financial advisor leads to a whole host of benefits, including:

1. Rational decision-making

When clients do not trust their financial advisor or the plan that advisor has created, they can end up making bad decisions. I had one client lose trust in the financial plan I built for him because he was inundated with doom-and-gloom news at the start of the COVID-19 pandemic. His fear outweighed his trust, and he ended up pulling all his money from the stock market . . . right before it changed direction, and we experienced one of the most robust bull markets of all time.

When clients trust, they have faith in their financial advisor to lead them down the right path, even when they are feeling nervous. Trust overrules trepidation. As Brodie said in my interview with him, "If we trust our financial advisor, we can accept higher levels of risk in the portfolio without anxiety."*

2. Open communication and honesty

When you trust your financial advisor, you're unafraid to come to them with questions, concerns, or ideas. A trusted advisor will listen, ask questions, and provide professional counsel. They will take you seriously.

On the other hand, if you do not trust your financial advisor, you may withhold information, refrain from asking questions, or keep ideas to yourself (out of fear of looking foolish or being reprimanded). A trusted advisor will always act with professionalism and encourage open communication.

3. Saving time and energy

If you trust your financial advisor to always act in your best interest, that saves a tremendous amount of time and energy. You won't have to conduct independent research to see if the advisor's guidance is *actually* right. You won't have to waste time worrying, or second-guessing, or calling up your brother-in-law for a second opinion. Most importantly, if you have faith in your financial advisor, you won't have to spend precious hours searching for a new one.

Trust is a core component of the professional relationship between a financial advisor and their client. Without trust, this relationship can deteriorate quickly, and the client will inevitably start turning to other sources of advice or looking for another advisor. When seeking a financial advisor, make sure they are qualified and provide a fiduciary standard of care, but also pay attention to "warmth signals," such as attentive listening, good communication, and a genuine desire to attend to your best interests.

---

* Brodie, interview by author, August 7, 2022.

Afterword by Dan Allison:

You've Read the Book. Now What?

When I was asked to write the afterword of this book, I thought about closing chapters and new beginnings. Though you've reached the end of the text, your real-life financial story is still unfolding. You likely have many days, and many decisions, ahead of you, and after reading this book you should be better equipped to find a trustworthy financial advisor to guide you through those days and decisions. Or, perhaps, you've reached the end of this book and realized, "You know what, I already have a great financial advisor. This person ticks all the boxes."

In either case, you may be wondering where to go from here. How can you *live* the lessons you've learned from this book, rather than letting them wither in some dusty corner of your mind?

If you haven't yet landed your dream advisor, your next steps could include reviewing what you've learned from these pages, highlighting the areas that are relevant to you, and initiating your search for a financial advisor based on the information and approaches discussed in this book.

But what happens once you *do* find and hire a superb financial advisor? What then? Alternatively, what happens if you realize you're already working with an exceptional financial advisor? You could pat yourself on the back, pour yourself a beverage of choice, and call it a day. Or you could pay it forward.

If we find an outstanding restaurant, doctor, travel destination, or auto mechanic, we naturally feel compelled to pass this information along to our loved ones and acquaintances. We don't do this for a commission or other financial incentives; rather, we do it because we genuinely care about these people and want what's best for them. So why wouldn't we make recommendations about one of the most important aspects of our lives? Why wouldn't we help our friends and family create a better financial future by directing them toward a well-qualified, trustworthy financial advisor? We want the people in our lives to live comfortably, free themselves from money worries, and have a plan in place for when they will inevitably depart from this world. Referring them to an excellent financial advisor is a gift that can help them to achieve these goals (and more).

If your neighbor is dealing with cancer, and you happen to know a top-rated oncologist, wouldn't you do everything in your power to connect them? While financial planning may not seem quite as urgent as that example, sometimes it *becomes* urgent. In my own life, I have had to help family members whose loved ones passed away without a comprehensive financial plan in place. Picking up the pieces and moving forward was an exceedingly difficult and distressing process during an already painful period. If a comprehensive plan (put together by a reputable financial advisor) had already been in place, all this heartache could have been avoided.

"Sure," you might be saying. "Paying it forward is important. I've already told a few friends about my amazing financial advisor. What more do you want?"

That's a great start, to be sure, but did your coworker, golfing buddy, or mother-in-law actually call your financial advisor based on an off-handed recommendation? If they're like most people, they probably did not. Over the past twenty years, an in-depth study of tens of thousands of individual investors found that the vast majority of referrals people make—about 80 percent—are casual and do not inspire action. These referrals might be framed like this, "I hear you'll be selling your business soon. You should call my advisor." While well-intentioned, this type of referral does not usually materialize into anything. Financial advisors, such as the author of this book, have told me that they get about three to five referrals per year for every one hundred clients they have, even though dozens of clients tell them they've encouraged a friend or family member to call.

What is the disconnect here? Why do so many people *think* they've given a referral, when nothing ever results from their suggestion?

As the president and founder of Feedback Marketing Group, I study the art of referral-making in the financial industry. Through my research and conversations with advisors, I've learned a lot about the mentalities of both consumers and financial advisors. On the consumer side, if someone is told to call a financial advisor, they will likely think of a dozen reasons not to do it.

I can wait a while—no need to call now.

Can I really *trust this financial advisor?*

The whole process intimidates me. I'm not even sure where to begin.

I don't know much about investing; how will I know if I'm being taken for a ride?

I'm doing fine right now. Looking for a financial advisor can wait.

A lot of these excuses boil down to two main factors: a lack of education and a lack of urgency. Through no fault of their own, many consumers know very little about the world of financial planning and investment management. As David has articulated in this book, we typically do not learn much about these subjects in school, so it's up to us to self-educate. Additionally, it benefits many investment firms to keep the financial planning industry a bit muddy and hard to decipher. The average consumer is not going to know the difference between a fee-only and a fee-based financial advisor or know how to identify a true fiduciary. They also won't necessarily understand fee structures and commissions and won't know what's honest and fair.

And then there's urgency. Unfortunately, many people delay seeking and hiring a financial advisor until the floodwaters have risen and the dam is about to burst. In other words, they wait until they're in crisis mode before taking action. We can plan for other aspects of our lives, so why not do the same when it comes to hiring a financial advisor? The time to plan your wedding is not the day of the wedding. The time to plan a trip is not when your airplane lands. Similarly, financial planning should not be reactive, but proactive. If you care about someone, you'll want to encourage them to find a financial advisor sooner rather than later. Build up the levees *before* the floodwaters start rising.

On the financial advisor side, I have found that those who are best at turning a lukewarm referral into a client are those with sales experience *and* an inclination to sell. This is a blanket statement, of course, but it is remarkable to me how the best, most trustworthy financial advisors are often the worst at touting their services and ushering in new clients. This reluctance to self-promote may stem from their deep commitment to reject anything sales-related when it comes to offering financial planning. They are service oriented, not sales oriented. But when you have an excellent set of services, it's crucial to talk about them. You might be the most skilled filmmaker in the world, for example, but if you don't advertise your movie, no one will see it (and that is doing a disservice to yourself and your would-be audience).

When we think about the hang-ups for both consumers and financial advisors (especially those who are non-salesy), it's no wonder we find a chasm between referrals and contacting, and eventually hiring, an advisor. We have two sides that are reluctant to reach out to each other for various reasons. In the meantime, the clock is ticking, and the consumer may be approaching a crisis point in their life (whether they see it coming or not).

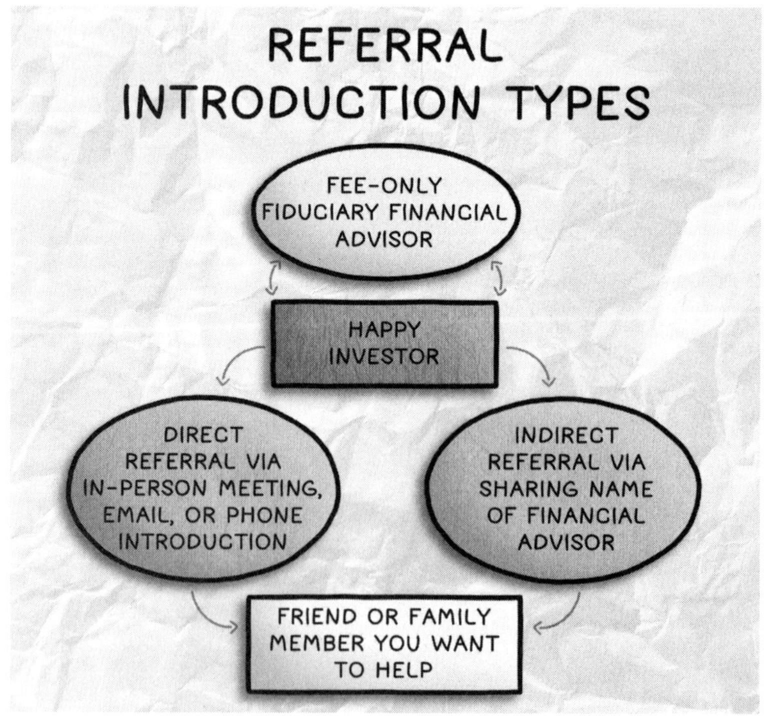

You are now in a unique position to help bridge that chasm. After reading this book, you have a deeper knowledge of the financial advising and investment management industry than the average American. You understand what to look for in a financial advisor, what to avoid, and how to conduct a search for a reputable advisor. You also understand why it's crucial to start searching for a financial planner today, rather than putting it on some future to-do list. How do you transfer that education and urgency to others?

I can think of a few ways, including the following:

Talk openly about how your current advisor has helped you on your financial journey (if, indeed, this is true).

Encourage your loved ones to read this book and other similar educational publications.

Give specific examples of how your financial advisor has helped you. (Have they minimized your taxes? Set up your estate plan? Helped define your path to retirement?)

Ask others about their roadblocks—their reasons for not yet connecting with a financial advisor.

Make a "warm" referral by connecting your friends and family with your financial advisor through an introductory email, a low-pressure lunch, or a phone call.

Invite a friend to an event at your current financial advisory firm and introduce them to your financial advisory team.

I tend to take an optimistic view of humanity. At our core, I believe we are empathetic and want to help our loved ones as best we can. Although connecting someone with a trustworthy financial advisor may seem like a practical, commonsense act, it is really an act of love. What is more important than making sure our friends and family members are secure, comfortable, and supported for the rest of their days, no matter what life throws at them? What is a greater gift than giving our loved ones peace of mind?

Dan Allison
President and founder
Feedback Marketing Group
August 22, 2023

Appendix 1
Allodium Educational Resources

The one-page resources that appear in the following fifteen pages were designed by Allodium Investment Consultants and are copied here with their permission. They are meant to supplement some of the topics discussed in this book. Some of these one-page resources are also available on the Allodium website at www.allodium.com.

1. Comparison Worksheet
2. External Team
3. Fee-Only Financial Advisor Pyramid
4. Fiduciary Oath Handout
5. Financial Planning Goals
6. Financial Planning
7. Individual Investors—WM Services
8. Service Menu Worksheet
9. Sharpen Your Investment Focus
10. Value of Advice
11. Advice Providers
12. New Client Intake Process
13. Individual Investors—WM Diagram
14. Investing Consulting
15. NAPFA Membership

Comparison Worksheet

Comparing investment advisors can be difficult when services and fees vary and advisors affiliated with broker/dealers or banks claim to be "independent." Since advisors differ, comparing cost alone is often not enough to select the very best for your needs. To make a fully informed choice, we encourage you to compare advisors using the factors listed below.

ADVISOR VALUES & CAPABILITIES	NEW ADVISOR	YOUR ADVISOR
Registered Investment Adviser with regulatory obligation to always act in clients' best interests. (Note: Broker/dealers do not have this obligation.)	●	
Not affiliated with any investment product provider to avoid conflicts of interest.	●	
Investment practices based on the Global Fiduciary Standard of Excellence (Fi360.com).	●	
Multiple financial planners are NAPFA-Registered Financial Advisors.	●	
Over 25 years of professional investment experience.	●	
Understands the unique needs of both individual and institutional investors.	●	
Experienced with alternative investment strategies to reduce risk.	●	
Credentials include respected professional designations (AIF®, CFP®, etc.)	●	

ADVICE FACTORS	NEW ADVISOR	YOUR ADVISOR
Performs comprehensive cash flow assessment and goal clarification.	●	
Provides comprehensive financial risk assessment and recommendations.	●	
Drafts formal investment policy statement to guide investment decisions.	●	
Recommends appropriate asset allocation and investment options to manage risk.	●	
Offers unconstrained investment options that are not limited to certain product providers.	●	
Uses third-party due diligence research on investment managers.	●	
Provides quarterly reports incorporating investments held across multiple custodians.	●	
Detailed performance reports that compare each individual holding to its benchmark.	●	

SERVICE FACTORS	NEW ADVISOR	YOUR ADVISOR
Conducts comprehensive annual investment review meetings with clients.	●	
Negotiates custodian and investment manager fees on behalf of clients where possible.	●	
Provides comprehensive tax reporting.	●	
Provides client access to secure investor portal for sharing sensitive documents.	●	
Directly collaborates with clients' other advisors (accountant, attorney, etc.) as needed.	●	
Provides education and presentations about investment and fiduciary best practices.	●	
Meets with and surveys clients to assess their satisfaction with the firm.	●	

ADVISOR COMPENSATION	NEW ADVISOR	YOUR ADVISOR
One advisory fee for investment advice and financial planning/fiduciary consulting services.	●	
Only source of advisor's income are fees from clients to avoid conflicts of interest.	●	
Receives no sales commissions for products and services used with clients.	●	
Fully discloses compensation paid by client to advisor. No hidden fees.	●	

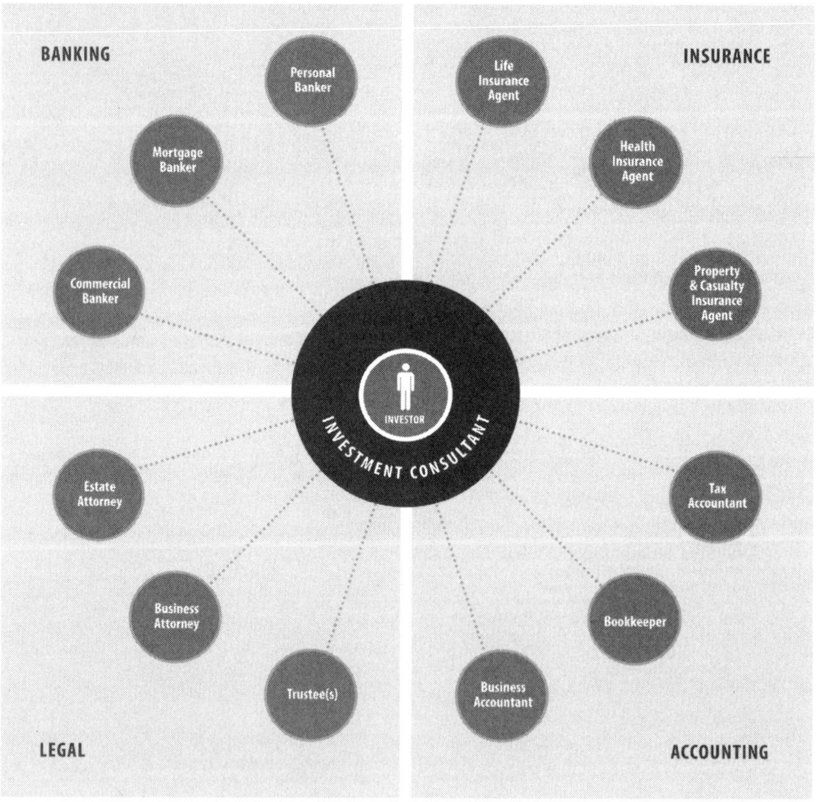

Fee-Only Advisors

There are about 283,060 personal financial advisors in the United States.[1] Less than 2% of those are NAPFA-Registered Financial Advisors. How can a NAPFA-Registered Financial Advisor help you?

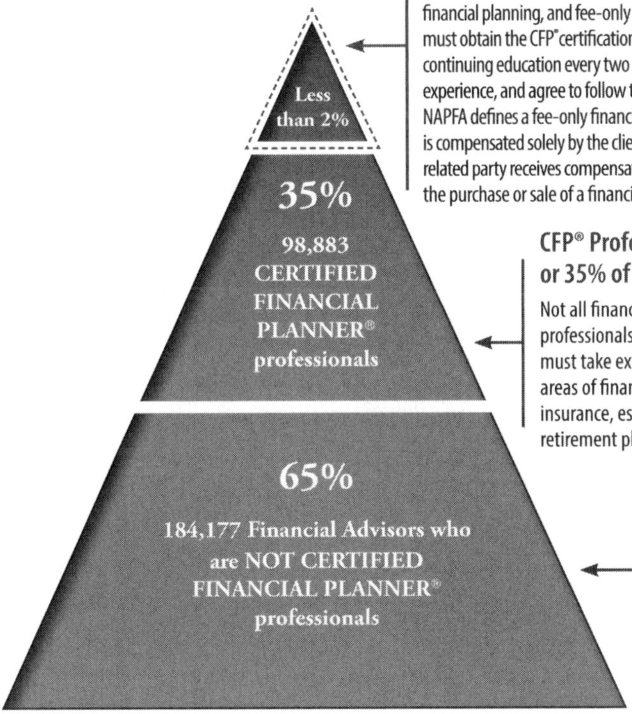

Less than 2%

35%

98,883 CERTIFIED FINANCIAL PLANNER® professionals

65%

184,177 Financial Advisors who are NOT CERTIFIED FINANCIAL PLANNER® professionals

NAPFA-Registered Financial Advisors: 4,600 or less than 2% of financial advisors[2]

Financial professionals who meet the highest membership standards for professional competency, client-focused financial planning, and fee-only compensation. They must obtain the CFP® certification, complete 60 hours of continuing education every two years, have three years of experience, and agree to follow the NAPFA fiduciary oath. NAPFA defines a fee-only financial advisor as one who is compensated solely by the client. The advisor nor any related party receives compensation that is contingent on the purchase or sale of a financial product.

CFP® Professionals: 98,883 or 35% of financial advisors[3]

Not all financial planners are CFP® professionals. A CFP® professional must take extensive exams in the areas of financial planning, taxes, insurance, estate planning, and retirement planning.

Financial Advisors: 184,177 or 65% of financial advisors

Financial advisors who are not CFP® professionals.

1. U.S. Bureau of Labor Statistics, https://www.bls.gov/oes/current/oes132052.htm (2022)
2. NAPFA, https://www.napfa.org/about-us (April 3, 2024)
3. CFP Board, https://www.cfp.net/knowledge/reports-and-statistics/professional-demographics (April 3, 2024)

www.allodium.com

Fiduciary Oath

Our firm is proud to commit to the following five fiduciary principles:

1. We will always put ***your*** best interests first.

2. We will act with ***prudence***—using the skill, care, diligence, and good judgment of a professional.

3. We will provide ***full*** disclosure of all important facts.

4. We will avoid conflicts of interest and strive to provide ***unbiased*** advice.

5. We will manage any unavoidable conflicts in ***your*** favor.

www.allodium.com

Financial Planning Goals

The secret of wealth is to spend less than you earn and invest the difference.

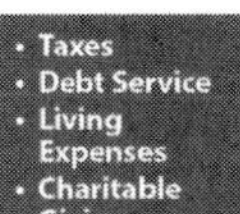

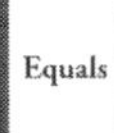

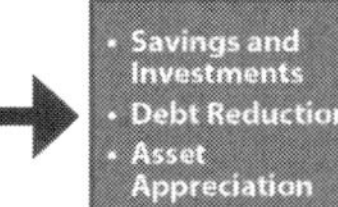

Equals

Comprehensive Financial Planning

Financial Position

- Personal Financial Statement
- Cash Flow Management
- Debt Reduction Strategies
- Identity Theft Protection

Asset & Income Protection

- Life Insurance
- P & C Insurance
- Health Insurance
- Disability Insurance
- Long-Term Care Insurance

Income Tax Planning

- Income Tax Strategy
- Asset Placement Strategy
- Tax-Advantaged Investments

Investment Planning

- Asset Allocation
- Due Diligence Research
- Selecting Managers
- Monitor Investments

Estate Planning

- Asset Titling
- Wealth Transfer
- Family Education
- Trust Management
- Charitable Planning

Retirement Planning

- Short- & Long-Term Goals
- Retirement Income Projection

The role of the Financial Planner is to find ways to help you increase your net worth and to help you to accomplish all of your financial objectives.

Define the purpose of your money: what is the purpose of your wealth?

- ☐ Attain Financial Security
- ☐ Provide Retirement Income
- ☐ Reduce or Eliminate Debt
- ☐ Fund College Expenses
- ☐ Fulfill Lifestyle Desires
- ☐ Start a New Business
- ☐ Establish Financial Independence
- ☐ Support a Charitable Giving Plan
- ☐ Wealth Transfer to Family
- ☐ Other Purpose (s):

Notes:

Financial Planning

"Financial planning is a collaborative process that helps maximize a client's potential for meeting life goals through financial advice that integrates relevant elements of the client's personal and financial circumstances."

Certified Financial Planner Board of Standards, Inc. (CFP Board)

A CERTIFIED FINANCIAL PLANNER® professional can provide you with a personalized, written financial plan based on the major financial planning subject areas published by the CFP Board of Standards.

Financial Statement Preparation and Analysis

Develop a summary of your current financial position including net worth statement, cash flow summary, and debt review. Includes cash flow analysis/planning and budgeting.

Insurance Planning and Risk Management

Provide a risk management analysis to protect your assets and your income, which may include life insurance, medical insurance, disability, long-term care, property and casualty, liability, and identity theft.

Employee Benefits Planning

Review employer retirement plans, business group benefits, executive benefits, and other employer-provided benefits.

Investment Planning

Establish a formal investment policy, asset allocation recommendations, and investment selection and monitoring.

Income Tax Planning

Identify tax-deferred and tax-efficient investing strategies to optimize your financial position. This may include a review of retirement benefits available to you.

Retirement Planning

Prepare financial projections and assist you in developing a savings and/or withdrawal plan incorporating other financial goals as applicable.

Estate Planning

Review your estate plan, your wealth transfer plan, and the coordination of your estate plan with asset titling and beneficiary designations.

www.allodium.com

Wealth Management Services

Wealth management combines investment management, financial planning and specialized financial services, which can include personal retail banking services, estate planning, legal and tax advice. A CERTIFIED FINANCIAL PLANNER® professional can provide you with a personalized, written financial plan based on the major financial planning subject areas published by the CFP Board of Standards.

Financial Planning Services

1. Financial Position Analysis
2. Investment Planning
3. Retirement Planning
4. Financial Goal Setting and Prioritization
5. Income Tax Planning
6. Asset & Income Protection
7. Estate Planning & Wealth Transfer

In addition to traditional financial planning services, wealth management services may also include:

Wealth Management Services

1. ***Maintaining your comprehensive financial plan with an annual review:***
   - Creating and maintaining an action plan with reminders when appropriate
   - Introducing you to outside professionals (accountants, attorneys, etc.)
   - Reviewing proposals for health, life and property and casualty insurance
   - Reviewing your social security to maximize your benefits
   - Reviewing your insurance policies (life, disability, health, etc.)
   - Reviewing your income tax returns and estate plan documents
2. ***Integrating your financial plan with your investment portfolio:***
   - Implementing a recommended investment portfolio(s)
   - Rebalancing your investment portfolio back to target when appropriate
   - Harvesting capital losses for income tax benefits when appropriate
3. ***Introducing tax advantaged investment strategies:***
   - Establishing tax advantaged accounts (HSA & 529 plans) when appropriate
   - Establishing qualified retirement plans (IRA, Roth IRA, etc.) when appropriate
   - Analyzing the opportunities to convert IRA accounts to Roth IRA accounts
4. ***Integrating your financial plan and estate plan with related entities:***
   - Coordinating with your company retirement plan accounts, charitable trusts, etc.
   - Identifying your beneficiaries and updating your documents
5. ***Educating your family members:***
   - Helping your children to learn about investing and personal finance
   - Helping fiduciary decision-makers learn about fiduciary investment management
6. ***Collaborating with other professional advisors:***
   - Meeting with your professional advisors such as accountants, attorneys, etc.

Service Menu Worksheet

Purposeful individual investors are proactive in selecting the specific services that truly add value. Use this worksheet to identify the specific investment advisory services that will help you to accomplish your financial goals.

INVESTMENT MANAGEMENT	NEED	WANT	PASS
Comprehensive cash flow assessment.	✓		
Comprehensive goal clarification.			
Comprehensive financial risk assessment.			
Strategic asset allocation policy to manage investment risk.			
Portfolio construction analysis and written investment plan.			
Due diligence research on investment managers.			
Negotiation with custodians and investment managers to minimize fees.			
Full disclosure of all fees and compensation paid to investment advisors and money managers.			
Implementation of the recommended investment portfolio.			
Periodic rebalancing of investment portfolio.			
COMPREHENSIVE PERFORMANCE REPORTING	**NEED**	**WANT**	**PASS**
Comprehensive quarterly portfolio performance evaluation reports.			
Comprehensive monthly portfolio performance evaluation reports.			
Comprehensive tax reports on investment portfolio holdings.			
Quarterly meetings to review your investment portfolio.			
Quarterly conference calls to review your investment portfolio.			
Comprehensive annual investment review meeting to review your investment strategy and policy.			
Online access to portfolio holdings with daily valuation, gain/loss data and year to date performance.			
FINANCIAL PLANNING SERVICES	**NEED**	**WANT**	**PASS**
Personal Financial Statement (Net Worth Statement).			
Cash flow analysis and budget planning.			
Retirement income planning.			
Income tax planning.			
Asset and income protection planning.			
Estate planning.			
Philanthropic planning.			
Annual Review Meeting.			
Annual Review Booklet with Letter of Understanding and updated Personal Financial Statement.			
Collaboration with your other advisors (accountant, attorney, banker, insurance agent, etc.) as needed.			
Coordination with related entities and related portfolios.			
INVESTOR EDUCATION	**NEED**	**WANT**	**PASS**
Educational presentations on wealth management for individual investors.			
Educational presentations on personal finance for children and young adults.			
Educational presentations on fiduciary investment management for foundations, endowments, and trusts.			
Optimal investment structure for the efficient governance of your investment portfolios.			

Sharpen Your Focus

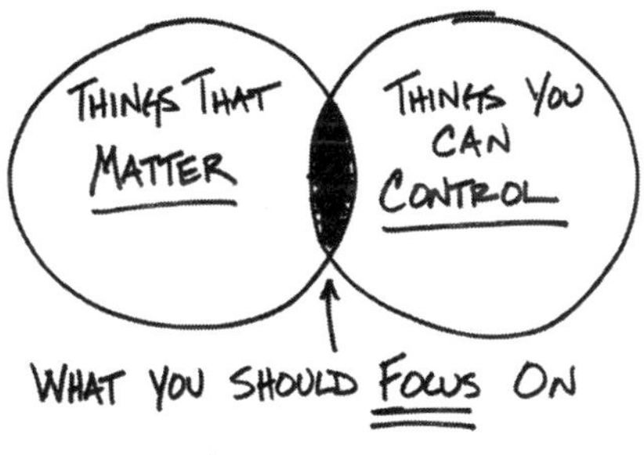

Many investors waste time and energy trying to beat the market.

More enlightened investors learn to relax and focus on both the things that matter and the things that they can control. They let the markets work for them.

Matter		Control	
	Focus		
Things That Do Not Matter	Things That Matter	Things That You Can Control	Things That You Can't Control
Hot Stock Tips	Your Unique Aspirations	Your Investment Philosophy	Natural Disasters
Your Friend's Performance	Your Decisions	Your Investment Decisions	The Stock Market
Market Forecasts	Your Future	Your Savings Rate	The Economy
Financial Media	Your Security	Your Investment Policy	Interest Rates
Watching the Market Daily	Achieving Your Goals	Your Time Horizon	The Government

www.allodium.com

Value of Advice

You may be seeking a financial advisor for various reasons. Some reasons may include help with planning for your retirement, minimizing your tax liability, saving for a specific financial goal, or navigating the stock market. You may be looking for help with life's questions, such as: What is your life vision? How do you define success? What legacy do you want to leave? No matter why you seek a financial advisor, ideally, you want to get to a place where you feel financially secure. The first step is deciding what type of advice you need and how much you are willing to pay for it. Common questions that investors ask themselves are: What will I get for my money? How will it benefit me? In other words—what is the value of advice?

What Financial Advisors Do

- Financial position analysis
- Income tax planning
- Asset and income protection planning
- Estate planning
- Investment planning
- Manage investment risk and preserve capital
- Investment performance evaluation
- Provide expertise related to investment strategies
- Provide education about various strategies
- Financial goal-setting and prioritization
- Guidance with difficult investment decisions
- Retirement planning
- Establish a future income stream from the portfolio
- Responsible investing
- Provide third-party endorsement of investment decisions and actions

How Financial Advisors Help

A good financial advisor will help you get organized and stay focused. Together, you and your financial advisor can build a plan that reflects your goals as they change over time.

You Don't Have to Manage Your Portfolio by Yourself: You are not alone. Your financial advisor will walk beside you. You may not have the time or desire to manage your own portfolio. You don't have to worry about the details of your investments or your financial plan. In addition, investors often tell us they don't know what they don't know. Financial advisors can provide financial coaching and advice with a fiduciary standard of care in a trusting and transparent environment.

Big-Picture Perspective: Experienced professionals can help you stay on course with a long-term comprehensive strategy. They can help you avoid the pitfalls of emotional biases that often plague investors during times of market volatility. A financial advisor will help you stay disciplined, reducing the emotional component in the decision-making process. Financial advisors can help you articulate your long-term investment goals and strategies, select tax-efficient investments, and manage your portfolio and asset allocations. They can also provide ongoing investment monitoring and risk analysis.

Accessible and Responsive Client Service: You deserve great communication from your financial professionals. A financial advisor will take the time to really listen to you and respond to your requests in a timely manner. Financial advice works best when built on a strong advisor-client relationship. Life is not always perfect, but as far as possible, a relationship with a trusted financial advisor could help you achieve peace of mind.

Advice Providers

ADVISOR TYPES		
ADVISOR	**"HYBRID BROKER/ADVISOR"**	**BROKER**
Advice	Advice AND/OR Sales	Sales
Relational	Relational AND/OR Transactional	Transactional
Relationship Retainer	Account Contract AND/OR Security Transactions	Security Transactions
COMPENSATION		
Fees	Fees AND/OR Commissions	Commissions
Fee-Only	Fee-Based	Commission-Based
Fee-Only Advice	Fee-Based Products AND/OR Commission-Based Products	Commission-Based Products
REGULATION AND STANDARD OF CARE		
Firms Registered with Securities and Exchange Commission (SEC)	Firms Dually Registered with the SEC AND Also Affiliated with a Broker-Dealer	Banks, Brokerage Firms, and Insurance Companies Selling Investment Securities
Investment Adviser Representatives (IAR)	Investment Adviser Representatives (IAR) AND Registered Representatives (RR)	Registered Representatives (RR)
Website Disclosure: "SEC-Registered Investment Adviser..."	Website Disclosure: "SEC-Registered Investment Advisor..." AND "Securities Offered by..."	Website Disclosure: "Securities Offered by..."
Fiduciary Standard	Fiduciary Standard AND/OR Suitability Standard	Suitability Standard

www.allodium.com

New Client Intake Process

1 VALUES MEETING	2 DIAGNOSTIC MEETING	3 PROPOSAL MEETING	4 IMPLEMENTATION MEETING
OUR PURPOSE: Determine if we may be a match	**OUR PURPOSE:** Understand you and your financial goals	**OUR PURPOSE:** Share the investment proposal with you	**OUR PURPOSE:** Align and initiate your investment strategy
WHAT WE DO: • We learn what's important to you • We learn why you are seeking an advisor	**WHAT WE DO:** • We ask questions to learn your story (background, goals, family, work, etc.) • We assess your risk profile	**WHAT WE DO:** • We present your investment proposal and financial planning opportunities • We explain fees and any tax implications	**WHAT WE DO:** • We clarify any investment strategy modifications • We gather your communications preferences
WHAT YOU DO: • You learn about our investment philosophy • You learn how we are compensated	**WHAT YOU DO:** • You provide your financial documents • You share your financial goals	**WHAT YOU DO:** • You ask questions • You are able to request modifications to the proposal	**WHAT YOU DO:** • You confirm your investment plan • You sign implementation paperwork
MEETING DETAILS: • Meet with chief investment officer • Meeting Length: 1 hour	**MEETING DETAILS:** • Meet with chief investment officer and investment consultants • Meeting Length: 2 hours	**MEETING DETAILS:** • Meet with chief investment officer and investment consultants • Meeting Length: 2 hours	**MEETING DETAILS:** • Meet with investment consultants • Meeting Length: 2 hours

www.allodium.com

Wealth Management

Wealth Management is a financial advisory service for individual investors that provides investment management, comprehensive financial planning, and the coordination of financial planning activities with your other professional advisors. The continuous discretionary management of your investment portfolio is a core service that supports all of the other components of your comprehensive financial plan. A Wealth Manager (typically having obtained the CERTIFIED FINANCIAL PLANNER® certification) is the professional advisor responsible for developing, managing, and monitoring all of the various aspects of your comprehensive financial plan. The Wealth Manager considers your income and expenses and all aspects of your personal financial statement (including both assets and liabilities) in the management of your personal wealth.

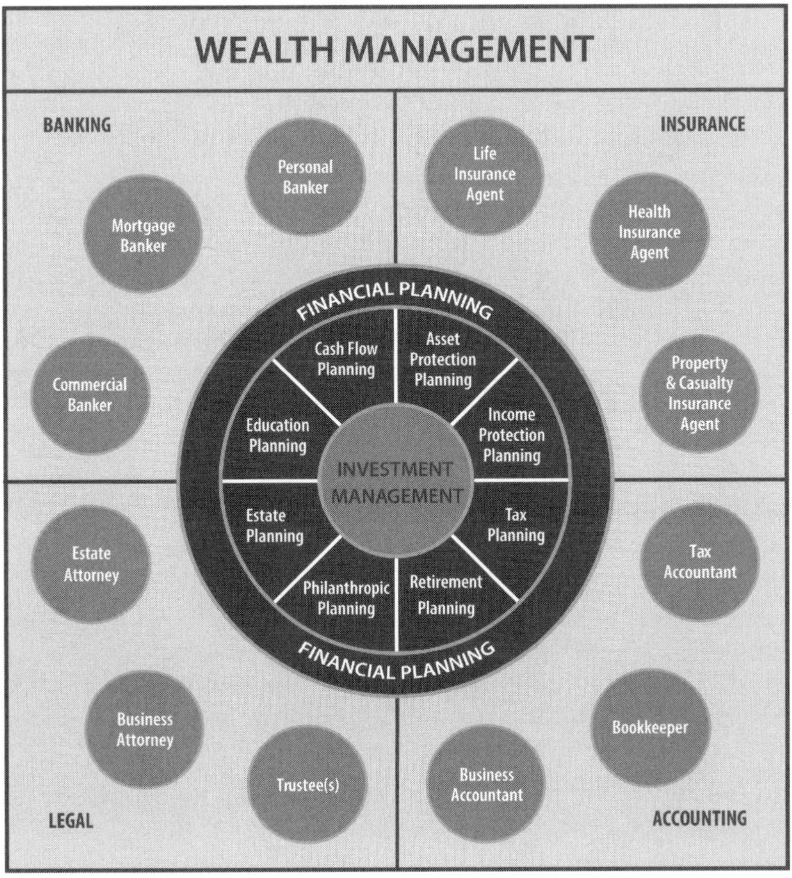

WEALTH MANAGEMENT

BANKING
Personal Banker
Mortgage Banker
Commercial Banker

INSURANCE
Life Insurance Agent
Health Insurance Agent
Property & Casualty Insurance Agent

FINANCIAL PLANNING
Cash Flow Planning
Asset Protection Planning
Income Protection Planning
Tax Planning
Retirement Planning
Philanthropic Planning
Estate Planning
Education Planning
INVESTMENT MANAGEMENT
FINANCIAL PLANNING

LEGAL
Estate Attorney
Business Attorney
Trustee(s)

ACCOUNTING
Tax Accountant
Bookkeeper
Business Accountant

Investment Consulting

Investment management consulting defines the specific roles and responsibilities of the various investment service providers that help the investor to build a broadly diversified investment portfolio. This institutional governance approach to investment management emphasizes the use of an investment management consultant to help the investor to develop a comprehensive investment plan. In effect, this investment management consulting model allows the investor to control the high-level investment policy decisions while delegating the granular investment decisions to professional investment managers.

Primary Roles in the Institutional Investment Management Consulting Model

1. **Investor:** The primary responsibilities of the investor are to develop and document financial goals and to define the risk profile of the portfolio. The investor should be prepared to monitor and supervise all service vendors and investment options and avoid prohibited transactions and conflicts of interest.
2. **Investment Advisor:** The investor retains an objective, third-party investment advisor, often referred to as an investment management consultant, to assist in managing the overall investment process. Investment advisors can help investors with their fiduciary responsibilities by guiding them through a disciplined investment process. The investment advisor educates the investor and assists in the preparation, implementation, and maintenance of the investment policy statement. In addition, the investment advisor conducts asset allocation studies, offers investment options with supporting research, helps implement diversification and asset allocation strategies, coordinates investment manager search processes, and provides ongoing investment manager reporting and evaluation.
3. **Investment Manager:** Unlike trustees and investment advisors who manage the investment process, investment managers make investment decisions regarding security selection and price. They oversee the assets under their supervision according to the guidelines and objectives outlined in the prospectus, service, or trust agreements. Investment managers exercise full investment discretion with regards to buying, managing, and selling assets held in the portfolios and promptly vote all proxies.
4. **Custodian:** Custodians are responsible for the safekeeping of the portfolio's assets. They maintain separate accounts by legal registration, value the holdings, collect all income and dividends owed to the portfolio, and settle all transactions initiated by the investment managers. Custodians also provide monthly reports that detail transactions, cash flows, securities held and their current value, change in value of each security, and the overall portfolio since the previous report.

An investment management consultant is an investment professional who helps investors set and meet long-term financial goals. There are three important reasons for hiring an investment management consultant:

- *Knowledge that the client/investor does not have or cannot afford to develop internally.*
- *Guidance and help with difficult decisions.*
- *Third-party endorsement or validation of decisions and actions.*

NAPFA Membership

The National Association of Personal Financial Advisors (NAPFA) is a professional association of fee-only financial advisors, providing support and education for its members. NAPFA-Registered Financial Advisors must meet specific educational standards to be eligible for membership. For instance, they must obtain the CFP® certification and complete 60 hours of continuing education every two years. Members must also abide by the NAPFA code of ethics, comply with all federal and state statutes and regulations, and make all required regulatory filings. In addition, members must also be fee-only financial advisors.

NAPFA defines fee-only compensation as a financial advisor "who is compensated solely by the client with neither the advisor nor any related party receiving compensation that is contingent on the purchase or sale of a financial product."[1] In other words, NAPFA members may not receive commissions, fees, bonuses, rebates or any other type of compensation derived from the recommendations that are given to the client. They are also prohibited from owning or being employed by a financial industry services firm that receives these commissions or rebates.

There are many benefits to working with fee-only NAPFA-Registered Financial Advisors. They can offer objective, independent advice, free from the conflicts of interest that occur from the sale of commission-based products. NAPFA-Registered Financial Advisors are fiduciaries, bound to act in the investor's best interest, not their own interests. Investors are becoming more educated about financial advisors and understand the benefits of objective financial advice. NAPFA-Registered Financial Advisors are meeting the investor demand for a fiduciary standard of care.

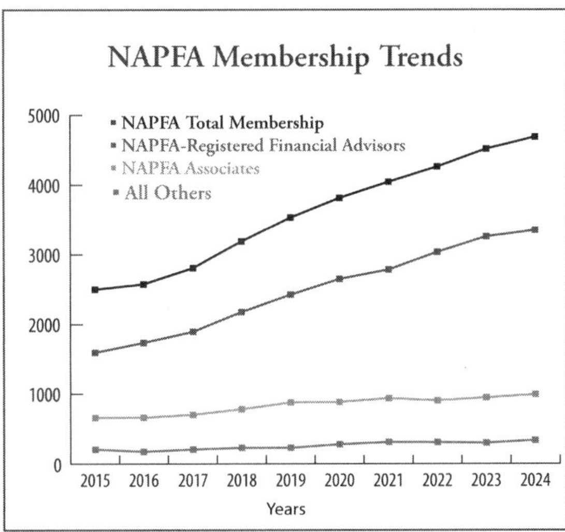

By joining NAPFA, financial advisors demonstrate to potential clients that they strive to offer the fiduciary standard of care.

NAPFA membership has grown between 2015 and 2024, as shown in the chart. NAPFA serves as a resource that can help investors find advisors who value objective financial advice.

Membership data provided by NAPFA

1. Retrieved from https://www.napfa.org/membership/our-standards

Appendix 2
AdvisorSmart® Educational Resources

Our goal is to help you as an individual investor.

To educate yourself about objective financial advice, go to www.AdvisorSmart.com/Resources where you will find a wealth of free resources related to financial advice and financial advisors.

These one-page resources on the following pages were designed by AdvisorSmart® for you, the reader. They are meant to supplement some of the topics discussed in this book.

1. Financial Advisor Registration Matrix
2. Sample Selection Criteria: Needs, Wants, and Nice-to-Haves
3. Selection Criteria: Needs, Wants, and Nice-to-Haves (blank template)
4. Evaluation Matrix (scoring sheet)
5. Sample Advisor Selection Process
6. Sample Elimination Factors
7. Sample Advisor Selection Process Timeline

Visit the AdvisorSmart® website at www.AdvisorSmart.com/Resources for a free download of all of these documents, as well as additional educational resources.

www.AdvisorSmart.com/Resources

AdvisorSmart®

Financial Advisor Registration

Financial Adviser Type	FINRA Registration License	Examination*	Permitted Activities	Compensation Model	Typical Employer
Registered Representative (RR)	Series 6	**Series 6** Investment Company and Variable Contracts Products Representative Exam	Sell Products (Annuities and Mutual Funds)	Commission-Based	Investment Securities Brokerage Firm
	Series 7	**Series 7** General Securities Representative Exam	Sell Products (General Investment Securities)	Commission-Based	
	Series 63	**Series 63** Uniform Securities Agent State Law Exam	Sell Product (General Investment Securities – State Licensing)	Commission-Based	
Registered Representative (RR) AND Investment Adviser Representative (IAR)	Series 66	**Series 66** Uniform Combined State Law Exam	Deliver Financial Advice AND Sell Products	Commissions AND Fees (Fee-Based)	Dually-Registered Firm
Investment Adviser Representative (IAR)	N/A	**Series 65** Uniform Investment Adviser Law Exam	Deliver Financial Advice	Fee for Advice (Fee-Only)	Registered Investment Adviser (RIA) Firm

*Examination requirements may vary by state. There are potential examination waivers for certain professional designations.

www.advisorsmart.com

AdvisorSmart®

Sample Selection Criteria

Financial Advisory Firm for Individual Investors

Our Needs — We NEED the financial advisory firm to have these traits:

1	**RIA Firm:** Registered Investment Adviser (RIA) with the Securities and Exchange Commission (SEC)
2	**Retirement Planning Experience:** Years of experience in developing retirement income plans
3	**Retirement Planning Expertise:** Specialized knowledge with developing retirement income plans
4	**Fiduciary Oath:** Willing to acknowledge a fiduciary relationship in writing
5	**Comprehensive Performance Evaluation Reporting:** Monthly and quarterly reports
6	**Reasonable Fees & Transparency:** Competitive compensation with full disclosure
7	**CERTIFIED FINANCIAL PLANNER™:** A team with professional financial planning expertise.
8	**Personnel Size:** Staff has at least ten employees and five professionals

Our Wants — We WANT the financial advisory firm to have these traits:

1	**Independent Advice:** Independent of banks, brokerage firms, and insurance companies
2	**Comprehensive Advice:** Balance sheet, taxation, insurance, cash flow, financial planning, risk management
3	**Disciplined Advice:** Firm follows the Global Fiduciary Standards of Excellence (Broadridge/Fi360)
4	**CEFEX Certification:** Firm certification from the Centre for Fiduciary Excellence (CEFEX)
5	**Quality Fiduciary Advice:** Comprised of professionally trained Accredited Investment Fiduciary® (AIF®) staff
6	**Investment Philosophy:** Evidence-based investment approach using low-cost index funds
7	**Investment Policy:** Assistance with developing our investment policy statement
8	**Investment Strategy:** Asset allocation and periodic portfolio rebalancing to manage investment risk
9	**Investment Management:** Discretionary investment portfolio management service
10	**Tax Expertise:** Familiarity with tax compliance for individual investors
11	**NAPFA Membership:** Firm is a member of the National Association of Personal Financial Advisors (NAPFA)
12	**Good Fit:** Firm has at least three accounts of similar or greater size

Our "Nice-to-Haves" — It would be "NICE" for the financial advisory firm to have these traits:

1	**Local Office:** Provides for more frequent in-person (face-to-face) meetings
2	**Size of Firm:** A financial advisory firm that is AT LEAST 10 times bigger than our current investment portfolio
3	**Trust Management:** Experience helping with a special needs trust
4	**Organizational Assistance:** Help to organize financial documents
5	**Family Education:** Assistance in educating clients about investing, including younger family members
6	**Personalized Service:** Customized service plan
7	**Socially Responsible Investing:** Assistance with ESG factors and responsible investment strategies
8	**Estate Planning:** Collaboration with our estate planning attorney to implement the estate plan
9	**Collaboration:** Coordination with our professional advisors (accounting, legal, banking, insurance, etc.)
10	**Estate Settlement:** Assistance in settling the estate of a family member
11	**Philanthropic Planning:** Helping our family to clarify our charitable giving strategies

www.advisorsmart.com

AdvisorSmart®

Sample Selection Criteria Template

Financial Advisory Firm for Individual Investors

Our Needs — We NEED the financial advisory firm to have these traits:

1	
2	
3	
4	
5	
6	
7	
8	

Our Wants — We WANT the financial advisory firm to have these traits:

1	
2	
3	
4	
5	
6	
7	
8	
9	
10	
11	
12	

Our "Nice-to-Haves" — It would be "NICE" for the financial advisory firm to have these traits:

1	
2	
3	
4	
5	
6	
7	
8	
9	
10	
11	

www.advisorsmart.com

AdvisorSmart®

Financial Advisor Evaluation Matrix

for Individual Investors

Use these questions to determine if the vendor meets your predetermined selection criteria. The best possible response is 12 affirmative (yes) answers. Choose to eliminate the vendors with the most NO answers.

CRITERIA	QUESTION	VENDOR 1	2	3	4	5
1. RIA Firm	Are you a Registered Investment Adviser (RIA) firm?	Y				
2. Fee-Only	Do you qualify to be a NAPFA fee-only firm?					
3. Fiduciary	Will you acknowledge your fiduciary obligations in writing?					
4. Independent	Are you independent from banks, brokerage, and insurance firms?					
5. Comprehensive	Will you advise on both our assets and our liabilities?					
6. Disciplined	Do you have a defined and repeatable investment process?					
7. Experienced	Do you have experience and expertise serving clients like us?					
8. Personalized Service	Will you tailor your investment services to meet our needs?					
9. Cost	Can you provide the annual cost in dollars to retain your firm?					
10. Conflicts of Interest	Will you manage any conflicts of interest in our favor?					
11. Third-Party Verification	Is your firm certified by any third-party verification services?					
12. Fiduciary Education	Will you provide fiduciary education to our family members?					
	Total Number of YES Answers					

AdvisorSmart®

Advisor Selection Process

Individual Investor — Process to Select a Financial Advisor					
A		B		C	
YOUR INTERNAL PREPARATIONS		DEVELOPING YOUR SELECTION PROCESS		SELECTING YOUR ADVISOR	
1.	Decision to Look for an Advisor	1.	Design Your Advisor Selection Process	1.	Review Request for Information (RFI) and Complete RFI Response Summary
2.	Decision to Use Request for Information (RFI) Process	2.	Determine Advisor Selection Process Timeline	2.	Complete Scoring Worksheet and Evaluate RFI Responses Relative to Criteria
3.	Clarify Your Needs, Wants, and Desires	3.	Develop Advisor Selection Criteria	3.	Select Three Finalists and Schedule Finalist Presentations
4.	Update Internal Documents—IPS and Net Worth Statement	4.	Develop Scoring Worksheet	4.	Generate Specific Interview Questions
5.	Identify Advisor Pools	5.	Develop Evaluation Procedure	5.	Meeting Preparation
6.	Start Process of Elimination by Sector	6.	Develop Advisor Candidates List	6.	Interview Finalists
7.	Choose Advisor Type	7.	Prepare Preliminary Request for Information (RFI)	7.	Select Advisor and Check References
8.	Decide to DIY or Outsource Advisor Selection Process	8.	Select RFI Recipients	8.	Transition Account(s)

www.advisorsmart.com

AdvisorSmart®

Sample Financial Advisory Firm Elimination Factors to Consider

for Individual Investors

Sample Elimination Factors
1. Firms that are ***not regulated*** by the government to provide financial advice.
2. Firms already having been fined for selling toxic investments.
3. Firms selling ***commission-based*** bank products.
4. Firms selling ***commission-based*** insurance products.
5. Firms selling ***commission-based*** investment brokerage firm products.
6. Firms selling ***fee-based*** investment brokerage firm products.
7. RIA firms ***affiliated with*** a bank.
8. RIA firms ***affiliated with*** an insurance company.
9. RIA firms ***affiliated with*** an investment securities brokerage firm.
10. RIA firms ***affiliated with*** a custodian.
11. RIA firms with ***no experience*** with individual investors.
12. RIA firms with ***no expertise*** working with individual investors.
13. RIA firms that are ***NOT*** CEFEX certified.

www.advisorsmart.com

AdvisorSmart®

Sample Selection Process Timeline

for Individual Investors

Stage	Week	Tasks
Your Internal Preparations	1	Decision to look for an advisor. Clarify your needs, wants, and desires.
	2	Update your internal documents (investment policy statement and net worth statement). Identify advisor pools.
	3	Start process of elimination by sector; choose advisor type. Decide to DIY or to outsource the advisor selection process work.
Developing Your Selection Process	4	Develop your advisor selection criteria.
	5	Develop your advisor selection scoring worksheet, develop your evaluation procedure, and develop your financial advisor candidates list.
	6	Select final candidates, generate specific questions, and issue your request for information (RFI).
Selecting Your Advisor	7	Collect and review responses. Complete your response summary.
	8	Select three finalists; schedule finalist presentations. Prepare for face-to-face meetings. Interview three finalists, complete your scoring worksheet, and evaluate proposals relative to criteria.
	9	Select an advisor, check references, and transition accounts.

www.advisorsmart.com

Glossary

Accredited Investment Fiduciary® (AIF®): a designation conveyed to individuals by Fi360 (a Broadridge company) who have met educational, competence, conduct, and ethical standards to carry out a fiduciary standard of care and serve the best interests of their clients.

Accredited Investment Fiduciary Analyst® (AIFA®)**:** a designation conveyed to individuals by Fi360 (a Broadridge company) who have met educational, competence, conduct, and ethical standards to evaluate a fiduciary's compliance with fiduciary best practices and qualifies them to certify an organization's conformance with a "fiduciary standard of excellence," as defined by the organization.

Advice: guidance or recommendations offered with regard to prudent future action.

Advice—comprehensive: financial planning that considers the entirety of your financial life, including your assets, your liabilities, your taxes, your income, your business—these interrelated aspects of your financial life are never isolated from each other.

Advice—disciplined investment management: a rational and logical investment decision-making process based on prudent investment practices using an academic, evidence-based investment philosophy and approach.

Advice—independent: financial advice from a financial advisor that is not affiliated with or employed by an investment product provider such as a bank, investment securities brokerage firm, or an insurance company.

Advice—objective: financial advice from a financial advisor that is not biased by the financial compensation provided to the financial advisor from their employer.

Advice-only: a growing area of financial planning that focuses on providing financial.planning services for those seeking advice without investment management.

AdvisorSmart®: an investor advocate that helps investors to find fee-only financial advisors.

Allodium Investment Consultants: an independent, fee-only investment management consulting firm that provides investment advice to individual and institutional investors.

American Institute of Certified Public Accountants® (AICPA®): the national professional organization for all Certified Public Accountants that is working to ensure that the public remains confident in the integrity, objectivity, competence, and professionalism of CPAs.

Annuity: a series of payments made at equal intervals.

Asset management: a systematic process of developing, operating, maintaining, upgrading, and disposing of assets in the most cost-effective manner.

Assets under management (AUM): the market value of the investments managed by a person or entity on behalf of clients.

Behavior gap: the difference between the rates of return that investments produce when an investor makes rational decisions and the rates of return investors actually earn when they make choices based on emotions.

Broadridge: a global Fintech company that owns both Fi360 and the Center for Fiduciary Studies.

Broker: one that acts as an agent for others, as in negotiating contracts, purchases, or sales in return for a fee or commission.

BrokerCheck: a free service provided by the Financial Industry Regulatory Authority (FINRA) to help investors investigate the records of brokers and brokerage firms, including information about their credentials, qualifications, employment history, and disciplinary events.

CEFEX certification: a third-party assessment conducted by CEFEX to certify that a financial service firm is conforming to fiduciary best practices and required standards detailed by the *Prudent Practices.*

Center for Fiduciary Studies: a division of Fi360 (a Broadridge Company) that offers the designations of Accredited Investment Fiduciary® (AIF®) and Accredited Investment Fiduciary Analyst® (AIFA®) to give financial advisors the opportunity to enhance their fiduciary knowledge and demonstrate that they are serious about their fiduciary responsibilities.

Centre for Fiduciary Excellence (CEFEX): a global assessment organization that develops and administers a variety of programs that help investment stewards, such as foundation, endowment, and charitable organization trustees, achieve the Global Fiduciary Standard of Excellence in their investment management, governance, and operational processes.

Certified Financial Planner® (CFP®): a designation awarded by the Certified Financial Planner® Board of Standards, Inc., (CFP Board) to individuals who successfully complete the CFP Board's initial exams then continue ongoing annual education programs to sustain their skills and certification.

Certified Investment Management Analyst® (CIMA®): a certification issued by the Investments and Wealth Institute to individuals who successfully complete the Institute's initial exams then continue ongoing annual education programs to sustain their skills and certification.

Certified Public Accountant (CPA): an accounting professional who has met certain education, exam, and experience requirements for licensure by a state board of accountancy.

CFA Institute: a professional trade association for investment professionals directly involved in or supporting the investment decision-making process.

CFP Board of Standards: a nonprofit organization that sets and enforces the requirements for Certified Financial Planner® certification to uphold standards of competency and ethics for financial planners.

Chartered Financial Analyst® (CFA®): a globally recognized professional designation awarded to individuals by the CFA Institute that measures and certifies the competence and integrity of financial analysts.

Chartered Financial Consultant® (ChFC®): a financial planning designation awarded by the American College of Financial Services (an accredited private education institution) to individuals who successfully complete their multiple exams.

Chartered Life Underwriter® (CLU®): a professional designation awarded by the American College of Financial Services (an accredited nonprofit educational institution) for individuals who wish to specialize in life insurance and estate planning.

Commission: a payment to someone who sells goods that is directly related to the amount sold, or a system that uses such payments.

Committee for the Fiduciary Standard: a committee formed in May 2009 to advocate for the authentic fiduciary standard as established under the Investment Advisers Act of 1940.

Compensation—commission-based financial advisory firm: commission-based financial advisory firms receive sales commission compensation from the consumer based on the specific financial products they sell to you.

Compensation—fee-based financial advisory firm: fee-based financial advisory firms receive sales commission compensation from the consumer based on the specific fee-based financial products they sell to you.

Compensation—fee-only financial advisory firm: fee-only firms are compensated directly by their clients for advice, plan implementation, and the ongoing management of assets and do not accept sales commission compensation for their work.

Comprehensive advice (see Financial advice)

Conflict of interest: some financial advisors (commissioned and dually registered fee-based advisors who receive compensation based on the specific financial products they sell to you) may have difficulty putting the client's interest above their own due to the conflict of interest inherent in these sales transactions.

Customer Relationship Summary (Form CRS): a mandatory written disclosure which provides the consumer with a financial advisory firm relationship summary that tells you about the types of services the firm offers; the fees, costs, conflicts of interest, and required standard of conduct associated with those services; whether the firm and its financial professionals have reportable legal or disciplinary history; and how to get more information about the firm.

Dimensional Fund Advisors (DFA): a private investment management firm headquartered in Austin, Texas, that has a long history of applying academic research to practical investing. (*See* Evidence-based investing.)

Disciplined advice (see Financial advice)

Discretionary investment management: a firm has discretionary authority (or manages assets on a discretionary basis) if it has the authority to decide which securities to purchase and sell for the client.

Dual registration (dually registered financial advisor): a dually registered financial advisor (also known as a dual hat advisor) is registered both as a Registered Representative (broker) of their firm brokerage division as well as an Investment Adviser Representative (IAR) of their firm's Registered Investment Adviser (RIA) division.

Dual registration (dually registered financial advisory firm): a dually registered financial advisory firm (also known as a hybrid advisory firm) has two divisions and is registered both as an investment securities brokerage firm and as a Registered Investment Adviser (RIA).

ESG investing: an approach to investing that considers environmental, social, and governance factors alongside financial factors in the investment decision-making process.

Evidence-based investing: an investment philosophy based on the process of systematically reviewing, appraising, and implementing academic research findings to aid the delivery of optimum investment solutions to investors.

Federal Deposit Insurance Corporation (FDIC): an independent agency created by Congress to maintain stability and public confidence in the nation's financial system. The FDIC insures deposits; examines and supervises financial institutions for safety, soundness, and consumer protection; makes large and complex financial institutions resolvable; and manages receiverships.

Fee-based financial advisory firm compensation (see Compensation)

Fee-only financial advisory firm compensation (see Compensation)

Fee schedule: a chart highlighting the fee rates for the financial advisory firm's various services which lets customers know what to expect when working with the firm.

Fees—asset-based financial advisory firm: an asset-based fee is an advisory fee that an investor pays to the financial advisory firm based on a percentage of the investor's assets managed by the financial advisory firm.

Fees—hidden (see Hidden fees)

Fees—hourly rate financial advisory firm fees: a fee-only financial planner may offer to provide either limited or comprehensive financial planning services for an hourly fee (typically in the range of $100 to $300 per hour) for one-time or ongoing financial planning engagements.

Fees—project-based financial advisory firm fees: a fee-only financial planner may offer to provide either limited or comprehensive financial planning services for a project-based fee (typically by estimating the number of hours required for the project) for one-time or ongoing financial planning engagements.

Fees—retainer, flat retainer financial advisory firm fees: a financial planner pricing structure characterized by ongoing fixed retainer fees as the primary (or sole) compensation for the provided advisory services as opposed to a commission-based model, assets-under-management fee, or one-time financial planning fee.

Fi360: a subsidiary company of Broadridge that helps financial intermediaries use prudent fiduciary practices.

Fiduciary: a relationship involving trust, especially with regard to the relationship between a trustee and a beneficiary.

Fiduciary best practices: best practices for fiduciary investment advisors related to a prudent investment decision-making process based on laws and regulations that set minimum expectations for fiduciary investment advisors. Standards-setting bodies that grant professional certifications, such as CFP Board, CFA Institute, AICPA®, and Fi360 promulgate codes of ethics and standards of conduct that may exceed certain legal and company compliance obligations based upon best practices for those with special expertise.

Fiduciary duty: the relationship between a fiduciary and the principal (or beneficiary) on whose behalf the fiduciary acts.

Fiduciary duty of care: the responsibility to inform oneself as completely as possible to exercise sound judgments that protect a beneficiary's interests. The fiduciary duty of due care requires that fiduciaries use that amount of care which ordinarily careful and prudent people would use in similar circumstances and consider all material information reasonably available in making business decisions.

Fiduciary duty of good faith: the responsibility to always act within the law to advance the interests of the beneficiary. At no time should the fiduciary take actions that are outside of legal constraints.

Fiduciary duty of loyalty: the responsibility to always act in the best interest of the beneficiary, putting their well-being first and foremost. It includes the duty of the fiduciary to excuse themselves from taking actions when there's a conflict of interest with the beneficiary's welfare. At the most fundamental level, the duty of loyalty requires fiduciaries to act in the best interests of the beneficiary and to place the interests of the beneficiary ahead of their own interests and the interests of third parties.

Fiduciary duty of prudence: to administer matters and make decisions concerning the interests of beneficiaries with the highest degree of professional skill, caution, and critical awareness of risk.

Fiduciary duty to obey: the responsibility to abide by the legal norms of both the fiduciary entity and external law.

Fiduciary oath: an oath declaring a financial advisor's commitment to adhere to a fiduciary relationship and, in so doing, be accountable for the advice to their clients. Investors have a right to know whether their advisor is acting in their best interests and can request that advisors provide a signed copy of a fiduciary oath every time they enter an advisory relationship with a financial advisor. Investors can and should insist the fiduciary oath be signed by their financial advisor before entering a relationship.

Fiduciary oath—Committee for the Fiduciary Standard: I believe in placing your best interests first. Therefore, I am proud to commit to the following five fiduciary principles: 1. I will always put your best interests first. 2. I will act with prudence; that is, with the skill, care, diligence, and good judgment of a professional. 3. I will not mislead you, and I will provide conspicuous, full, and fair disclosure of all important facts. 4. I will avoid conflicts of interest. 5. I will fully disclose and fairly manage, in your favor, any unavoidable conflicts.*

Fiduciary oath—NAPFA: The advisor shall exercise their best efforts to act in good faith and in the best interests of the client. The advisor shall provide written disclosure to the client prior to the engagement of the advisor, and thereafter throughout the term of the engagement, of any conflicts of interest, which will or reasonably may compromise the impartiality or independence of the advisor.

*** The Committee for the Fiduciary Standard, "Fiduciary Oath: Individual."**

The advisor, or any party in which the advisor has a financial interest, does not receive any compensation or other remuneration that is contingent on any client's purchase or sale of a financial product. The advisor does not receive a fee or other compensation from another party based on the referral of a client or the client's business. Following the NAPFA Fiduciary Oath means I shall: 1. Always act in good faith and with candor. 2. Be proactive in disclosing any conflicts of interest that may impact a client. 3. Not accept any referral fees or compensation contingent upon the purchase or sale of a financial product.*

Fiduciary standard of care: the overriding standard for a fiduciary financial advisor is called the fiduciary standard of care, which requires that a financial advisor act solely in the client's best interest when offering personalized financial advice.

Financial advice: advice, recommendation, guidance, projection, or proposal relating to a financial product or financial service provided by a financial services provider to a person under the applicable establishing legislation provided by any means, irrespective of whether or not such advice, recommendation, guidance, projection, or proposal is sought by the person or whether such advice, recommendation, guidance, projection, or proposal has resulted in a transaction being affected.

Financial advisor: a professional who provides financial services to clients based on their financial situation. In many countries, financial advisors must complete specific training and be registered with a regulatory body to provide advice.

Financial Industry Regulatory Authority (FINRA): a private American corporation that acts as a self-regulatory organization that regulates member brokerage firms and exchange markets.

Financial plan: a document that details a person's current financial circumstances and their short- and long-term monetary goals. It includes strategies to achieve those goals.

Financial planner: a financial advisor that advises their clients on investments, insurance, tax, retirement, and estate planning.

Financial planning: a process that involves looking at a client's entire financial picture and then advising them on how to achieve their short- and long-term financial goals.

Financial Planning Association® (FPA®): the leading membership organization for Certified Financial Planner® professionals and those engaged in the financial planning process.

Form ADV: a form that all professional investment advisors are required to file annually with the Securities and Exchange Commission (SEC). Form ADV is the uniform form used by investment advisors to register with both the SEC

---

* The National Association of Personal Financial Advisors, "Fiduciary Oath."

and state securities authorities. Form ADV consists of two parts, both of which are available to the public on the SEC's Investment Adviser Public Disclosure (IAPD) website.

Form ADV Part 1: a form that all professional investment advisors are required to file annually with the Securities and Exchange Commission (SEC). Form ADV Part 1 requires information about the investment advisor's business, ownership, clients, employees, business practices, affiliations, and any disciplinary events of the advisor or its employees. Part 1 is organized in a check-the-box, fill-in-the-blank format. The SEC reviews the information from this part of the form to manage its regulatory and examination programs.

Form ADV Part 2: a form that all professional investment advisers are required to file annually with the Securities and Exchange Commission (SEC). Form ADV Part 2 requires investment advisers to prepare narrative brochures that include plain English disclosures of the adviser's business practices, fees, conflicts of interest, and disciplinary information. The brochure is the primary disclosure document for investment advisers and must be delivered to advisory clients. Part 2 of Form ADV includes two subparts, Part 2A and Part 2B. Part 2A contains eighteen disclosure items to be included in the investment adviser's brochure. In addition, investment advisers are required to deliver annually to clients a summary of material changes to the brochure along with either a revised brochure or an offer to deliver a copy of the revised brochure. Part 2B is called the "brochure supplement" and includes information about specific individuals acting on behalf of the investment adviser who provide the investment advice and interact with the client.

Foundation for Fiduciary Studies: a now-defunct not-for-profit [501(c)(3)] organization established in September 2000 to develop and advance registered standards for investment fiduciaries, which included trustees, investment committee members, brokers, bankers, investment advisers, and money managers. The registered standards were designed to provide the details of a procedurally prudent process based on existing fiduciary legislation, regulations, regulatory opinion letters and bulletins, and case law. The Foundation was independent of any ties to the investment community and therefore positioned to be a crucible for advancing registered fiduciary standards throughout the industry and to the public. It maintained and updated the standards and practices as changes occurred in legislation, regulation, and industry practices. It contributed to the development of the *Prudent Practices* that were later published by the Center for Fiduciary Studies at Fi360.

Global Fiduciary Standard of Excellence: a series of fiduciary handbooks published by Fi360 as reference guides for knowledgeable investment professionals, stewards, and investors who serve in a fiduciary capacity, also known as "investment fiduciaries." The handbooks assume some experience and familiarity with basic investment management concepts and procedures and are not how-to manuals for beginners.

Hidden fees: extra hidden or undisclosed fees and charges that the consumer may not necessarily be aware of at the time of purchase and often may appear in fine print on a contract. These fees can often be deceptive because they muddy the purchase price for consumers.

Hybrid broker advisors (see Dual registration [dually registered financial advisors])

Independent advice (see Advice)

Institute for the Fiduciary Standard (IFS): a research and education institution—a think tank—whose single purpose is to promote the vital importance of the fiduciary standard in investment and financial advice.

Insurance agent: a person employed to sell insurance policies.

Internal Revenue Service (IRS): the revenue service for the United States federal government, which is responsible for collecting US federal taxes and administering the Internal Revenue Code, the main body of the federal statutory tax law.

Investing: the process of committing money with the expectation of achieving a profit or material result by putting it into financial plans, shares, or property, or by using it to develop a commercial venture.

Investment Adviser Representative (IAR): any of a Registered Investment Adviser (RIA) firm's supervised employees is an Investment Adviser Representative if they have more than five clients and regularly solicit, meet with, or otherwise communicate with the firm's clients.

Investment advisor (IA): the US Securities and Exchange Commission defines an investment advisor as a person or business that receives compensation for providing investment advice or issuing reports on individual securities.

Investment broker: a person or institution who facilitates buying and selling investments, including stocks, bonds, mutual funds, commodities, real estate, and other securities. (*See* Series 7)

Investment consultant: the US Securities and Exchange Commission (SEC) subsumes investment consultants under the term *investment advisers*: "a person that advises as to the selection or retention of an investment manager."*

Investment management: the professional asset management of various securities, including shareholdings, bonds, and other assets, such as real estate, to meet specified investment goals for the benefit of investors.

Investment management consulting: investment advisors who advise their clients (which can include asset owners, fund managers, and trustees) on which funds, asset classes, and countries to invest into as a part of the investment and

---

* The IC Research Institute, "Approach."

asset allocation strategy and portfolio construction process.

Investment manager: a person or company responsible for managing investments on behalf of a financial institution or its clients.

Investment securities license (see Series 7)

NAPFA Code of Ethics: these are the eight ethical requirements for the fee-only financial planners who are members of NAPFA: objectivity, confidentiality, competence, fairness and suitability, integrity and honesty, regulatory compliance, full disclosure, professionalism.

NAPFA-Registered Financial Advisor: fee-only Certified Financial Planners® (CFPs®) who are members of NAPFA and who have also met all necessary requirements of NAPFA membership have earned the right to call themselves NAPFA-Registered Financial Advisors. This prestigious title is recognized by those in the field and in the media as identifying those who are professional, ethical financial advisors.

National Association of Personal Financial Advisors (NAPFA): a professional trade association for fee-only financial planners. For more than forty years, NAPFA has been the standard bearer for fee-only, fiduciary financial advisors advocating for high professional and ethical standards. Working in a strict fee-only fiduciary capacity, NAPFA-affiliated financial planners are committed to maintaining the highest level of competency with a client-centered focus that means aligning solely with their client's interests.

Non-discretionary investment management: a firm has non-discretionary authority (or manages assets on a non-discretionary basis) if it *does not* have the authority to decide which securities to purchase and sell for the client and instead needs to ask the client for decisions on every transaction to buy or sell individual securities and/or to hire and fire investment managers.

North American Securities Administrators Association (NASAA): an association of state securities administrators who are charged with the responsibility to protect consumers who purchase securities or investment advice. Founded in Kansas in 1919, it is the oldest international investor protection organization.

Objective advice (see Advice)

Personal Financial Specialist (PFS™): a certification for Certified Public Accountants (CPAs) that allows them to expand their expertise and offerings to include financial planning and wealth management. The American Institute of Certified Public Accountants® (AICPA®) established the PFS™ credential, which is reserved for CPAs, meaning holding a CPA is a prerequisite.

Ponzi scheme: a fraudulent investing scam promising high rates of return with little risk to investors. A Ponzi scheme is a fraudulent investing scam which generates returns for earlier investors with money taken from later investors.

This is similar to a pyramid scheme in that both are based on using new investors' funds to pay the earlier backers. Both Ponzi schemes and pyramid schemes eventually bottom out when the flood of new investors dries up and there isn't enough money to go around. At that point, the schemes unravel.

Process of elimination: a logical method to identify an entity of interest among several ones by excluding all other entities. In educational testing, it is a process of deleting options whereby the possibility of an option being correct is close to zero or significantly lower compared to other options. In selecting a financial advisor, if you want to work with a financial advisor that acknowledges a fiduciary relationship, you will delete any of the possible options where there is any chance that the financial advisor will not be operating with a fiduciary standard of care.

Profession: a disciplined group of individuals, professionals, who adhere to ethical standards and who hold themselves out as and are accepted by the public as possessing special knowledge and skills in a widely recognized body of learning derived from research, education, and training at a high level, and who are prepared to apply this knowledge and exercise these skills in the interest of others.

Professional: a member of a profession or any person who works in a specified professional activity. The term also describes the standards of education and training that prepare members of the profession with the particular knowledge and skills necessary to perform their specific role within that profession. In addition, most professionals are subject to strict codes of conduct, enshrining rigorous ethical and moral obligations.

***Prudent Practices*:** a handbook officially published by Fi360 in 2003, the *Prudent Practices* comprise a step-by-step process that ensures a fiduciary investment strategy is properly developed, implemented, and monitored according to both legal and ethical obligations.

***Prudent Practices for Investment Advisors*:** this publication is part of a series of fiduciary handbooks published by Fi360 to define the Global Fiduciary Standard of Excellence. The handbooks are reference guides for knowledgeable investment professionals, stewards, and investors who serve in a fiduciary capacity, also known as "investment fiduciaries." The handbooks are not how-to manuals for beginners. They assume some experience and familiarity with basic investment management concepts and procedures. This handbook was published in 2019 to provide a reference guide of fiduciary practices for professionals who provide investment advice, including wealth managers, financial advisors, trust officers, investment consultants, financial consultants, financial planners, and fiduciary advisors.

Registered Investment Adviser (RIA): a firm that is an investment adviser in the United States, registered as such with the Securities and Exchange Commission or a state's securities agency.

Registered representative (RR): a person who works for a client-facing financial firm such as a brokerage company and serves as a representative for clients who are trading investment products and securities. Registered representatives may be employed as brokers, financial advisors, or portfolio managers. Registered representatives must pass licensing tests and are regulated by the Financial Industry Regulatory Authority (FINRA) and the Securities and Exchange Commission (SEC). RRs must furthermore adhere to the suitability standard. An investment must meet the suitability requirements prior to being recommended by a firm to an investor. The following question must be answered affirmatively: "Is this investment appropriate for my client?" In addition, on June 5, 2019, the Securities and Exchange Commission adopted a package of rulemakings and interpretations designed to enhance the quality and transparency of retail investors' relationships with investment advisers and broker-dealers, bringing the legal requirements and mandated disclosures in line with reasonable investor expectations, while preserving access (in terms of choice and cost) to a variety of investment services and products. Specifically, these actions include new Regulation Best Interest, the new Form CRS, and two separate interpretations under the Investment Advisers Act of 1940. Individually and collectively, these actions are designed to enhance and clarify the standards of conduct applicable to broker-dealers and investment advisers, help retail investors better understand and compare the services offered and make an informed choice of the relationship best suited to their needs and circumstances, and foster greater consistency in the level of protections provided by each regime, particularly at the point in time that a recommendation is made.

Securities and Exchange Commission (SEC): an independent agency of the United States federal government, created in the aftermath of the Wall Street Crash of 1929. The primary purpose of the SEC is to enforce the law against market manipulation.

Securities broker: individuals who advise customers who want to make financial investments. Securities brokers supply institutional and individual clients with pertinent facts to assist them in buying or selling stocks, bonds, commodities, and options. They may develop or maintain a diversified selection of securities known as a portfolio. Securities brokers are also called securities, commodities, and financial services sales agents. (*See* Series 6 and Series 7)

Series 6 Investment Company and Variable Contracts Products Representative Examination: financial advisors are required to pass this exam to be licensed to buy and sell investment and insurance products, including mutual funds, variable annuities, variable life insurance, municipal fund securities, and unit investment trusts. Investment advisors and private bankers may also take this exam. Series 6 is administered by the Financial Industry Regulatory Authority (FINRA), a government nonprofit organization that deals with the oversight of broker-dealers in the US.

Series 7 General Securities Representative Examination: financial advisors are required to pass this exam to be registered and licensed to buy and sell a large variety of investment and insurance products. This license gives the financial advisor permission to sell almost any type of security—including public and private stocks and bonds, mutual funds, money market funds, ETFs, UITs, real estate investment trusts (REITs), hedge funds, government securities, direct participation programs (DPPs), options on mortgage-backed securities, venture capital, rights, warrants, repos, and certificates of accrual on government securities and municipal securities. This series is best for stockbrokers, some financial planners, and advisors as well as some insurance agents. Series 7 is administered by the Financial Industry Regulatory Authority (FINRA), a government nonprofit organization that deals with the oversight of broker-dealers in the US.

Series 63 Uniform Securities State Law Examination: financial advisors are required to pass this state law test for broker-dealer representatives. The exam is a North American Securities Administrators Association (NASAA) exam administered by FINRA.

Series 65 NASAA Investment Advisers Law Examination: financial advisors are required to pass this exam to become registered as an Investment Adviser Representative of a Registered Investment Adviser (RIA) firm. The exam is a North American Securities Administrators Association (NASAA) exam administered by FINRA.

Series 66 Uniform Combined State Law Examination: this exam qualifies an individual as if they had passed both the Series 63 and Series 65. However, to register as an Investment Adviser Representative based on the Series 66, an individual must also have passed the FINRA Series 7 exam and the exam must be valid (i.e., not expired).

Socially responsible investing (SRI): an investment discipline that considers environmental, social, and corporate governance criteria to generate long-term competitive financial returns and positive societal impact.

Stockbroker (see both Investment Broker and Series 7)

Sustainable Investment Forum, the (US SIF): the US membership association for professionals, firms, institutions, and organizations engaged in sustainable and responsible investing. US SIF and its members advance investment practices that consider environmental, social, and corporate governance criteria to generate long-term competitive financial returns and positive societal impact.

Trust: assured reliance on the character, ability, strength, or truth of someone.

Wall Street: an eight-block-long street in the Financial District of Lower Manhattan in New York City. It runs between Broadway in the west to South Street and the East River in the east. The term "Wall Street" has become a metonym for the financial markets of the United States as a whole, the American financial services industry, New York–based financial interests, or the Financial District itself. Anchored by Wall Street, New York has been described as the world's principal financial and fintech center.

Wealth advisor: financial advisors who provide both financial planning and investment management services to individual investors. Many wealth advisors also provide tax planning and estate planning services that benefit individual investors. (*See* Wealth manager)

Wealth management (WM): a financial advisory service that provides a combination of both investment management and financial planning services to help individual investors manage and protect their wealth from market volatility. It is a discipline which incorporates structuring and planning wealth to assist in growing, preserving, and protecting wealth, whilst passing it on to the family in a tax-efficient manner and in accordance with their wishes. Wealth management brings together investment planning, investment management, tax planning, wealth protection, estate planning, succession planning, and family governance.

Wealth manager: financial advisors who offer a combination of both investment management and financial planning services to help individual investors to manage and protect their wealth from market volatility. (*See* Wealth advisor)

Wirehouse brokerage firm: a wirehouse investment securities brokerage firm is a term used to describe a full-service investment broker-dealer firm and can be a full-service investment broker-dealer firm of any size. Modern-day wirehouses range from small regional brokerage firms to large institutions with global footprints. The term *wirehouse* recalls a period in which investment broker-dealer firm offices were connected by private telephone or telegraph lines so that all branches would have immediate access to the same financial market information as one another. Although virtually every financial institution has moved beyond these "wires" in daily practice, the term remains one used to describe these institutions today.

Sources: Merriam-Webster, Cambridge Dictionary, The Free Dictionary, Legal Dictionary, Securities and Exchange Commission, Financial Industry Regulatory Authority (FINRA), North American Securities Administrators Association (NASAA), Internal Revenue Service, Investopedia, Wikipedia, National Association of Personal Financial Advisors, Nerd Wallet, Fi360, Centre for Fiduciary Excellence (CEFEX), Institute for the Fiduciary Standard, Committee for the Fiduciary Standard, *Prudent Practices for Investment Advisors*, etc.

Acronyms

This is a list of some common acronyms that you will encounter when learning about financial advice and financial advisors.

ADV—Form ADV that all Registered Investment Advisers are required to file annually with the SEC

AICPA—American Institute of Certified Public Accountants® (AICPA®)

AIF—Accredited Investment Fiduciary® (AIF®)

AIFA—Accredited Investment Fiduciary Analyst® (AIFA®)

AUM—Assets under management

CEFEX—Center for Fiduciary Excellence (CEFEX)

CFA—Chartered Financial Analyst® (CFA®)

CFP—Certified Financial Planner® (CFP®)

ChFC—Chartered Financial Consultant® (ChFC®)

CIMA—Certified Investment Management Analyst® (CIMA®)

CLU—Chartered Life Underwriter® (CLU®)

CPA—Certified Public Accountant

CRS—Customer Relationship Summary (Form CRS) which is a mandatory written disclosure

DFA—Dimensional Fund Advisors

DIY—Do It Yourself

ESG—Environmental, Social, and Governance

FDIC—Federal Deposit Insurance Corporation

Fi360—a Broadridge company that helps financial intermediaries use prudent fiduciary practices

FINRA—Financial Industry Regulatory Authority

FPA—Financial Planning Association® (FPA®)

IA—Investment Advisor

IAR—Investment Adviser Representative (IAR)

IFS—Institute for the Fiduciary Standard

IPO—Initial Public Offering

IRA—Individual Retirement Account

IRS—Internal Revenue Service

NAPFA—National Association of Personal Financial Advisors

NASAA—North American Securities Administrators Association

PFS—Personal Financial Specialist (PFS™)

REIT—Real Estate Investment Trust

RIA—Registered Investment Adviser

RR—Registered Representative

SEC—Securities and Exchange Commission

SRI—Socially Responsible Investing

US SIF—The Sustainable Investment Forum

WM—Wealth Management

Bibliography

Adamczyk, Alicia. "This Is When People Start Saving for Retirement—And When They Actually Should." *CNBC*. September 4, 2019. https://www.cnbc.com/2019/09/04/the-age-when-americans-start-saving-for-retirement.html.

Allison, Dan. Interview by author. August 15, 2023.

Allodium Investment Consultants. "Allodium Name." *Allodium Investment Consultants*. 2018. https://www.allodium.com/images/pdf/Allodium-Name-Description-and-Meaning.pdf.

Allodium Investment Consultants. "Manager Screening: Investment Process." *Allodium Investment Consultants*. 2018. https://www.allodium.com/images/pdf/Allodium-Investment-Process-Manager-Screening.pdf.

American Bankers Association. "Americans Trust Banks Most to Keep Their Information Safe." *American Bankers Association*. October 29, 2020. https://www.aba.com/news-research/analysis-guides/americans-trust-banks-most.

Atkinson, Steve. Interview by author. August 10, 2023.

Backman, Maurie. "Most Americans Don't Trust Their Financial Advisors. Should They?" *Motley Fool*. July 11, 2017. https://www.fool.com/retirement/2017/07/11/most-americans-dont-trust-their-financial-advisors.aspx.

Better Markets. "Special Report: Wall Street's Crime Spree 1998–2020: 395 Major Legal Actions and $195+ Billion in Fines and Settlements Over the Last 20 Years." *Better Markets*. January 13, 2021. https://img1.wsimg.com/blobby/go/c5ca56b0-518d-4372-b123-d655e524002c/downloads/2021%20Better%20Markets%20report%20-%20Wall%20Street%20Crime.pdf?ver=1686183418755.

Bloomenthal, Andrew. "Warren Buffett's Investing Strategy: An Inside Look." *Investopedia*. December 26, 2022. https://www.investopedia.com/investing/warren-buffetts-investing-style-reviewed/.

Booth, David. "Trust the Financial Advisor Who Trusts the Market." *Dimensional Fund Advisors*. October 28, 2022. https://www.dimensional.com/us-en/insights/trust-the-financial-advisor-who-trusts-the-market.

Boyson, Nicole M. "The Worst of Both Worlds? Dual-Registered Investment Advisers." *Northeastern University, D'Amore-McKim School of Business*. May 3, 2019. https://papers.ssrn.com/sol3/papers.cfm?abstract_id=3360537.

Bradshaw Law Group. "Duty of Care and Duty of Loyalty Owed by Directors in Delaware." *Corporate Securities Legal, LLP.* June 10, 2015. https://bradshawlawgroup.com/duty-of-care-and-duty-of-loyalty-owed-by-directors-in-delaware/.

Brodie, Herman. Interview by author. August 7, 2022.

Brodie, Herman, and Klaus Harnack. *The Trust Mandate: The Behavioral Science Behind How Asset Managers* Really *Win and Keep Clients*. Hampshire, Great Britain: Harriman House, 2018.

Brown, Geoffrey. Interview by author. May 24, 2022.

Browning, Lynnley. "Advisors Have a Serious Trust Problem with Consumers, Research Shows. Here's Why and What to Do." *FinancialPlanning.com*. May 25, 2021. https://www.financial-planning.com/news/amid-rise-of-digital-finance-americans-lack-trust-in-investment-advisors-morning-consult-research-shows.

Business Wire. "Webster Bank Explores Current State of Financial Inclusion with Its Inaugural Financial Empowerment Study." *Business Wire*. October 16, 2023. https://www.businesswire.com/news/home/20231015982107/en/Webster-Bank-Explores-Current-State-of-Financial-Inclusion-with-its-Inaugural-Financial-Empowerment-Study.

Butler, Dave. Interview by author. August 30, 2023.

CEFEX. "How Clients Benefit from Their Advisor's CEFEX Certification." *Centre for Fiduciary Excellence, LLC (CEFEX)*. 2014. https://www.allodium.com/images/pdf/benefits-to-cefex-advisor-clients.pdf.

CFP Board. "10 Questions to Ask Your Financial Advisor." *Certified Financial Planner Board of Standards, Inc. (CFP Board)*. Accessed May 2023. https://www.letsmakeaplan.org/how-to-choose-a-planner/10-questions-to-ask-your-financial-advisor.

CFP Board. "CFP® Certification 2021 Principal Knowledge Topics." *Certified Financial Planner Board of Standards, Inc. (CFP Board)*. March 2021. https://www.cfp.net/-/media/files/cfp-board/cfp-certification/2021-practice-analysis/2021-principal-knowledge-topics.pdf.

CFP Board. "Personal Financial Planning: A Guide to Starting Your Personal Financial Plan." *Certified Financial Planner Board of Standards, Inc. (CFP Board)*. 2014. https://www.allodium.com/images/pdf/CFP_Board_Consumer_Guide_to_Financial_Planning.pdf.

Chapman, Tyler. Interview by author. March 12, 2023.

Committee for the Fiduciary Standard. "Committee Names Kathleen M. McBride Chairman." February 9, 2015. *The Committee for the Fiduciary Standard.* http://www.thefiduciarystandard.org/.

Committee for the Fiduciary Standard. "Fiduciary Oath: Individual." *The Committee for the Fiduciary Standard.* Accessed September 2022. http://www.thefiduciarystandard.org/wp-content/uploads/2015/02/fiduciaryoath_individual.pdf.

Consumer Federation of America. "A Framework for Addressing Broker-Dealer and Investment Adviser Conflicts of Interest When Providing Retail Investment Advice." *Consumer Federation of America (CFA).* Accessed April 2022. https://consumerfed.org/wp-content/uploads/2019/04/CFA-Conflict-of-Interest-Framework.pdf.

Contreras, Oscar, and Joseph Bendix. "Financial Literacy in the United States." *Milken Institute.* 2021. https://milkeninstitute.org/sites/default/files/2021-08/Financial%20Literacy%20in%20the%20United%20States.pdf.

Cook, Wendy. Interview by author. November 14, 2022.

Cook, Wendy. "Who Is 'the Media'?" *Wendy J. Cook Communications.* April 27, 2023.

Corbin, Kenneth. "Yikes! Clients Still Don't Trust Their Advisors, CFA Institute Finds." *FinancialPlanning.com.* April 6, 2018. https://www.financial-planning.com/news/financial-advisors-face-high-levels-of-mistrust-from-their-clients-cfa-institute-finds.

Corkery, Michael. "Wells Fargo Fined $185 Million for Fraudulently Opening Accounts." *New York Times.* September 8, 2016. https://www.nytimes.com/2016/09/09/business/dealbook/wells-fargo-fined-for-years-of-harm-to-customers.html.

Data USA. "Personal Financial Advisors." *Data USA.* Accessed March 2022. https://datausa.io/profile/soc/personal-financial-advisors.

Davis, Chris, and Sam Taube. "Robinhood Review 2023: Pros, Cons and How It Compares." *Nerdwallet.* February 14, 2023. https://www.nerdwallet.com/reviews/investing/brokers/robinhood.

Ellwood Associates. "Ellwood Viewpoint: Why We Think Independence Matters." May 12, 2019. https://cdn2.hubspot.net/hubfs/5191015/Ellwood_March2019_Theme/PDF/Why%20We%20Think%20Independence%20Matters_May2019_FINAL.pdf.

Ely, Guerdon. Interview by author. March 28, 2022.

FeeOnlyNetwork. "FeeOnlyNetwork.com is Different by Design." Accessed September 30, 2024. https://www.feeonlynetwork.com/about-fee-only-network.

Fi360. "What We Do." Accessed 2022. https://www.fi360.com/what-we-do.

Financial Industry Regulatory Authority. "FINRA Rule 2111 (Suitability) FAQ."

Financial Industry Regulatory Authority (FINRA). Accessed April 2022. https://www.finra.org/rules-guidance/key-topics/suitability/faq.

Financial Planning Association. "Choosing a CFP® Professional: Questions to Ask." *Financial Planning Association (FPA)*. Accessed August 2022. https://www.allodium.com/images/pdf/FPA_on_Choosing_a_CFP.pdf.

Fischer, Michael S. "The 10 Most-Fined Financial Services Firms." *Think Advisor*. March 9, 2021. https://www.thinkadvisor.com/2021/03/09/the-10-most-fined-financial-services-firms/.

The Free Dictionary by Farlex. S.v. "Fiduciary." Accessed September 2022. https://legal-dictionary.thefreedictionary.com/Fiduciary.

Ganti, Akhilesh. "Wealth Management: What It Is and What Wealth Managers Charge." *Investopedia*. July 9, 2022. https://www.investopedia.com/terms/w/wealthmanagement.asp.

Geddes, Patrick. Interview by author. July 5, 2022.

Godin, Seth. "Good Advice . . ." *Seth's Blog*. May 15, 2014. https://seths.blog/2014/05/good-advice/.

Good Jobs First. "The $160 Billion Bank Fee: What Violation Tracker 2.0 Shows about Penalties Imposed on Major Financial Offenders." June 2016. https://www.goodjobsfirst.org/wp-content/uploads/docs/pdf/160billionbankfee.pdf.

Hamburger, Brian. Interview by author. August 9, 2023.

Hannah, Colonel (Ret.) Sean. "Toward a Noble Profession." *Thayer Leadership*. January 1, 2017. https://www.thayerleadership.com/blog/2017/toward-a-noble-profession.

Henriques, Allan. Interview by author. June 1, 2022.

Horsager, David. "Trusted Leader: 8 Pillars that Drive Results." https://davidhorsager.com/speaking/.

Hutchens, Eric. Interview by author. December 2022.

Iacurci, Greg. "Here's How Investors Can Spot the Next Bernie Madoff." *CNBC*. April 15, 2021. https://www.cnbc.com/2021/04/15/heres-how-investors-can-spot-the-next-bernie-madoff.html.

The IC Research Institute. "Approach." Accessed September 30, 2024. https://www.ic-research.com/research-approach-on-investment-consulting.

Investec Wealth & Investment. "What Is Wealth Management?" *Investec Wealth & Investment* [now part of Rathbones Group Plc]. Accessed January 2022. https://www.investec.com/en_gb/wealth/private-clients/wealth-management-services/what-is-wealth-management.html.

InvestmentNews. "Ever Hear of a 'Lay Fiduciary'? There Are 17.5 Million of Them." *InvestmentNews*. June 16, 2021. https://www.investmentnews.com/ever-hear-of-a-lay-fiduciary-there-are-17-5-million-of-them-207802.

Jaffe, Chuck. *Getting Started in Finding a Financial Advisor.* New York: Wiley, 2010.

Kagan, Julia. "Investment Advisers Act of 1940: Definition, Overview." *Investopedia*. October 28, 2021. https://www.investopedia.com/terms/i/investadvact.asp.

Kitces, Michael. "Financial Adviser Vs Advisor—What's the Difference?" *Kitces.com*. August 18, 2016. https://www.kitces.com/blog/financial-adviser-vs-advisor-vs-financial-planner-whats-the-difference/.

Kitces, Michael. Interview by author. July 24, 2023.

Krueger, Pam. Interview by author. August 7, 2023.

Lemke, Tim. "What Is Wealth Management?" *The Balance*. June 8, 2022. https://www.thebalancemoney.com/wealth-management-4772460.

Loveland, Keith. Interview by author. August 16, 2023.

Lynch, Richard. Interview by author. July 20, 2022.

Martin, Asia. "Advisors Rank Almost as Low as Mechanics on Trustworthiness." *WealthManagement.com*. May 7, 2020. https://www.wealthmanagement.com/industry/advisors-rank-almost-low-mechanics-trustworthiness.

McBride, Kate. "Did You Know That There's More Than One Type of Fiduciary?" *Fiduciary Path*. March 2022. https://fiduciarypath.com/did-you-know-that-theres-more-than-one-type-of-fiduciary/.

McBride, Kate. Interview by author. March 29, 2022.

McBride, Kate. Interview by author. September 6, 2022.

McNair, Kamaron. "Survey: Consumers Trust Banks More Than the Federal Government." *DepositAccounts.com*. July 6, 2021. https://www.depositaccounts.com/blog/consumers-trust-bank-more-than-federal-government.html.

Merriam-Webster. S.v. "Fiduciary." Accessed September 2022. https://www.merriam-webster.com/dictionary/fiduciary.

Minnesota Legislature. *Notice of Breach of Fiduciary Duty*. 336.3-307, c 565, s 35. MS 1992. https://www.revisor.mn.gov/statutes/cite/336.3-307.

Mitchell, Aaron, and Deborah Korenstein. "Drug Companies' Payments and Gifts Affect Physicians' Prescribing. It's Time to Turn Off the Spigot." *STAT News*. December 4, 2020. https://www.statnews.com/2020/12/04/drug-companies-payments-gifts-affect-physician-prescribing/.

Morse, Gardiner. "Decisions and Desire." *Harvard Business Review*. January 2006. https://hbr.org/2006/01/decisions-and-desire.

The National Association of Personal Financial Advisors. "About Us." *The National Association of Personal Financial Advisors (NAPFA)*. Accessed March 2022. https://www.napfa.org/about-us.

The National Association of Personal Financial Advisors. "Our Standards." *The National Association of Personal Financial Advisors (NAPFA)*. Accessed May 2022. https://www.napfa.org/membership/our-standards.

The National Association of Personal Financial Advisors. "Fiduciary Oath." *The National Association of Personal Financial Advisors (NAPFA)*. Accessed September 2022. https://www.napfa.org/mission-and-fiduciary-oath.

Panksep, Carlos. Interview by author. July 6, 2022.

Peters, Katelyn. "Everything You Need to Know about the DOL Fiduciary Rule." *Investopedia*. September 30, 2022. https://www.investopedia.com/updates/dol-fiduciary-rule/.

Pillai, Marie. Interview by author. March 28, 2022.

Powell, Robin. "Robin Powell: The Voice with Nothing to Sell Is Hardest to Hear." *Money Marketing*. July 10, 2023. https://www.moneymarketing.co.uk/opinion/robin-powell-the-voice-with-nothing-to-sell-is-hardest-to-hear.

Prince, Russ Alan. "What Is Wealth Management?" *Forbes*. May 16, 2014. https://www.forbes.com/sites/russalanprince/2014/05/16/what-is-wealth-management/.

Psychology Today. "Intuition." *Psychology Today*. Accessed November 2022. https://www.psychologytoday.com/us/basics/intuition.

Simon, W. Scott. "Why I'm a Fiduciary." *Morningstar*. October 3, 2013. https://fiduciary-experts.com/why-im-a-fiduciary-2/.

Slider, Allan. Interview by author. August 30, 2023.

SmartAsset. "Find a Financial Planner." *SmartAsset*. Accessed December 2023. https://smartasset.com/retirement/find-a-financial-planner.

Solin, Daniel. *Does Your Broker Owe You Money?* 2nd ed. Bonita Sprints, FL: Silver Cloud, 2004.

Statista Research Department. "Share of Americans Who Work with a Financial Advisor in 2022." *Statista*. September 8, 2022. https://www.statista.com/statistics/1176393/financial-advisor-usa/.

Steele Capital Management. "Home Page." *Steele Capital Management*. Accessed September 2022. https://www.steelecapital.com/.

Stotz, Andrew. "ISMS 27: Larry Swedroe—Familiar Doesn't Make It Safe and You're Not Playing with the House's Money." *MyWorstInvestmentEver.com*.

July 25, 2023. https://myworstinvestmentever.com/isms-27-larry-swedroe-familiar-doesnt-make-it-safe-and-youre-not-playing-with-the-houses-money/.

Swedroe, Larry. "How to Find an Advisor You Can Trust." *Buckingham Strategic Wealth.* Accessed November 2022. https://buckinghamstrategicwealth.com/resources/family-life-transitions/how-to-find-an-advisor-you-can-trust.

Thinkbox. "Introduction to TV Sponsorship." *Thinkbox.* July 14, 2023. https://www.thinkbox.tv/how-to-use-tv/sponsorship-and-content/tv-sponsorship/introduction-to-tv-sponsorship/.

Thorp, Brian. Interview by author. August 12, 2023.

Tretina, Kat. "Best Retirement Plans of 2023." *Forbes.* September 2023. https://www.forbes.com/advisor/retirement/best-retirement-plans/.

Tun, Zaw Thiha. "Investment Adviser vs. Broker: What's the Difference?" *Investopedia.* August 29, 2021. https://www.investopedia.com/articles/investing/071515/investment-advisor-versus-broker-how-they-compare.asp.

US Department of Justice: Office of Public Affairs. "BNP Paribas Agrees to Plead Guilty and to Pay $8.9 Billion for Illegally Processing Financial Transactions for Countries Subject to U.S. Economic Sanctions." *US Department of Justice: Office of Public Affairs.* June 30, 2014. https://www.justice.gov/opa/pr/bnp-paribas-agrees-plead-guilty-and-pay-89-billion-illegally-processing-financial.

US Department of Justice: Office of Public Affairs. "Credit Suisse Agrees to Pay $5.28 Billion in Connection with Its Sale of Residential Mortgage-Backed Securities." *US Department of Justice: Office of Public Affairs.* January 18, 2017. https://www.justice.gov/opa/pr/credit-suisse-agrees-pay-528-billion-connection-its-sale-residential-mortgage-backed.

US Department of Justice: Office of Public Affairs. "JPMorgan Chase & Co. Agrees to Pay $920 Million in Connection with Schemes to Defraud Precious Metals and U.S. Treasuries Markets." *US Department of Justice: Office of Public Affairs.* September 29, 2020. https://www.justice.gov/opa/pr/jpmorgan-chase-co-agrees-pay-920-million-connection-schemes-defraud-precious-metals-and-us.

US Securities and Exchange Commission. "Updated Investor Alert: Social Media and Investing—Stock Rumors." *US Securities and Exchange Commission (SEC).* November 5, 2015. https://www.sec.gov/oiea/investor-alerts-bulletins/ia-rumors.

Velasquez, Francisco. "Americans Are Changing Who They Turn to for Financial Advice." *CNBC.* August 28, 2021. https://www.cnbc.com/2021/08/28/americans-are-changing-who-they-turn-to-for-financial-advice.html.

Veres, Bob. Interview by author. June 2, 2022.

Watkins III, James W. "Battle of the Best Interests: Why the Financial Services Industry Opposes a True Fiduciary Standard and Genuine Investor Protection." *CommonSense InvestSense.* June 12, 2023. https://investsense.wordpress.com/.

Watkins III, James W. Interview by author. April 15, 2022.

List of Contributors

We are thankful for the generous contributions of a long list of financial experts who helped us in the development of this book. We appreciate their time and talent in helping the individual investor to find better financial advice. I appreciate all the contributions from this group of experts; any errors in the book are solely my responsibility, as the author.

The following individuals contributed quotations and insights to this book, through either online interviews or written correspondence:

Allison, Dan (Afterword)

Atkinson, Steve (Chapters 2, 19)

Brodie, Herman (Chapter 38)

Brown, Geoffrey (Chapters 14, 15)

Butler, Dave (Chapter 17)

Chapman, Tyler (Chapter 30)

Cook, Wendy (Chapters 7, 23, 31)

Ely, Guerdon (Chapter 21)

Geddes, Patrick (Chapters 3, 16)

Hamburger, Brian (Chapter 8)

Henriques, Allan (Chapters 20, 21)

Hutchens, Eric (Chapter 26)

Kitces, Michael (Chapters 5, 19)

Krueger, Pam (Chapters 5, 9, 27)

Loveland, Keith (Chapter 37)

Lynch, Rich (Chapter 18)

McBride, Kate (Chapters 20, 21, 22)

Panksep, Carlos (Chapters 18, 20)

Pillai, Marie (Chapter 20)

Simon, W. Scott (Chapter 22)

Slider, Allan (Foreword, Chapters 14, 27)

Swedroe, Larry (Chapters 6, 23)

Thorp, Brian (Chapters 5, 19)

Veres, Bob (Chapter 7)

Watkins, James (Chapters 20, 21)

Index

U

V

W

X

Acknowledgments

For their support and encouragement, I would like to thank all the members of the team at Allodium Investment Consultants for their encouragement as I worked on this project.

Allodium also was kind to allow me to share insightful Allodium educational materials to help explain the importance of objective financial advice, the value provided by a professionally trained financial advisor, the importance of comprehensive financial planning, and many other concepts that enlighten the consumer with financial advice and help the individual investor to find objective financial advisors.

While researching the book, we interviewed national experts to gain their perspectives on the various topics we addressed in the development of the text. We really appreciate their contributions and thank them for sharing their time and expertise. All the individuals we quoted in the book have been listed in the List of Contributors at the end of this book.

Many thanks to Kate Leibfried at Click Clack Writing, who was able to extract my thoughts on this arcane subject and put them into readable sentences to help the reader to understand the obscure concepts that encompass the world of financial advice. Her organizational skills, willingness to listen, patience, attention to detail, and masterful editing skills were incredibly helpful in completing this book.

Kudos to Michael Boorman at Wisdom Made Easy for providing the creative visuals to bring the text to life. A picture is worth a thousand words.

My appreciation to my Wise Ink team, who helped me to get this book published: Dara Beevas, Lindsay Bohls, Caitlin Fultz, Kellie

Hultgren, Hanna Kjeldjerg, Emily Mahon, Zenyse Miller, Shannon Plunkett, Crown Shepherd, and Vivian Steckline.

I appreciate all the help I have received over the years from the small group of passionate investor advocates who are shining light on the benefits of fee-only financial advice and the companion fiduciary standard of care. You all know who you are, and rest assured you are all helping to make the world a better place.

And a special thank-you to my wife Kay, the love of my life, for allowing me the large amount of free time that I needed to pursue writing this book.

About the Author

David Bromelkamp is the founder of Allodium Investment Consultants, an independent, fee-only Registered Investment Adviser (RIA) firm in Minneapolis, Minnesota which oversees hundreds of millions in investment portfolio assets. Allodium is the first ever Minneapolis-based firm to earn the esteemed CEFEX certification, which demonstrates fiduciary excellence for a firm based on a fiduciary best practice standard. Bromelkamp is an Accredited Investment Fiduciary® (AIF®) with over forty years of real-world financial experience. His career in finance has included working in his early years as a Certified Public Accountant (CPA) for various public accounting firms, in his middle years at a New York Stock Exchange–member investment securities brokerage firm, and more recently owning and managing a NAPFA-member, fee-only financial planning firm. Bromelkamp is a member of the National Association of Personal Financial Advisors (NAPFA) and has been a member of the Minnesota Society of Certified Public Accountants (MNCPA) for almost four decades.

After serving investors as a financial advisor for more than thirty years, Bromelkamp established AdvisorSmart® in 2018 with a mission to educate investors to find better, more objective financial advice. As an investor advocate organization, AdvisorSmart® aims to help millions of individuals gain a better understanding of today's financial advisory industry so they can seek and hire a trustworthy financial advisor.

David Bromelkamp is a public speaker and speaks frequently to professional trade associations on the best practices of fiduciary investment management. He has taught continuing professional education courses on fiduciary investment management for the Minnesota Society of Certified Public Accountants (MNCPA) and the Minnesota State Bar Association (MSBA). Additionally, Bromelkamp has taught graduate courses as an adjunct instructor in finance at the Opus College of Business at the University of St. Thomas in St. Paul, Minnesota.

David has served as a director on the nonprofit boards of both the Minnesota Society of Certified Public Accountants and Catholic Charities of St. Paul & Minneapolis. He is currently a member of the Planned Giving Committee at Saint John's University in Collegeville, Minnesota.

To book David Bromelkamp for a speaking engagement, or to learn more about the AdvisorSmart® book, visit AdvisorSmartBook.com.

Scan this QR code with your phone to access the AdvisorSmartBook.com website to find more information about the book

AdvisorSmart® Discussion Group Questions

"Asking questions is the first way to begin change."
—Kubra Sait

AdvisorSmart® is an investor advocate focused on improving financial literacy for investors related to the selection of financial advisors. Our vision is to help millions of investors to get better financial advice. Asking good questions is often the start of any important change. We envision a better world for investors in the future by having all of us learn to ask better questions.

If you want to learn, you should never feel dumb asking questions. We learn more by asking good questions than by not asking them. As you finish this book, we challenge you to discuss the book with your groups to continue the learning. Your groups might include book clubs, investment clubs, schools, libraries, professional trade associations, nonprofit organizations, consumer advocacy organizations, investor advocacy organizations, journalists, regulators, politicians, and any other groups focused on improving financial literacy.

These discussion group questions are provided to help you lead a group discussion about some of the ideas presented in this book:

1. **Investor Confusion:** Why are individual investors so confused about the different types of financial advisors?

2. **Investor Hurdles:** What are the biggest impediments to objective financial advice for the average investor?

3. **Fiduciary Advice:** Why should the government require a fiduciary standard of care to be provided to individual investors by all financial advisors?

4. **Dual Registration:** How (and why) did the government regulators allow financial firms to be dually registered as both investment advisors and brokers?

5. **Characteristics of Good Advice:** What are some of the most important characteristics of quality financial advice to look for when selecting a financial advisor?

6. **Free Financial Advice:** What are some examples of free financial advice in your life, and how has this advice helped or hurt you?

7. **Biased Financial Advice:** Why do you feel that objective financial advice is an important characteristic for the individual investor?

8. **Avoiding Bad Financial Advice:** What are some of the things that you can do as an individual investor to avoid being taken advantage of by a financial advisor?

9. **Better Financial Advice:** What are some of the specific things that we can do to improve the quality of financial advice that our investors get from financial advisors?

10. **Trust:** Why do some investors distrust financial advisors?

11. **Helping Your Family Members:** What advice would you give your family members about the process of selecting a financial advisor?

12. **Fee-Only Financial Advisors:** What are the pros and cons of working with an independent fee-only fiduciary financial advisor?

13. **Conflicts of Interest:** What are the potential conflicts of interest with the consumer that are present when a brokerage firm owns a Registered Investment Adviser firm?

14. **Brokerage Firm Management:** What do the senior managers of an investment securities brokerage firm think about the conflicts of interest inherent in the fee-based compensation model?

15. **Regulation:** If the average investor is confused about the various job titles used by financial advisors, why do you think that the US government does not standardize the job titles that can be used by financial advisors?

16. **Regulation—Dual Registration:** What are some of the conflicts of interest that are inherent in the relationship between dually registered "two-hat" broker/advisors and the consumer that are not present with a fee-only financial advisor?

17. **Regulation—Self-Regulation:** Why is the US government allowing brokerage firms to be self-regulated via FINRA when the major Wall Street firms are fined with regularity for selling toxic investments to the average consumer?

18. **Fiduciary:** Why should the US government require financial advisors to acknowledge their fiduciary obligations in writing?

19. **History of Regulation:** What is the meaning of the Merrill Lynch rule in the context of the dually registered financial advisor?

20. **Political Pressure:** How much does FINRA spend every year lobbying the United States Congress?

21. **Advisor Compensation:** What is the problem with investment brokerage firms paying bonuses to financial advisors to get the brokers to move from one firm to another?

22. **Sales Culture:** What is the problem with investment brokerage firms marketing their financial advisors as "top producers" based on the amount of sales commissions they generate for the firm?

AdvisorSmart® is continuing our research to identify the correct questions for all of us to ask. For a longer list of additional group discussion questions, please visit www.AdvisorSmartBook.com/BeyondTheBook.

If you would like to contribute a new question to our list, please send your question to us directly via email at David@AdvisorSmart.com and use the email subject heading "New Group Discussion Question."

www.AdvisorSmartBook.com/BeyondTheBook

Scan this QR code with your phone to access additional AdvisorSmart® Discussion Group Questions.

AdvisorSmart® Images

The readers of *AdvisorSmart®* are encouraged to use the illustrated images in the book to promote the concepts that will lead to better financial advice. The beautiful images in the book were designed by Michael Boorman at Wisdom Made Easy (www.WisdomMadeEasy.com).

These images are available to you for free download at www.AdvisorSmart.com/images.

Please feel free to use these images created for AdvisorSmart® by Wisdom Made Easy to further enlighten the individual investor about financial advice and financial advisors. Financial advisors are also welcome to use these images to educate their clients about financial advice and financial advisors.

If you have a specific request related to the use of AdvisorSmart® images, please send your question to us directly via email at David@AdvisorSmart.com and use the email subject heading "AdvisorSmart Image Permission Request."

www.AdvisorSmart.com/Images

Scan this QR code with your phone to access free AdvisorSmart® Images

AdvisorSmart® Beyond the Book Bonus Materials

For exclusive resources and special offers developed for the readers of this book, visit www.AdvisorSmartBook.com/BeyondTheBook

We have developed a Financial Advisor Selection Checklist that is available free to you as a reader of this book. To access your free checklist for selecting a financial advisor, send an email to us directly at David@AdvisorSmart.com and use the email subject heading "Free Financial Advisor Selection Checklist."

www.AdvisorSmartBook.com/BeyondTheBook

Scan this QR code with your phone to access free AdvisorSmart® Beyond the Book educational resources.

If you enjoyed this book, please consider writing a review on Amazon.

AdvisorSmart® Custom Editions and Bulk Orders

Educating the consumer about financial advisors is an important goal for AdvisorSmart®, so we are providing two opportunities for organizations to purchase additional copies of the book for their communities.

Bulk Orders and Custom Editions:

For information about special custom editions or book price discounts for bulk book purchases please visit:
www.AdvisorSmartBook.com/TheBook

Scan this QR code with your phone to obtain information about AdvisorSmart® bulk orders.

Or contact us at David@AdvisorSmart.com

For more information:

Email: David@AdvisorSmart.com
www.AdvisorSmart.com
www.AdvisorSmartBook.com

If you enjoyed this book, please consider writing a review on Amazon.

Join the AdvisorSmart® Community

AdvisorSmart® was established in 2018 with the mission to provide investors with the education they need to access better financial advice. AdvisorSmart® is an investor advocate focused on improving financial literacy related to the selection of financial advisors. Our vision is to help millions of investors get better financial advice.

While we might be able to help an individual investor to find better financial advice in about twenty minutes, we believe that changing the way that most investors approach Wall Street might take more than twenty years. We have a lot of work to do as a group to help investors get better financial advice.

Scan this QR code with your phone to access a newsletter subscription sign up form for the AdvisorSmart newsletter.

Stay Connected

Connect with AdvisorSmart® on social media:

- LinkedIn/Company/AdvisorSmart
- Facebook/AdvisorSmartBook
- Instagram/AdvisorSmartBook
- Pinterest/AdvisorSmartBook
- YouTube/AdvisorSmart
- X/AdvisorSmartCom

Let's continue the conversation. Stay connected with us on social media.

For more information:

Email: David@AdvisorSmart.com

www.AdvisorSmart.com

Scan this QR code with your phone to find the AdvisorSmart social media links so you can follow us on social media.

If you enjoyed this book, please consider writing a review on Amazon.

About the Type

This book was set in Baskerville MT Pro, a classical, readable, and approachable font. The accent font is Franklin Gothic, another classically readable font.